Lies Empowering International Criminal Reasoning

nova
science publishers
www.novapublishers.com

Human Rights: Contemporary Issues and Perspectives

More information about this series can be found at
https://novapublishers.com/product-category/series/human-rights-contemporary-issues-and-perspectives/

Law, Crime and Law Enforcement

More information about this series can be found at
https://novapublishers.com/product-category/series/law-crime-and-law-enforcement/

Farhad Malekian

Lies Empowering International Criminal Reasoning

nova
science publishers
www.novapublishers.com

DOI: https://doi.org/10.52305/IKRG5425

Additional color graphics may be available in the e-book version of this book.

Library of Congress Cataloging-in-Publication Data

ISBN: 979-8-89530-903-2 (Hardcover)
ISBN: 979-8-90134-000-4 (eBook)

Published by Nova Science Publishers, Inc. † New York

To dearest Ruby
To dearest Elsie
To dearest Braghe

Contents

Preface xi

Introduction xiii

Chapter 1 **The Supremacy of Reasoning Over Justice** 1
1. What Does Justice Look Like? 1
2. Adherence to a Unified Mandate 3
3. Foundation of Legal Duty 6
4. Necessity of Securing Assurance of Protection 8
5. Exacerbating Injustice 10
6. Objective of Justice 12
7. Glorified Awards to Immoral Offenders 14
8. Profound Failure in Our Institutional Morality 17

Chapter 2 **Self-Effacing Lies Manipulating Sound Justice** 21
1. The Misrepresentation of Accountability 21
2. Moral Dilemmas 23
3. Confronting Tensions 26
4. Self-Created Justice 29
5. Games Rooted in the Reasoning of Injustice 32
6. Deteriorating Justice 36
7. Spirit of Authoritarian Injustice Infringing Justice 38

Chapter 3 **A Legacy of Shame: The Disgrace of International Justice** 45
1. Marginalised Lifeboat of Justice 45
2. Dissenting Toward True Forms of Justice 49
3. Logic of Injustice 51
4. Resisting Against the Barbarity of Disingenuous Justice 53
5. Metaphorical Consumption of Justice 57

6. Desperate Justice 60
7. Scrutiny of the Values of Justice 62

Chapter 4 **Lying with Precedent: Distorting International Criminal Justice** 65
1. Selective Observation in the Imposition of Justice 65
2. Elevating Lies Over Victims 68
3. Justice Encouraging the Superiority of Lies 71
4. Institutional Framework for Distorting International Justice 74
5. Determining Who Wields Authority Over Justice 76
6. Subservience of Justice to Political Lies 78
7. Standardisation of Barbaric Coercive Force 82

Chapter 5 **Disequilibrium Empowering International Criminal Reasoning** 87
1. Describing the Equilibrium of Justice 87
2. Presenting Unattainable Views of Justice 90
3. Shaping the Shifted Moral Reasoning of the ICC 92
4. Lobbies of Characteristic Lies 95
5. Manufacturing False Evidence 97
6. Privatised Definition of International Crimes 100
7. Empowering Lies Through the Abandonment of Justice 103

Chapter 6 **Empowering the Monopolisation of International Criminal Justice** 107
1. Justice as the Monopoly of Lies 107
2. Negotiating the Consequences of the Injustices Derived from Lies 110
3. Advocacy of Justice by Colonial Governments 112
4. Precarious Positioning of Justice 116
5. Exceedingly Frangible Inclination of Justice 119
6. Lack of Accountability for Violations of Human Rights 122
7. Lies Rendering Legal Values 125

Chapter 7 **Empowering Reasoning of the Lies Interpreted in ICC Procedure** 129
1. Closing Any Genuine Opportunity of the Court 129
2. Lies Empowering Extensive Obliteration 130
3. Articulating Justice with the Reasoning of Lies 134
4. Illusion of Balance Between Justice and Lies 138
5. Security Council Supervising the Law of ICC 140
6. Empowering Reasoning Based on Immorality 143
7. Widespread Backbone Deficiencies in ICC Parties 145

Chapter 8 **Criminal Governments Orchestrating Their Bongos of Justice** 149
1. Bongos of Injustice 149
2. Lies Denying Validity to the Norms of Justice 153
3. Ignoring the Rationale Behind Virtue 156
4. Conflation of Fabrications Predicated for Self-Interests 159
5. Discounting Political and Legal Personalities 161
6. Contradiction with Rightful Criminal Reasoning 164
7. Mendacious Rhetoric and the Subversion of International Criminal Justice by the ICC Council 166
8. New Scenarios Empowering Reasoning of Lies 168

Chapter 9 **Conclusion** 173

Appendix 181
Chapter VII. Monopolizing the Power of the United Nations Organisation for Equality 181
Action with Respect to Threats to the Peace, Breaches of the Peace, and Acts of Aggression *181*

Bibliography 185

Index 205

Preface

Justice can be described as a construct that often conceals falsehoods, or at times, serves merely as a façade for such falsehoods. Regardless of how justice may be defined, it is evident that it does not emanate from the intentions of virtuous individuals; rather, it is shaped by the artistry of those who are dishonest. This observation aptly reflects the current state of international criminal justice. It would not be an exaggeration to assert that the definition of international justice has been historically manipulated, dictated, and promoted by those who have held positions of power while engaging in egregious international crimes. Consequently, the concepts of injustice and the massacre of innocent civilians cannot be relegated to mere footnotes in the evolution of international relations among various civilisations; instead, they reveal the brutality inherent in our more powerful natures. Regrettably, the existing system of international criminal justice suffers from a significant distortion of truth and an overwhelming infusion of deception - perpetrated through coercive means within the discussions held at the United Nations Security Council. Thus, we find ourselves governed by a “law” founded on lies, which must be adhered to by all individuals regardless of their varying inclinations. It is imperative to engage with this discourse and remain cognisant of one’s own nature.

Introduction

Addressing the influence of falsehoods within the context of international criminal justice is not merely important to me; it ought to be recognised as essential by all individuals involved in upholding the principles and standards of international criminal law. Falsehoods have infiltrated numerous facets of international criminal law, evolving into a framework that is challenging to contest due to the significant power that supports these deceptions. Moreover, individuals who dare to oppose these falsehoods may find themselves branded as terrorists or corrupt, potentially facing lethal consequences from intelligence operatives linked to political authorities.

Treaties signed and ratified under any title aimed at promoting the system of international criminal law are classified as law-making treaties. However, an alternative characterisation of the current state of international criminal law emerges due to the infiltration of lies within its scope, which might be described as lie-making sanctions. This scenario presents a morally ambiguous discourse on norms and interpretations that embrace unclear or unconventional methodologies for defining international criminal law in a manner favourable to autocratic regimes globally. As such, predicting the ultimate ramifications arising from these falsehoods remains elusive. I have aptly designated this phenomenon as "Lies Empowering International Criminal Reasoning," which effectively underscores how such untruths reinforce the ambitions and malign interests of powerful nations.

The reality is that doctrines founded on deceit exist within the domain of international criminal law, facilitating the continuation of fabrications propagated by dominant governments aimed at consolidating their political power through unscrupulous means. It is apparent that numerous compromised international criminal lawyers align their views with the imposed falsehoods enforced by political autocrats within the United Nations Organisation. These doctrines are fundamentally utipolitianist in nature, relying on moral and legal authority derived from treaties that have been interpreted and deduced by influential political actors within the Security

Council. This suggests that only a select few members can dictate what is regarded as the true essence of international criminal law and justice.

It is imperative not to conflate utipolitianism with utilitarianism; while utilitarianism encompasses elements based on utility and enjoyment alongside certain moral considerations that should not be overlooked, utipolitianism focuses solely on leveraging power for self-serving purposes without regard for ethical principles.

For instance, resolutions drafted and adopted by the Council concerning military interventions in Iraq were rapidly legitimised based on misrepresentations put forth by the United States and British governments; subsequent inquiries revealed that allegations regarding unlawful weapons were unfounded. It was through this collective impact of fabrications that international criminal reasoning was fortified, enabling aggression resulting in the deaths of over half a million children. The concept of "Lies Empowering International Criminal Reasoning" encapsulates a vision held by utipolitianist governments which intend to achieve global supremacy through militarised control. This indicates that integrating international criminal law into resolutions and powers governed by Chapter VII of the United Nations must adhere to entirely different principles - essentially predicated upon layers of deception.

This suggests that utipolitianism constitutes a theory grounded in deception, which permits those in positions of authority to retain control through the application of force. Such deceptions are frequently articulated with an imperative quality, implying that the principles of utipolitianism ought to be upheld and enforced without exception. The execution and enforcement of the authority wielded by utipolitianist governments, particularly in relation to theories of international criminal law, are improbable to materialise absent the falsehoods that form the basis of international criminal reasoning.

At its inception, the United Nations effectively aligned itself with imperialist powers characterised by criminality and their stipulations. This alignment signifies that military influence was officially incorporated into the United Nations following World War II, thereby converting military forces into legal authorities. If comprehending international criminal justice is attained through coercive measures, then resultant outcomes may be distorted by arbitrary influences. This again underscores the detrimental effect that deception has on the integrity of international criminal reasoning.

The role of deception utilised by political authorities is to improperly broaden the scope of international criminal justice principles in order to counter and dismiss the assertions made by governments or nations advocating for their traditional, cultural, ethnic, or sovereign rights. Efforts by victims of international crimes lack authoritative recognition, and the enforcement of these untruths through coercive means, as delineated in Chapter VII of the United Nations Charter, is well-documented. Consequently, no repudiation of these untruths can be justified based on the exercise of veto power. While it may be necessary to elucidate the rationale behind what might occasionally appear as essential falsehoods, this consideration bears no relevance to those powers that disseminate such inaccuracies. Therefore, the justification for disregarding the rights of other nations or governments originates from these powers' stances, which signify a fundamental failure within the international community.

As previously indicated and as will be elaborated upon throughout this book, the falsehoods articulated by political authorities during their meetings and discussions do not accurately represent an understanding of international criminal justice. When foundational positions and substantive principles within this system are compromised, it becomes apparent that not only are these principles treated unjustly but they are also systematically undermined in relation to moral precepts governing international criminal jurisdiction. We contend that deceptions perpetuated by powerful and oppressive governments within both the Security Council and on battlefields are closely linked to specific adjudicative circumstances underpinned by claims to justice.

The ramifications of these untruths portray militaristic actions as being those undertaken by an army considered one of the most moral in the world. Through various artistic representations, they inflict immense suffering, resulting in the loss of millions of innocent lives - predominantly children.[1] Furthermore, when principles of international criminal justice are selected while insisting on adherence to tenets rooted in international humanitarian law during armed conflicts, it leads to a significant erosion of credibility regarding

---

[1] For instance "the UN initially estimated that 5,000 children were born of rape in the 1994 genocide, but the Survivors' Fund – a British charity working in Rwanda – believes the number might be nearer 20,000. Unlike genocide orphans, children of rape do not qualify for government assistance and many live in poverty. Aid programmes have tended to concentrate on the plight of the raped women, paying little attention to the children, who have grown up feeling rejected by their mothers and stigmatised by the wider community. In Rwanda, ethnicity comes through the father's line, so Tutsi survivors call the children *Interahamwe* and "son of a snake," while the relatives of the Hutu rapists often tell the children that their mothers are wicked for testifying against their fathers and putting them in jail." Rwanda 20 years on: the tragic testimony of the children of rape https://www.theguardian.com/world/2014/jun/08/rwanda-20-years-genocide-rape-children. See also See *also* Farhad Malekian, *International Criminal Law of Children* (New York: Nova Sciences Publishers, 2021).

conceptions of justice. This occurs under the rationale that opposing entities are categorised as terrorists and pose a threat to the existence of human civilisation, while simultaneously justifying their own actions and dismissing resistance movements as violent and aggressive. Consequently, any notion of self-defence is rejected within the context of international criminal justice, along with a complete disregard for the use of armed force. Such falsehoods further reinforce flawed international criminal reasoning in regions such as the Middle East and Latin America.

A conception of justice based on deception is evidently counterproductive and facilitates the normalisation and acceptance of dishonest norms within international relations. It seems reasonable to assert that norms founded on fabricated evidence and testimonies have become more deeply entrenched than ever before. Consequently, an equitable understanding of justice has been eradicated from discussions among judges or prosecutors at the International Criminal Court, who remain beholden to directives from dominant powers within the Security Council.[2] While it is highly desirable for an international criminal justice system to be rooted in legal principles and genuine wisdom, such a shared understanding remains unacknowledged due to lies stemming from the authority exercised by powerful governments, which serve critical functions.

In summary, falsehoods that empower international criminal reasoning are irrational; they embody autocracy, tyranny, despotism, and hypocrisy within a justice system inherently characterised by complex dimensions. Throughout this discourse, I have argued that both the foundational position and underlying aspects of international criminal justice must be scrutinised not only through general judicial systems but also specifically through international criminal jurisprudence. Furthermore, I contend that many practitioners in international human rights law and international criminal law must recognise that our engagement with legal study should not centre on achieving positions or superficial titles but rather on ensuring alignment with legal integrity while refraining from enabling criminals and perpetuating their fabrications. This requires an awareness among legal professionals regarding their duties and responsibilities to act rationally and maintain open-mindedness without yielding to deceit due to concerns about job security. They face a choice between upholding justices versus injustices, adhering to

---

[2] Farhad Malekian, *Conscience of Prosecutors in International Criminal Law, the Heart of the Matter* (New York: Nova Science Publishers, 2021); Farhad Malekian, *Conscience of Lawyers in International Criminal Law, the Burden of Doppelgängers* (New York: Nova Science Publishers, 2021).

lawful authority over reliance on coercive power, as well as between maintaining ethical standards in their knowledge versus compromising principles for personal gain at the expense of international human rights and criminal justice systems.

Farhad Malekian
Uppsala, Sweden,
12th September 2025
f.malekian.in.crim.l@telia.com
f.malekian.in.crim.l@gmail.com

Chapter 1

The Supremacy of Reasoning Over Justice

1. What Does Justice Look Like?

Justice is a complex and intricate topic to address. In essence, justice cannot be classified merely as a theory or a non-theory; it encompasses both tangible and intangible actions. An individual who seeks justice inevitably encounters a framework of valuable and less valuable thoughts, actions, reactions, and numerous explanations that extend beyond conventional notions of justice. This complexity arises because the components of justice are not inherently fixed, leading to diverse objections stemming from varying interpretations of what is deemed right or wrong. The primary reason for these differing interpretations lies in the fact that each person assesses justice based on their own understanding, personal needs, and divergent assumptions. It is at this juncture that the interests of individuals intersect with the concept of "justice," which fundamentally relates to determining who possesses rights or who offers more acceptable justifications regarding matters of rightness - culminating in what we ultimately define as justice.[1] Consequently, when engaging with issues of rights and wrongs, we must evaluate them within a broader context that transcends personal understandings to arrive at a clearer definition of justice that aligns with moral principles concerning rights.

The examination of the foundational principles of justice is essential for comprehending the theoretical framework of the science of justice, which is closely intertwined with an understanding of human existence and the fundamental shared interests that underpin the concept of "human rights."

---

[1] Farhad Malekian, 'Emasculating the Philosophy of International Criminal Justice in the Iraqi Special Tribunal,' *Cornell International Law Journal*, 58/5 (2005), pp. 675-725; Farhad Malekian, *Gravity of Wisdom in International Criminal Law* (New York: Nova Science Publishers, 2021); Farhad Malekian, *Orchestrating Diversity in International Criminal Justice* (New York: Nova Science Publishers, 2021); Farhad Malekian, *Trading Virginity of International Criminal Justice* (New York, Nova Science Publishers, 2020); Farhad Malekian, *Paralysing International Criminal Justice* (New York: Nova Science Publishers, 2021); Read also Baum L. M., 'Pursuing Justice in a Climate of Moral Outrage: An Evaluation of the Rights of the Accused in the Rome Statute of the International Criminal Court,' 19 *Wisconsin International Law Journal* (2001), 197; Hoover Joseph, Moral Practices: Assigning Responsibility in the International Criminal Court, 76 *Law and Contemporary Problems* (2014), pp. 263-86.

These rights encompass the right to life, ownership of personal property, freedom of expression, and the liberty to seek justice in pursuit of happiness within a domain that respects both individual and collective rights. Consequently, in our quest for justice, we encounter limitations defined by certain principles. It is important to note that referencing a collection of rights does not justify infringing upon the rights of others - whether visible or not. Justice, therefore, is a broad concept in nature that simultaneously adheres to specific definitions and facts relevant to diverse community interests. Thus, justice can be regarded as a science that elucidates for individuals what constitutes a limitation and where deception reaches its boundaries. This underscores the necessity of avoiding conflicts so as not to violate the dignity associated with others' rights, thereby clarifying what actions are permissible and impermissible.

It is evident that justice is intrinsically linked to the realm of peaceful resolutions. This suggests that justice opposes conflicts and the mistreatment of any of its subjects. As aptly stated, justice embodies the principles of peace and serves as the fundamental basis for fostering harmonious relations in the future. If this fundamental requirement of justice is not met or is violated during negotiations between parties, then justice cannot be attained, resulting in the absence of peace for those who seek a form of justice that promotes harmony and goodwill. Consequently, justice represents an essential concept that can elucidate the conditions under which humanity may coexist peacefully. It should be noted that true justice cannot exist without the genuine acknowledgement by all involved parties. Therefore, it is important to emphasise that the components of justice do not equate to mere self-satisfaction among conflicting parties; rather, they signify the fulfilment of the core needs associated with peace, which encompasses righteousness and valid justification for establishing or maintaining peaceful relations.

These conditions are not only prerequisites for realising the principles of justice but also ensure equitable treatment for both present and future subjects. This indicates what is necessary to achieve the foundational condition of justice related to peace. Consequently, peaceful justice cannot manifest if one unjustly and inhumanely infringes upon another's rights while claiming to pursue peace. Such actions do not constitute peace; instead, they initiate profound conflicts and ultimately extinguish any potential for attaining peace, thereby exacerbating the brutality of wars among various nations. It is essential to the principles of justice that each individual refrains from actions that are unjustified and violate the fundamental rights of others. This means that whether from a national or international perspective, we must avoid engaging in behaviours that infringe upon the rights of others. We must consciously refrain from actions that ultimately lead to violations, infringements, corruption, misconduct, intentional wrongdoing, or criminal behaviour.

2. Adherence to a Unified Mandate

The question often arises regarding the recognition of violations: what truly leads to the disrespect of justice, and why do we witness so many violations that ultimately escalate into serious conflicts and wars? It is also worth considering whether these violations are the result of greater injustices driven by greed, or if they are not violations at all, but rather acts of self-defence against severe and prolonged abuses. Furthermore, some actions may not be perceived as violations but as necessary defences against the brutality of certain authorities that act inhumanely toward their own citizens or specific races and ethnic groups. A clear example of this can be seen in the movements in France against authoritarian political powers. The French Revolution, for instance, was organised to disarm those whose brutality threatened the entire French nation. In this context, the elements of justice were not violated; instead, the intention was to foster peace, reciprocity, integrity, and equality among nations.

In other words, as long as there are no violations and the authorities uphold the principles of justice, society remains at peace and should continue to foster harmony among all its members, including those tasked with maintaining peace and justice on behalf of the government. Consequently, the essence of justice lies in its intention rather than its actions. If the intention behind justice is noble and aims for positive outcomes that promote peace and prosperity for all individuals, then true justice can ultimately be realised. It is important to note that while various codifications, constitutions, protocols, conventions, agreements, treaties, and declarations, as well as statutes, may contain sound principles, their effectiveness is compromised when hypocrites hide the intentions behind them. In such cases, the true purpose of justice becomes obscured, and the ideals of justice and peace become stagnant.[2]

[2] Consult Robert F. Kennedy, Why the Arabs don't want us in Syria: They don't hate 'our freedoms.' They hate that we've betrayed our ideals in their own countries - for oil in http://www.politico.eu/book/why-the-arabs-dont-want-us-in-syria-mideast-conflict-oil-intervention/; Washington's Secret Agendas – Truth is being Disguised to Suit, available online at http://www.oneworldofnations.com/2014/09/washingtons-secret-agendas-truth-

When either of these fundamental conditions - peace or justice - is violated, nations find themselves in conflict.[3] This indicates that the realm of evil, wrongdoing, and crime persists in severe and bloody confrontations until justice is restored.[4]

Another example is Irish republicanism, the political movement advocating for an Irish republic without British rule under utipolitianist authority. Throughout its centuries-long existence, it has been a political gathering that has been both elected and militant, and has been equally supported and criticised. However, the modern emergence of democracy, nationalism, and radicalism, groups across the Island formed a movement aimed at independence from British brutal colonialist power. Thus, the revolutions in France and Ireland represented a step toward establishing peace and eliminating the crimes committed by those in power. This indicates that the intentions behind these movements were fundamentally good, aimed at preventing further harm to the principles of justice.

The evidence throughout human history suggests several uncomfortable truths. It indicates that, as the histories of various nations reveal and as the brutality of colonialism continues to demonstrate, humanity struggles to coexist peacefully when malevolent intentions dominate our thoughts. In our pursuit of justice, we must tap into the innate instincts and collective wisdom of the human race, which are essential for establishing enduring justice and peace. Therefore, it is imperative to adhere to a unified order and to fulfil a singular universal obligation: that each individual should treat every other person with honesty and integrity. It is here that we encounter justice as a symbol of peace and happiness for all, rather than as a tool wielded by powerful individuals or governments. This is why we strive to pursue justice in the name of peace - justice that is not harmful and does not create victims through its processes, but rather liberates individuals from the shackles of inhumanity and wrongdoing.[5]

---

is.html; 'Former Liberian dictator Charles Taylor had US spy agency ties' available online at http://www.bostonglobe.com/metro/2012/01/17/mass-escapee-turned-liberian-dictator-had-spy-agency-ties/DGBhSfjxPVrtoo4WT95bBI/story.html.

[3] *Id.*

[4] *Id.*

[5] "We do understand that justice is very difficult to uphold, and that justice may take different perspectives. What is peculiar to human beings concerning the proper definition of justice is not the definition itself, or principles, but the manner of treatment by nations with different vocabularies for the definition of justice. If the definition of international human rights is torment, misery, destruction of our homes, and the killing of our children, then all nations should share the same principles. We should not only kill the Afghan, Syrian,

The pertinent question then arises: what, functionally speaking, is achieved by classifying certain individuals as victims of violations against the principles of peace? Several motivations can be envisioned for the creation of such classifications. One reason may stem from our personal interests, which lead us to categorise certain individuals as inferior. Another reason could be our desire to position ourselves within a group that we perceive as more legitimate than others. Consequently, we may categorise individuals according to national or international standards, even placing certain nations above others by using terms such as developed, underdeveloped, terrorists, Black or other problematic terms.

Our interpretation of rights and duties significantly influences the outcomes of justice, as well as the maintenance of peace and prosperity. This is particularly evident in situations where there is a profound conflict between true justice and false justice. Although both may present themselves as justice, there is a fundamental difference in their adherence to the principles of justice, which in turn affects the development and understanding of peace. It is a fact that the principles of peace are inherently linked to behaviours that align with the principles of justice. When the elements of justice are compromised, the foundations of genuine peace are immediately undermined. Moreover, it is difficult to support the rights of victims while simultaneously endorsing the oppressors. The acknowledgement of peace and the recognition of rights for all individuals can become a deceptive facade that distorts the reality of true justice, ultimately disenfranchising victims of their rights. Authentic peace relies on a justice system that is fundamentally persuasive and normative. However, we often conflate the justice system with conditions of superiority, which are in constant conflict with the ideals of moral and philosophical justice.

Vietnamese, Iraqi, Libyan, but also the children of permanent members of the Security Council and their allies. Obviously, this is a very silly argumentation and has to be rejected immediately. However, if the definition of justice means heavenly rights, bliss, happiness, sincere commitment, and respect for all individuals of all nations that too should certainly be provided to our neighbours near and far." Farhad Malekian, *Classical Morality in International Peremptory Criminal Law* (Cambridge Scholars Publishing, 2018), pp. 211-2.

3. Foundation of Legal Duty

Undoubtedly, individuals owe numerous moral duties to their fellow human beings who require justice and peace. We assert that we are not only responsible for refraining from violating the inherent dignity of humanity, but we also have a duty to provide for the starving and homeless. Giving away what is essential for oneself to those in need is the essence of human rights. This obligation is not merely a moral one; it is fundamentally a legal duty. The rationale is straightforward: legal norms do not need to address every single issue that pertains to human duties or moral responsibilities. This implies that providing clothing to naked children or vulnerable citizens is an imperative duty for all individuals and their communities.

It is not without reason that we establish organisations to cooperate and assist those in need. This reflects our commitment to justice and peace for every individual. Therefore, presenting the truth is our established duty, just as providing shelter for the homeless and caring for the sick are essential responsibilities for all human beings. In fact, justice functions as an institutional system that relies heavily on protecting the defenceless and offering support to the vulnerable. We assert that the institution of justice is not a private entity; rather, it represents a collective understanding aimed at enlightening the uninformed. This implies a strong connection between our moral and legal obligations to achieve justice and prevent injustices. In other words, each of us must act as our own judges, striving to avoid wrongdoing and deceit in every situation. The proliferation of lies and the personal interpretation of interests undermine the integrity of justice, making the pursuit of peace seem like a utopian dream. These principles of justice are also linked to our personal capacities and the extent to which individuals are willing to prioritise self-interpretation over rightful interpretations of justice. Ultimately, the application of the fundamental principle of truth within the justice system is essential for ensuring the distribution of peace to every individual.

There is no doubt that we are responsible for presenting the truth and refraining from lying for the sake of justice and the establishment of peace. Additionally, we must consider our moral duties in relation to national and international standards. We cannot take the lives of individuals and then claim the high morality of our actions.[6] We cannot destroy the civilisations of other

[6] On morality role in justice consult Fuller Lon Luvios, *The Morality of Law* (Virginia: Yale Law University, 2nd, ed., 1969); A. R. C. Duncan, *Practical Reason and Morality* (Nelson,

nations and then speak about maintaining peace.[7] We cannot condemn the commission of wrongdoing or murder under national law as a crime while simultaneously engaging in the justification of killing millions of people from other nations in the name of peace.[8] Our policy is not only misguided but also constitutes a serious conspiracy against the international legal system. Justice, like peace, is not a personal matter; both are manifestations of moral truth.

With the aim of genuinely presenting justice and upholding its principles, we intend to address and honour the unified essence of humanity through a commitment to honesty towards our fellow beings. This commitment is fundamental to our identity and serves as a pathway to achieving social and international peace. Furthermore, it is crucial that throughout these processes, we maintain our collaboration with the elements of justice to ensure the protection of all individuals. If this interpretation of justice is erroneous, how can we effectively address the concept of peace, which cannot exist independently if justice does not prevail? This implies that we are compelled to pursue appropriate avenues for justice if the preservation of peace is deemed essential for the overall existence of humanity.

We may achieve these objectives through various means, whether through individual actions or collective efforts contributing to a framework of genuine justice. Such individual and collective commitment to advancing justice is so vital and impactful that it can yield either enduring and equitable justice or its opposite. Subsequently, we may inadvertently begin to construct a notion of just war, which equates to a peace born from conflict. This is ethically wrong and destructive. This scenario frequently arises, leading to an evident discourse on accountability; however, there is often a lack of definitive authority to delineate right from wrong since the administration of law and justice is frequently influenced by power dynamics - wherein those wielding power exploit their might against weaker or victimised nations through internationally wrongful conduct.

1957); M. J. Detmold, *The Unity of Law and Morality: A Refutation of Legal Positivism* (Canada: Law Book Co. of Australasia, 1984); Lea Brilmayer, *American Hegemony: Political Morality in a One Superpower World* (1994); Ahmad Haque Adil, *Law and Morality at War* (2017); Himma Kenneth and Brian Bix (eds), *Law and Morality* (2005); David Lyons, 'Moral Aspects of Legal Theory' in Kenneth Himma and Brian Bix (eds) *Law and Morality* (2005).

[7] *Id.*

[8] Farhad Malekian, *Powertionism in International Criminal Justice* (New York: Nova Science Publishers, 2022).

4. Necessity of Securing Assurance of Protection

What then is the role of justice and the regulations established in numerous international conventions aimed at preventing illegality, immorality, and violations? There may be various interpretations regarding this question, accompanied by differing rationales intended to persuade victims or social and international audiences alike. It is an inherent right of every victim, irrespective of nationality, to seek justice. This right should never be extinguished, and the authorities that purport to uphold justice must address all matters with due regard for the principles of justice and the establishment of genuine peace.[9] We acknowledge that every individual deserves to be treated fairly and to receive their rightful entitlements.[10] It is essential that no individual or group is regarded as inferior to another, regardless of ethnic background.[11]

The administration of justice should typically be pursued without resorting to any form of force. It is essential that individuals act and work in ways that do not infringe upon the rights of others. This means that we can freely and voluntarily engage in actions that uphold justice and promote peace, provided we do not violate our own rights or those of others. In essence, justice signifies protection rather than violation. It entails mutual safeguarding against wrongdoers, criminals, lawbreakers, and offenders. Furthermore, it is essential that we agree to judicial proceedings that are fair and equitable for all parties involved, regardless of their power or status. This highlights the importance of caution in matters of justice and its requirements. Consequently, courts cannot render judgments without a thorough investigation, as justice is not merely a reflection of our personal will but is rooted in the fundamental principles that govern its establishment and the true nature of each case. A comprehensive investigation is vital to ensure that the provisions of justice remain free from malevolent influences or immoral interpretations and desires of the parties involved. It entails freedom from deception or concealment, ensuring that international criminal reasoning remains sound and untainted.

The denial of justice constitutes a fundamental injustice, thereby necessitating the pursuit and realisation of justice. This principle must apply not only to those in positions of authority but also universally among all individuals. Consequently, we must consistently strive to eliminate any

---

[9] Consult Farhad Malekian, *Documents on the Principles of International Human Rights* (Stockholm: Norstedts Juridik AB, 2007).

[10] *Id.*

[11] *Id.*

potential errors in our judgments and accept accountability for mistakes stemming from haste and emotional impulses. Every individual aspires to witness justice being served and should not be subjected to inferior treatment or relegated to a position of insignificance within the realm of justice. Each person has the right to feel secure in the assurance of protection, which represents a foundational requirement for the principle of justice and, consequently, for achieving peace.

This is why we discuss justice as the maintenance of peace and truth for every individual within a secure framework, as well as for society as a whole, under the system of international procedures. Justice is not evaluated based on personal perspectives but rather through the understanding of the collective will of the judges in a court of law. A court in which judges exhibit bias is, therefore, recognised as lacking objectivity and cannot be considered a true representation of justice. This is particularly significant in criminal courts that impose severe punishments on victims or individuals who have not committed any violations, or who are fighting for their countries' freedom. In such cases, the theory of justice becomes essential and effective in establishing the rights of those who have been subjected to various violations. This suggests that the reasons for these violations are often related to cultural rights and norms. Consequently, the theory of justice evolves into a theory of culture, which, in turn, represents the natural rights of individuals, encompassing the collective and common rights of humanity within the realms of civil and criminal jurisdiction.

At the same time, it is essential for those responsible for delivering justice to exercise caution and ensure that their personal beliefs do not influence the court's judgment. The role of justice is not to create satisfaction for any party involved in a case, but rather to uncover the truth and render an appropriate and authentic judgment. Therefore, judgments should not focus on satisfying one party at the expense of another; instead, they should aim to reach the essence of the truth and provide restitution for those whose rights have been violated and who are considered victims of those violations. This necessitates recognising that when we speak of justice, we refer to pure justice - free from any form of political bias in court procedures. This highlights the importance of impartiality and integrity among those involved in the justice process, ensuring that they do not prioritise their own political affiliations. Although discussing objectivity in this context can be challenging and problematic when evaluating true justice, the fundamental principles necessary to achieve authentic justice remain unchanged and should not be regarded as secondary.

5. Exacerbating Injustice

In all situations, we are striving to develop our capacity for justice through various means.[12] This entails fulfilling the requirements for moral deliberation.[13] We only meet the principles of justice when we exercise the true faculty of justice, which reflects the comprehensive application of the criteria and knowledge within our understanding.[14] These principles cannot be upheld without acknowledging the moral essence of truth, as opposed to the distortion of justice. This indicates that our pursuit is not limited to the rights of our own culture or affiliations, but rather encompasses the rights of every individual whose rights have been violated due to erroneous or intentional misinterpretations.

It is not permissible for an individual to be legally compelled to join or support an organisation whose protection they do not desire. It is neither feasible nor reasonable for a person to affiliate with or endorse an association whose plans or methods they do not approve of. It is likely that they will achieve their stated goal of upholding justice and peace while also avoiding injustice. In their view, it would be absurd to join or support an entity that operates inefficiently. They believe that aligning with or endorsing someone who, in their opinion, would lead to injustice and criminality is unacceptable. It is crucial that they retain the freedom to choose whether to join or not. They must uphold their fundamental cultural rights in this regard, just as they do in all other matters, based on their own interests, judgment, or conscience. A government or court that prioritises the prevention of injustice is akin to a government that prioritises fire prevention. There is no justification for compelling any individual to join or support such associations against their will, judgment, or conscience. It is essential to respect individuals' autonomy and avoid forcing them to endorse ideas or organisations that they do not wish to support or whose purposes or methods they do not approve of.

---

[12] See *Issues in Contemporary Legal Philosophy: The Influence of H.L.A. Hart* (Ruth Gavison, ed., 1987); Heidi Hurd, '*Challenging Authority,*'100 *Yale Law Journal* 1611 (1991); G. Hughes, 'Validity and the Basic Norm,' 59 *California Law Review* 695 (1971); H.L.A. Hartart, *Essays in Jurisprudence and Philosophy* (1983); Joseph Raz, *The Morality of Freedom* (1986); J.W. Harris, *Legal Philosophers* (2ndedn.,1997); Johan Austin, *The Province of Jurisprudence Determined and the Uses of the Study of Jurisprudence* (1954); Postema Gerald J., *Bentham and the Common Law Tradition* (1986); Julie Dickson., *Evaluation and Legal Theory* (2001); H.L.A. Hart., *The Concept of Law* (1961). H.L.A. Hart., *The Concept of Law* (2ndedn., P.A. Bulloch and J. Raz eds., 1994).

[13] Examine *Id.*

[14] *Id.*

The inquiry must then be made regarding the meaning of the term "true justice." Is it merely a conventional expression associated with the definition of justice, or does it represent the significance of instilling specific substance within the concept of justice to adequately address its capacity in relation to the equitable distribution of rights, accompanied by a fully justifiable conscience? This perspective enables us to refute the argument suggesting a correlation between circumstances that necessitate granting rights to authentic justice and those pertaining to our individual interpretations. It is evident that there exists a robust connection among rights, despite our varying understandings of their essence. The issue at hand is not one of displacing personal interests but rather achieving and comprehending the certainty of rights that cannot be undermined by subjective interpretations but can only be realised through their fulfilment. This situation elucidates why numerous conflicts and frequent wars arise, during which stronger parties feel compelled to impose their own interpretations of rights based on personal or national conclusions. Consequently, this exacerbates problems and perpetuates warfare, resulting in the tragic loss of many innocent lives who are forcibly stripped of their rights. In this context, the definition of justice becomes inequitable; not only are victims deprived of their rights, but justice itself is also compromised in its foundational intentions.

This matter transcends the question of who possesses rights and who does not; it fundamentally concerns the respect afforded to the methods employed in administering justice regarding the rights of individuals seeking to solidify their entitlements appropriately. Justice should not merely reflect the imposition of specific viewpoints but rather strive for equitable outcomes. Consequently, it is essential, if not imperative, to honour the intentions of those subject to justice. However, these intentions must align with the fundamental principles of equality among all nations, which encompass a shared moral framework guiding decisions.[15] This underscores the importance of recognising objective realities rather than succumbing to subjective moral assertions that may be flawed, thereby overshadowing the true essence of morality - an acknowledgment rooted in an impartial understanding of

[15] Examine P. M. S. Hacker and J. Raz, (eds.), Law, *Morality and Society: Essays in Honour of H. L. A. Hart* (1977). See also Fuller Lon L., *The Morality of Law* (Yale Law University, 2nd ed., 1969); Kenneth Himma and Brian Bix (eds) *Law and Morality* (2005); M. J. Detmold, *The Unity of Law and Morality: A Refutation of Legal Positivism* (Canada: Law Book Co. of Australasia, 1984); Duncan A. R. C., *Practical Reason and Morality* (Nelson, 1957).

established legal norms rather than personal interpretations.[16] Thus, our focus should not revolve around a hierarchy of individuals but rather on the equality inherent in our perceptions of justice principles.[17] This perspective persists despite our inclination to impose or prioritise our opinions and their perceived success within the justice system. It is noteworthy that we are confronted not with a reiteration of our preconceived definitions of justice but with a conception that is markedly more realistic and equitable for each legal subject. Ultimately, the role of justice is not to conform to the desires of its constituents but to harness its capacity to fulfil genuine objectives associated with true justice.

6. Objective of Justice

True justice cannot exist unless we let go of our own personal desires. This is a fact and reality demonstrating that the definition of appropriate justice will work for everyone if there is no discrimination between men and women or among cultural and ethnic differences within nations. In other words, peace and justice can be achieved by transcending our personal undertones of justice and embracing a broad definition for the development of the rules and principles of justice. It is obvious that peace cannot be demanded during the process of injustice or during legal proceedings where our own demands and wills are presented. It is essential to distinguish the concept of utilitarianism from the notions of true justice and peace. This distinction arises from the fact that utilitarianism seeks to achieve a limited form of happiness for itself, rather than addressing the broader interests of all individuals. The objective of justice, therefore, lies in making decisions that are genuinely right, rather than those that we merely perceive as correct but do not serve the collective interest, instead catering to narrower interests.

Even when a higher degree of energy is exerted to enforce justice principles, it ultimately reveals itself to be monopolised as long as its independence is not assured. Much of the support for empowering appropriate justice stems from something more profound than mere personal or political will; I refer to this as transcendent power - an influence that surpasses conventional evaluations of justice. By contrast, we emphasise moral conscience as the most essential principle of justice. If justice is to be

---

[16] *Id.*
[17] *Id.*

recognised, we must seek it through the lens of morality - both in the actions taken, and in the principles, enforced by authorities wielding the power of law.[18] If the principles of justice are not enforced appropriately and are monopolised by those in power, justice will deviate from its moral foundation, leading to the prioritisation of the majority's interests.

Consequently, any discourse aimed at redefining justice proves challenging and often insurmountable. This difficulty stems from the understanding that justice is not merely a construct designed to fulfil our personal desires and interests; rather, it should encompass the interests of all without infringing upon public welfare. It is important to acknowledge that public discussions regarding the principles of justice may also reflect the personal interests of certain individuals. Thus, public interests must be evaluated alongside seemingly just rules to comprehend both unconscionable demands and those deemed reasonable. These considerations contribute significantly to debates surrounding an appropriate understanding of justice and highlight the potential drawbacks of misguided rules that could jeopardise equitable outcomes and disrupt the harmonious application of justice. Upon closer examination of contemporary standards of international criminal justice, it becomes evident that our judicial systems lack stability and fail to provide the necessary conditions for ensuring equality in the administration of justice.[19] Therefore, it is unsurprising that opponents of justice - who are often influenced by those in positions of power - invoke arguments about justice and its principles that diverge significantly from universally recognised natural rights.[20]

---

[18] On morality examine P. M. S. Hacker and J. Raz, (eds.), Law, *Morality and Society: Essays in Honour of H. L. A. Hart* (1977); Farhad Malekian, *Classical Morality in International Peremptory Criminal Law* (Newcastle: Cambridge Scholars Publishing, 2021); Joseph Raz, *Ethics in the Public Domain: Essays in the Morality of Law and Politics* (Oxford: Oxford University Press, 1994); Joseph Raz, *The Morality of Freedom* (1986); Robert Vischer K., *Martin Luther King Jr. and the Morality of Legal Practice: Lessons in Love and Justice* (2014).

[19] Consult Pardo Pilar Villanueva Sainz, 'Is International Criminal Law a Living Discipline?,' 3:4 The International Journal of Human Rights (1999), pp. 92-100; Farhad Malekian, *Tour de force of Moral Virtue in International Criminal Justice* (New York: Nova Science Publishers, 2022); Farhad Malekian, *Imperative Philosophy of International Criminal Justice: Visible Power – Invisible Essence* (New York: Nova Science Publishers, 2022); Farhad Malekian, *Powertionism in International Criminal Justice* (New York: Nova Science Publishers, 2022); M. Cherif Bassiouni, 'A Comprehensive Strategic Approach on International Cooperation for the Prevention, Control and Suppression of International and Transnational Criminality, Including the Establishment of an International Criminal Court,' 15 Nova Law Review 353 (1991).

[20] Consult views of Spooner Lysander, Natural Law; or the Science of Justice: A Treatise on Natural Law, Natural Justice, Natural Rights, Natural Liberty, and Natural Society;

Even when we present justice and its definition alongside a comprehensive array of norms and principles that appear stable and imperative, a significant issue persists: the stable provisions of the justice system are often not practically applicable due to their ornamental statutes and lack of enforceable power. However, under certain conditions, the presentation of justice can be genuinely free from political influence and can be trusted in all circumstances. At first glance, this seems promising and feasible; however, when we examine the practical measures and enforceability of justice principles, we find that these principles are like leaves caught in a hurricane, subject to the whims of those authorities who control the governing principles of justice that dictate when and how they should be applied. This indicates that justice remains a colony of powerful political interests, entirely under the sway of personal agendas.

The only way to achieve accountability is by maximising the principle of morality. This means that the common interests of all individuals should be prioritised in order to dismantle the power of authorities through necessary disobedience to certain laws. This requires a shared sense of empathy and a collective understanding of justice and its equitable enforcement, which are essential for establishing peaceful relations. It implies that we must put an end to greed, as it is a vice that blinds individuals to the suffering of others. This is the most serious issue contributing to unequal justice. When, in national or international contexts, we or our governments exploit certain populations, we confront the fundamental principles of injustice that hinder the establishment of peace. Our reasoning of lies overlays the ethical norms of justice with the purpose of empowering international criminal reasoning with those lies.

7. Glorified Awards to Immoral Offenders

The evaluation of justice is among the most complex and nuanced topics. This suggests that we may, at times, bestow prestigious medals or degrees upon individuals who have played a role in our unjust actions against other nations, all under the belief that our conduct is justifiable and even commendable. Consequently, military leaders, soldiers, or superiors may receive accolades during ceremonies for their actions, which may indeed constitute violations of

---

showing that all Legislation whatsoever is an Absurdity, a Usurpation, and a Crime. Part First. [1882], available at http://oll.libertyfund.org/titles/spooner-natural-law-or-the-science-of-justice-1882 (Accessed: on 18 December 2017).

international humanitarian law governing armed conflicts, as well as acts of war crimes, genocide, or crimes against humanity. This underscores the contentious nature of the term "war," which can be viewed as an affront to the natural rights of humanity. As such, definitions of justice and their implementation can vary significantly, potentially leading to the idolisation of those responsible for inflicting suffering on innocent children in other nations.

For example, following the Iraq War - during which over half a million children lost their lives - many soldiers were celebrated, and their actions were deemed just and morally acceptable from both a military and political standpoint. Numerous instances within the United States exemplify this phenomenon; soldiers who ought to have been condemned as criminals instead participated in celebratory events where their actions were sanctioned by the government. Examples include the murders committed during the Vietnam War and the appreciation of the United States government for their evil crimes. This illustrates how perceptions of justice can become distorted by self-interest and how such distortions can solidify into norms and definitions. Thus, it is evident that international legal standards have often been shaped and endorsed by individuals engaged in criminal behaviour. Consequently, this raises significant criticism regarding the foundation of justice itself and highlights how authoritarian governments' interests have influenced its development.

There exist comparable arguments regarding the leaders of various governments who have participated in the perpetration of grave international crimes on a significant scale while simultaneously endorsing and commending their military personnel or officials for such actions.[21] A pertinent illustration

---

[21] According to the provisions of international criminal law: International crimes and international delicts concerns:

"1. An act of a State which constitutes a breach of an international obligation is an internationally wrongful act, regardless of the subject-matter of the obligation breached.

2. An internationally wrongful act which results from the breach by a State of an international obligation so essential for the protection of fundamental interests of the international community that its breach is recognized as a crime by that community as a whole, constitutes an international crime.

3. Subject to paragraph 2, and on the basis of the rules of international law in force, an international crime may result, *inter alia,* from:

a serious breach of an international obligation of essential importance for the maintenance of international peace and security, such as prohibiting aggression;

a serious breach of an international obligation of essential importance for safeguarding the right of self-determination of peoples, such as that prohibiting the establishment or maintenance by force of colonial domination;

a serious breach on a widespread scale of an international obligation of essential importance for safeguarding the human being, such as those prohibiting slavery, genocide and apartheid;

of this can be observed in the government of the United Kingdom, which has nominated its Prime Minister for the highest honour bestowed by the monarchy. This reflects our approach to justice; we firmly believe that our assessments are correct and that there is nothing amiss with their foundational principles. Consequently, the standard framework for autonomous justice is not devoid of personal influences, and the impartiality of justice relies on interpretations articulated by those who wield authority over its discourse and possess the instruments of judgment at their disposal.

In contrast, as previously articulated, justice must derive its momentum from the principles of equality - an essential imperative that cannot be questioned by any individual, entity, or system. This assertion is grounded in the understanding that the essence of justice inherently respects universal validity or equality among all individuals, eschewing favouritism toward certain parties or monopolisation by others through its enforcement capabilities. Thus, any theory of justice assessed or measured by individuals acting as political authorities regarding what constitutes just or unjust actions fails to genuinely represent justice; rather, it delineates a perverse form of justice that opposes deeply ingrained criminal tendencies without substantial effect. This paradigm undoubtedly signifies a vulnerability within the judicial system and its operational conditions.

Beyond all else, the shortcomings of the justice system become evident when we assess the indications that true justice is often unattainable, and the intention behind justice is frequently disconnected from the rights of those it is meant to serve. Underlying principles are therefore distorted by those individuals who seek to impose rights rather than to ensure that they themselves are perceived as correct and that their version of justice is upheld.[22] A significant distinction lies in the fact that justice is named, honoured, flattered, and delivered in a manner that is accessible only to certain officials.

Consequently, the prevailing notion suggests that there is a fundamental cause of this disparity, and the assertion of equal justice is, in reality, a monopoly held by those wielding greater power - whether that be physical or

---

a serious breach of an international obligation of essential importance for the safeguarding and preservation of the human environment, such as those prohibiting massive pollution of the atmosphere or of the seas.

4. Any internationally wrongful act which is not an international crime in accordance with paragraph 2, constitutes an international delict." Text of Article 19; Report of the ILC on the work of its forty-eight session, A/51/10 (1996), 60.

[22] Consult Farhad Malekian, *Powertionism in International Criminal Justice* (Nova Sciences Publishers, 2022).

economic.[23] This is because the ultimate definition of justice is often, in practice, entrusted to those who possess financial or physical strength. Then, if the violation of justice is rooted in such power, it becomes decisive for those who hold it through their means and judgments.[24] This is why we often seek justice outside the conventional realm of the justice system, distancing ourselves morally from compelling principles.[25] All of these factors are interconnected with the pursuit of financial gain, which ultimately hinders us from achieving our moral or natural purposes.

8. Profound Failure in Our Institutional Morality

To acknowledge the moral function of the principle of justice is not merely to delineate what is right and what is wrong. When we discuss transcending justice, we refer to a profound moral virtue that must exist to ensure the equitable application of justice and to mitigate any conflicts with the theory of true justice. In some instances, we must conclude that the very principle of justice, which has been recognised as powerful and influential, may, in fact, be flawed and serve a decorative role in the presentation of justice. This leads us to trust in a principle whose true purpose may be the monopolisation of legal power.

That means that the principle appears to be aimed at repairing the problem of justice while, in reality, it brings more injustice because of its monopolisation of the power of the law or cheating the minds of certain individuals in order to manipulate their minds and common interests. It is also about the virtue relating to the creation and establishment of a philosophical theory that is fabricated to exploit the rights of others rather than the establishment and respect of the rights. That is why a few modern writers reduce the value of virtue and put more respect on the common validity of certain principles for all individuals in order to approach the most desirable ways of principles that function equally for all individuals - to the same level and degree.

It may be correct that most of our arguments around the principles of justice and their functions speak about promoting prosperity and respecting the rights of others, but this is, however, only possible when justice is based

---

[23] *Id.*
[24] *Id.*
[25] *Id.*

on the principle of moral understanding and underlies the basic principle of equality for all. The primary issue arises when we perceive justice merely as the distribution of rewards to individuals for the crimes they have committed. In this context, ambitious individuals often receive applause and are celebrated as brave and strong for executing the decisions of their governments or leaders. They may alter their course of action to align with what is widely recognised as valuable and important. This tendency encourages many to adjust their paths to gain approval from those in power.

Consequently, they become fervently driven to pursue their interests, often prioritising self-interest and allowing greed to cloud their judgment. However, the distinction between genuine justice and artificial justice is exceedingly narrow, often obscured from both deceivers and honourable individuals. The concept of failure is more prominently featured in discussions of equal justice and its interpretations. The belief that a person deserves rewards for successfully causing the deaths of millions is not only misguided but also distorts the fundamental understanding of justice. Ultimately, this perspective separates justice from the idea of peaceful resolutions, reducing it to merely a system of rewards. This represents a profound failure in the institutional comprehension of the origins and objectives of justice.

In summary, if one accepts that the theory of justice holds validity, there should be no need for explanations that ultimately lead to illegitimate infringements upon others' rights. It is only through instances of injustice in both national and international relations that discussions surrounding justice become relevant.[26] To attain genuine international justice, it is imperative that we prevent morally unjustifiable rules or expressions from taking hold; until such conditions are met, policies purportedly grounded in justice will falter.

---

[26] "But if, on the other hand, there be in nature no such principle as justice, no such principle as honesty, no such principle as men's natural rights of person or property, then all such words as justice and injustice, honesty and dishonesty, all such words as mine and thine, all words that signify that one thing is one man's property and that another thing is another man's property, all words that are used to describe men's natural rights of person or property, all such words as are used to describe injuries and crimes, should be struck out of all human languages as having no meanings; and it should be declared, at once and forever, that the greatest force and the greatest frauds, for the time being, are the supreme and only laws for governing the relations of men with each other; and that, from henceforth, all persons and combinations of persons - those that call themselves governments, as well as all others - are to be left free to practice upon each other all the force, and all the fraud, of which they are capable." Lysander Spooner, *Natural Law or the Science of Justice: A Treatise on Natural Law, Natural Justice, Natural Rights, Natural Liberty, and Natural Society; showing that all Legislation whatsoever is an Absurdity, a Usurpation, and a Crime*. Part First. [1882] Available online at http://oll.libertyfund.org/titles/spooner-natural-law-or-the-science-of-justice-1882.

Consequently, victims will continue to suffer under a political system favouring those with power, rendering any imposed notion of justice ineffective. The victims are, regrettably, deprived of their rightful claims. [27]

This indicates a disparity in the application of justice among individuals within the international community, where, under the guise of promoting universal rights, we impose the demands of occupying powers. As a result, we directly interfere with the freedoms and rights of weaker nations, leading to larger conflicts and ultimately wars driven by our political ideologies. Such actions manifest in various forms and expressions aimed solely at monopolising the rights of others while imposing our rationale, despite our awareness that such intentions involve a transaction of others' rights with a clear focus on dominating the legal and moral frameworks of justice.[28]

---

[27] Consult Francesca Albanese, From Economy of Settler-Colonial Occupation to the Economy of Genocide, Report of the Special Rapporteur on the situation of human rights in the Palestinian territories occupied since 1967; https://www.un.org/unispal/document/a-hrc-59-23-from-economy-of-occupation-to-economy-of-genocide-report-special-rapporteur-francesca-albanese-palestine-2025/.

[28] *Id.*

Chapter 2

Self-Effacing Lies Manipulating Sound Justice

1. The Misrepresentation of Accountability

The metaphor of a tsunami aptly illustrates the situation wherein justice yields fairness rather than peace. This implies that the pursuit of justice is often accompanied by fear among individuals regarding its attainment. When justice deviates from its true essence, it gives rise to destruction and significant disasters by its very nature. Justice that follows this path becomes unrestrained, leading to accountability for those at the helm of justice - whether they are political leaders or judicial authorities. It is noteworthy that many lawyers, judges, and politicians do not share this perspective; they maintain that their understanding of justice is correct or believe that any errors do not pertain to their practical application or interpretation of it.[1] In truth, these individuals who serve as interpreters or implementers of justice often fail to engage with public grievances because they do not perceive a connection between the improper execution of fundamental principles of justice and their approach to normative standards.[2] Consequently, they may hold divergent views regarding any form of criticism. Such positions are fundamentally rooted in self-interest.[3]

It is crucial to recognise that some of our discussions reflect misunderstandings about what constitutes the foundational principles of justice and our collective multilateral obligations in terms of comprehending and enforcing it. Furthermore, we must consider what implications exist for achieving equitable justice and how these should be integrated to ensure the rights of all individuals are upheld. While discussions on these topics extend beyond the questions posed, our duties and responsibilities must remain aligned with truth and righteousness.

---

[1] Farhad Malekian, *Conscience of Judges in International Criminal Law, the Heart of Judgements* (New York: Nova Science Publishers, 2021); Farhad Malekian, *Conscience of Lawyers in International Criminal Law, the Burden of Doppelgängers* (New York: Nova Science Publishers, 2021); Farhad Malekian, *Conscience of Prosecutors in International Criminal Law, the Heart of the Matter* (New York: Nova Science Publishers, 2021).

[2] *Id.*

[3] *Id.*

Consequently, the majority of individuals engage in work and seek a clear understanding of the principles of justice, which should treat all subjects equitably without favouring certain priorities. Nevertheless, discussions regarding interests often conflate personal and public concerns, leading individuals to contend for their rights within the framework of justice. If justice is improperly administered, whereby one party imposes its will and interests upon another through coercion or military force, supported by various authoritarian regimes, then justice itself remains perpetually at risk and fails to uphold peace. This implies that debates surrounding the philosophy of justice and peace only exacerbate violations; consequently, political philosophy struggles to resolve these conflicts in a manner that satisfies all parties involved. Thus, violations of rights persist.[4]

As the principles of justice fail to provide equitable interpretations of the collective will of those subjected to it, disputes fuelled by diverse arguments and significant transgressions continue unabated. This leads to considerations of what constitutes correct versus incorrect reasoning, ultimately contributing to serious societal disintegration that may culminate in conflict. This scenario reflects current global realities where the powerful impose their own interpretations of justice upon the vulnerable, who are compelled to acquiesce due to threats posed by superior military might capable of destroying their assets. Such circumstances shape our discourse and invoke moral imperatives regarding rights and the universality of justice - principles that must be equally accessible to all and not enforced through violent means.

This raises the question: How should we promote and define the distribution of justice to improve the standard of justice and foster peace? The entire argument revolves around how to avoid misleading interpretations of the theory of justice. Clearly, we need a starting point that is not dictated by political or economic growth but rather by the development and promotion of moral rights. This means we should not permit the principles of justice to be influenced by the mechanisms of force.

---

[4] Examine The Influence of H.L.A. Hart (Ruth Gavison, ed., 1987); Heidi Hurd, Challenging Authority, 100 Yale Law Journal 1611 (1991); G. Hughes, Validity and the Basic Norm, 59 California Law Review695 (1971); H.L.A. Hart, Essays in Jurisprudence and Philosophy (1983); Joseph Raz, The Morality of Freedom (1986); J.W. Harris, Legal Philosophies, 2ndedn. (1997); John Austin, The Province of Jurisprudence Determined and the Uses of the Study of Jurisprudence (1954); Postema, Gerald J, Bentham and the Common Law Tradition (1986); Julie Dickson, Evaluation and Legal Theory (2001); H.L.A. Hart, The Concept of Law (1961); H.L.A. Hart, The Concept of Law, 2ndedn., (P.A. Bulloch and J. Raz eds., 1994).

Such a requirement, as mentioned above, is not easily achievable in practical terms and necessitates a rational and independent consideration of justice, distinct from utilitarianism, which aims for the greatest happiness for the greatest number, but not for all. This implies that the concept of justice is cultivated, yet it primarily safeguards the rights of those who possess the means and resources to advocate for themselves. Consequently, justice not only suffers but is also articulated through the perspectives of those who prioritise individual rights, albeit under specific constraints they deem essential for maintaining justice - constraints that often reflect their own conditions and definitions of justice.

As I have stated, the scope of justice becomes inadequate to prevent severe conflicts between the weak and the strong. This situation forces the weak onto a path where peace is unattainable, leading to a cascade of disorder within justice. It suggests that, through the use of armed forces, the weak are cornered into a state of despair, where justice for them translates to enduring the aggression that fuels the happiness of others. This includes the ongoing use of force against them, resulting in a life marked by violence and destruction. This reality is evident in the current global landscape, dominated by the United States government. The situation reflects how various nations have been coerced into a harsh form of justice, imposed through the might of weaponry.

2. Moral Dilemmas

In addressing the concepts of justice and fairness, we inevitably encounter moral dilemmas that pertain to the significance of moral principles - if they exist - within the ongoing discourse on justice.[5] Consequently, the philosophy of justice cannot be dissociated from moral principles and their influence on both equitable and inequitable forms of justice.[6] This assertion is grounded in the reality that the boundaries of morality are not uniform; legal norms differ across jurisdictions and even among various courts, contingent upon interpretations and applications of statutory provisions. Moral reasoning serves as a means to align with natural law as well as legislative frameworks

---

[5] Joseph Raz, *Ethics in the Public Domain: Essays in the Morality of Law and Politics* (Oxford: Oxford University Press, 1994); Joseph Raz, *The Morality of Freedom* (1986); Farhad Malekian, *Classical Morality in International Peremptory Criminal Law* (Newcastle: Cambridge Scholars Publishing, 2021).

[6] *Id.*

in a constructive manner.[7] Furthermore, it also acts as a mechanism for structuring our thought processes and approaches to diverse issues. This highlights the moral convictions that inform our beliefs and rationales for argumentation. In all scenarios, whether in times of conflict or tranquillity, we confront the challenge of determining which behaviours, actions, decisions, or principles carry greater significance and are deemed more suitable under prevailing circumstances.[8]

Moral inquiries may often be dismissed or underestimated on a broader scale; however, they remain pivotal in all matters - even in conflicts perceived as critical to our understanding of personal justice or individual arguments aimed at achieving specific outcomes. It is asserted that a thorough analysis of morality is indispensable for navigating contingencies related to issues we have yet to encounter or may face in the future. Such considerations are vital for articulating notions of immoral versus moral justice. Although these discussions may be hypothetical in nature, it remains evident that just outcomes must anticipate all conceivable situations to effectively combat injustice through every possible means.

It is imperative that we exercise utmost caution to ensure that justice is not undermined in our actions or decisions, a concern that many individuals often overlook. Consequently, the concept of justice and its various dimensions are frequently called into question, whether in domestic contexts or within the frameworks of national, regional, or international courts. Courts endeavour to provide appropriate resolutions to cases at hand, which entails defining justice in a manner that is both fair and suitable. The primary responsibility of courts is not merely to resolve cases amicably but rather to do so justly. Judges typically reflect upon instances that have been handled unjustly.

This indicates that even amidst complex and challenging situations concerning the application of rightful decisions and safeguarding the essence of justice, we remain obligated to uphold certain principles without transgression. This situation presents a moral dilemma, placing individuals or authorities in a position where they must make a critical decision regarding the consequences of a case. We are compelled to make the right choice; otherwise, a poor decision could adversely affect the outcome. This issue

---

[7] Farhad Malekian, *Tour de force of Moral Virtue in International Criminal Justice* (New York: Nova Science Publishers, 2022); Farhad Malekian, I*mperative Philosophy of International Criminal Justice: Visible Power – Invisible Essence* (New York: Nova Science Publishers, 2022).

[8] *Id.*

transcends questions of justice alone, as it embodies an ethical or moral dilemma. The significance of this situation is particularly pronounced in conflicts that have substantial economic or political implications.

If our judgments regarding various matters suggest as much within the court of justice, then the outcomes of cases may influence the understanding of justice itself and necessitate a thorough examination of its provisions and applications. This implies that justice must be defined - by whatever means necessary - as an outcome derived from court rulings that warrant respect. However, the fairness of a court's decision may vary based on its autonomy or its subservience when rendering judgments. In this context, numerous ethical dilemmas may emerge, prompting the case to be assessed under prevailing circumstances. A crucial consideration is that irrespective of how justice is portrayed or defined, there must be a foundation of moral reasoning that should not be contested by those involved in the proceedings.

The situation raises the question of moral imperatives that prevent individuals or groups from engaging in actions that are fundamentally impermissible and contradict certain principles, without allowing such principles to overshadow other potential tenets of justice.[9] We can examine the case of Hitler by making slight modifications and drawing its parallels to the Palestinian situation, considering their cultural, traditional, and universal rights within their own territories.[10] This contemporary context involves a

---

[9] M. J. Detmold., *The Unity of Law and Morality: A Refutation of Legal Positivism* (Canada: Law Book Co. of Australasia, 1984); Lea Brilmayer, American Hegemony: *Political Morality in a OneSuperpower World* (1994); Adil Ahmad Haque, *Law and Morality at War* (2017); Kenneth Himma and Brian Bix (eds), *Law and Morality* (2005); David Lyons, 'Moral Aspects of Legal Theory' in Kenneth Himma and Brian Bix (eds) *Law and Morality* (2005).

[10] For example, the serious international criminal violations against Palestinian civilians in Sabra and Shatila in Beirut in 1982. See the Security Council Resolution 521 (1982), which reads, "*Condemns* the criminal massacre of Palestinian civilians in Beirut." Similar reaction can be seen in the General Assembly Resolution (37/123D). It reads that the General Assembly: "*Recalling* its resolution 95 (I) of 11 December 1946, *Recalling* also its resolution 96 (I) of 11 December 1946, in which it, inter alia, affirmed that genocide is a crime under international law which the civilised world condemns, and for the commission of which principals and accomplices - whether private individuals, public officials or statesmen, and whether the crime is committed on religious, racial, political or any other grounds - are punishable, *Referring to* the provisions of the Convention on the Prevention and Punishment of the Crime of Genocide, adopted by the General Assembly on 9 December 1948, *Recalling* the relevant provisions of the Geneva Convention relative to the Protection of Civilian Persons in Time of War, of 12 August 1949, *Appalled* at the large-scale massacre of Palestinian civilians in the Sabra and Shatila refugee camps situated at Beirut, *Recognising* the universal outrage and condemnation of that massacre, *Recalling* its resolution ES-7/9 of 24 September 1982, 1. Condemns in the strongest terms the large-scale

population that has suffered systematic persecution and genocide for over eight decades. Therefore, a similar argument can be made regarding the Palestinians as was historically made concerning the Jews during the Second World War.

We can approach the aforementioned issue from various angles and articulate it in different ways. This implies that there cannot be a moral distinction between the two cases. We cannot assert that defending the Jews during the Second World War was justified while claiming that defending the Palestinians is wrong simply because the latter lacks protection from Western countries. Clearly, our argument cannot be deemed moral or even legal, and it may ultimately fail. The dishonesty of powertionist governments has led to the theory of lies, which empowers international criminal reasoning.[11]

3. Confronting Tensions

Grasping the concept of appropriate justice is, overall, a challenging task that cannot be achieved without sacrificing the rights of all individuals. Rights are not gifts; they can be stripped away by the immoral actions and decisions of those who believe, and continue to believe, that their interpretations are correct. This has been demonstrated repeatedly throughout history in the evolution of the definition of justice and its enforceability. The reality is that, from a historical perspective and even in contemporary times, we have often strayed from the principles of justice. We have attempted to grant justice the power of enforceability, yet it is our own demands that have shaped its application. Consequently, a moral analysis of a case reveals that our understanding of justice and its principles is often skewed. This distortion can lead to the manifestation of injustice, which ultimately undermines the moral essence of individual rights and the rights of populations as a whole. Furthermore, the act of genocide represents not only the annihilation of a nation but also the obliteration of justice and moral integrity. While it is possible to present various arguments regarding this issue, the fundamental truth remains unchanged: genocide against a population is unequivocally genocide, and no further justification is required.

---

massacre of Palestinian civilians in the Sabra and Shatila refugee camps; 2. Resolves that the massacre was an act of genocide."

[11] Farhad Malekian, *Powertionism in International Criminal Justice* (Nova Sciences Publishers, 2022).

If our statements were not true, then moral persuasion would be inconceivable. Any consideration of justice, whether right or wrong, must therefore align with moral imperatives that aspire to truth, especially if the objective of justice is to uphold the rights of victims. In cases involving victims, we are compelled to accurately discern the facts amidst falsehoods and present them in a manner that supports the framework of equitable and fair justice. This is particularly evident when the rights of victims can be clearly identified and documented; the separation of rights from their rightful owners inflicts significant harm on the foundation of justice. In fact, what we present for international scrutiny regarding justice, criminal justice, and human rights is often mere affirmation, as long as rights are not granted to their rightful owners.

We assert that victims of violations must confront justice with tangible support, rather than merely dogmatic claims.[12] At its worst, international criminal politics, including human rights issues, can approach a perilous state,

---

[12] Francesca Albanese describes that:

"93. The overwhelming nature and scale of the Israeli assault on Gaza and the destructive conditions of life it has inflicted reveal an intent to physically destroy Palestinians as a group. The present report finds that there are reasonable grounds to believe that the threshold indicating the commission of the following acts of genocide against Palestinians in Gaza has been met: killing members of the group; causing serious bodily or mental harm to groups' members; and deliberately inflicting on the group conditions of life calculated to bring about its physical destruction in whole or in part. Genocidal acts were approved and given effect following statements of genocidal intent issued by senior military and government officials.

94. Israel has sought to conceal its eliminationist conduct of hostilities by defending the commission of international crimes as abiding with international humanitarian law. By distorting customary rules of international humanitarian law, including distinction, proportionality and precautions, Israel has de facto treated an entire protected group and its life-sustaining infrastructure as "terrorist" or "terrorist-supporting," thus transforming everything and everyone into either a target or collateral damage, hence killable or destroyable. In this way, no Palestinian in Gaza is safe by definition. This has had devastating, intentional effects, costing the lives of tens of thousands of Palestinians, destroying the fabric of life in Gaza and causing irreparable harm to its entire population. It constitutes a pattern of conduct from which the only reasonable inference to be drawn is that there is a State policy of genocidal violence against the Palestinian people in Gaza.

95. The Israeli genocide against the Palestinians in Gaza is an escalatory stage of a long-standing settler colonial process of erasure. For over seven decades this process has suffocated the Palestinian people as a group – demographically, culturally, economically and politically – seeking to displace it and to expropriate and control its land and resources. The ongoing Nakba must be stopped and remedied once and for all. This is an imperative owed to the victims of this highly preventable tragedy, and to future generations in that land." Anatomy of a Genocide: Report of the Special Rapporteur on the situation of human rights in the Palestinian territories occupied since 1967, p.3, https://www.ohchr.org/sites/default/files/documents/hrbodies/hrcouncil/sessions-regular/session55/advance-versions/a-hrc-55-73-auv.pdf. Footnotes omitted.

undermining the justice mechanism and elevating injustice, leading to catastrophic outcomes. This suggests that manipulating the concepts of justice or its provisions can erode the mechanisms of justice and result in various forms of victims' rights degradation. Consequently, we find ourselves engaged in ideological battles over the definitions of justice and its interpretative mechanisms, which often fail to connect with the true essence of justice.

However, the definition and interpretation of justice, as well as its dissemination, do not need to be this way. We cannot disregard the rights of others while claiming to negotiate justice and define its conditions. This approach transforms justice into a mere bargaining tool for our own advantage, rather than a principled framework. In doing so, we alter the fundamental understanding of justice and exert pressure on the opposing party to accept our interpretations of what justice entails. Consequently, whether the other party agrees or not becomes irrelevant; as long as one side holds the power of force, justice cannot be negotiated in good faith. Its outcomes will always be open to debate among the parties involved and future generations affected by these issues. A clear example of this is the situation in Palestine, where the rights of its people have been severely undermined by powerful nations. This indicates that the international political, legal, and human rights communities have reached a moral crisis regarding the definitions of justice and rights, a reality that can no longer be concealed on the global stage.

Some Western politicians, and perhaps nearly all of them, reject the definition of true justice. For them, justice is merely the implementation of the will of the powerful, while victims are expected to adapt to their circumstances as best as they can. This perspective suggests that justice is a pathway through which injustice can be transformed into justice. It implies that inequality prevails over the equality of rights and the inherent dignity of humanity. It is imperative to acknowledge that moral reflection often emerges and evolves logically from grappling with significant moral dilemmas, particularly when justice is consistently and egregiously undermined. This observation should not be misconstrued as mere opinion or a perplexing enigma; rather, it is a reality that when questions of justice are belittled and removed from genuine discourse and understanding, the foundations of true justice become paralysed.[13] *Consequently, our ability to critically evaluate the rationale for*

[13] Malekian, *Paralysing International Criminal Justice* (New York: Nova Science Publishers, 2021): Farhad Malekian, *Classical Morality in International Peremptory Criminal Law* (Newcastle upon Tyne: Cambridge Scholars Publishing, 2018, republished 2021); Martti Koskenniem, *The Politics of International Law* (Hart, 2011); Martti Koskenniemi, *The*

condemning those who have perpetrated injustice against victims becomes precarious. Faced with this tension, we may adopt various perspectives on justice and seek alternative avenues to uncover the truth. Nonetheless, as long as truth remains obscured and injustice persists unabated, the fundamental rights of individuals are relegated to the margins, rendering a clear comprehension of justice exceedingly complex and fraught with difficulties.

4. Self-Created Justice

In our quest to grasp the essence of justice and its appropriate definition, we may find ourselves reconsidering our circumstances and personal judgments alongside other principles. We oscillate between different rationales for justice while attempting to persuade opposing parties to relinquish their positions in light of the arguments we present. This process involves what can be termed moral recognition - engaging in moral reasoning that aligns with our ultimate conclusions. Thus, we navigate between substantiated facts and justifications deemed inappropriate, returning repeatedly to similar conditions aimed at undermining the stance of opposing parties - who are essentially the victims of our transgressions and have inflicted profound suffering upon them. Our moral attitudes towards the critical issue of injustices faced by victims are characterised by a consistent pattern of biases against their rights. It is evident that these moral perspectives are intertwined with our personal and collective interests, which we seek to promote and enforce through self-established rules and provisions. When these measures prove ineffective, we resort to resolutions, and ultimately, sanctions. *This suggests that we impose sanctions when weaker nations do not align with our interpretation of justice.*

Grasping the definition of justice is not straightforward; it requires a profound understanding of the political context of the time and its impact on the administration of justice by those who serve injustice. For such individuals, wrongful conduct often masquerades as justice. This situation implies that victims exist in the shadow of justice, rather than in its light. This shadow is not tangible; it offers not a true reflection but rather a mere illusion of justice, attainable only through tears and the longing for the realisation of rights and morality. A stark example of this is the plight of the Palestinian

---

Gentle Civilizer of Nations: the Rise and Fall of International Law, 1870-1960 (Cambridge University Press 2002); Farhad; Farhad Malekian, *Gravity of Wisdom in International Criminal Law* (New York: Nova Science Publishers, 2021).

population, exacerbated by the actions of the Zionist government and the complicity of many Western states.[14] When established rights are manipulated as political tools by malevolent governments, discussions of justice and equality become nearly impossible, even in their most abstract forms. *Consequently, the pursuit of genuine justice transforms into a utopian dream, rendering justice for the victims so elusive that it feels utterly unattainable.*[15]

Consequently, the pursuit of justice is not an isolated endeavour; rather, it is deeply entangled with national interests. Thus, in instances of significant violations of others' rights, we often seek broader support - support that is readily extended to both strong and weak entities. However, this support frequently becomes lost amid a cacophony of voices that operate without tangible impact, as the authority over justice lies predominantly with those

---

[14] "Yet, in the opinion of the Israeli government, all views expressed love for Zionism or love for Israel or love of one's own country. One can perceive all these possibilities in the actions of the country. The Nazi government expressed similar opinions when it started its infanticide against the innocent Jewish population, which had deep root of civilisation in Europe.6 Here, as we can see, such actions integrate three concepts of norms. These were the norms of legality, morality, and love. Nazism had its own concept of legality, morality, and expression of power to control human minds. It is true that Nazism and relevant integrated bodies changed the concept of morality in most of Germany. Their speeches show that the law was morality and morality the whole law, and the latter the presentation of the entire philosophy of how man should and should not behave and what the pure meaning of the term "need" was. We are cognisant of the fact that violations, decisions, or conducts, which are not based on the obvious reason of human beings' need, cannot be good choices for the structure of law and are therefore legally or philosophically invalid. One should not force human beings to accept conditions which are not fair and not based on the power of love for justice. Thus, we need a scrupulous examination of the growing improvement of international criminal law in order to understand why we have not succeeded by legal and moral codes in implementing the system among different civilisations and why the quality of criminal law and international criminal law has to be measured by the canon of love. *Unfortunately, the norms of international criminal law and human rights law and the entire structure of United Nations law are becoming a question of quantity rather than quality today*." Farhad Malekian, *Judgments of Love in Criminal Justice* (Switzerland: Springer: 2017, 2018), pp. 206-207.

[15] "The Palestinian population is facing the barbaric behaviour of the political Zionist government towards its children. Surprisingly, the barbarity of ignoring the provisions of human rights in the office of the prosecutor is taking the lives of innocent children. Moreover, mothers, fathers, and relatives are all being killed while the prosecutor of the ICC is sleeping in their bedrooms of political power. They are being killed not because they are Palestinians, but because they are human animals, and therefore should not enjoy the rules of proportionality, peremptory international criminal justice, or humanitarian law during. Consequently, judges and prosecutors of the ICC sit on their knees in order to protect their positions and there is no valiant lawyer present in the court of criminal justice. *Despite the prosecutor's recent activity in addressing accountability for certain Israeli leaders, it is clearly too late following the killing of forty thousand civilians."* Farhad Malekian, *International Crime of Blackboard-Barbarism* ((New York: Nova Science Publishers, 2025), p.83.

who possess the power to define what should be acknowledged and accomplished. As a result, meaningful dialogues regarding moral reasoning are supplanted by discussions dominated by military might. This situation opens the door to various challenges and reactions from victims, which may manifest as violence or destruction within their communities. Such dynamics indicate a failure of moral rights and principles to function effectively. *When moral considerations are disregarded, the erosion of the justice system becomes both evident and feasible. Consequently, victims - including myself - find ourselves engaged in internal conflicts. This illustrates our inability to reach a consensus on an appropriate definition of justice; instead, we encounter a notion of justice that resembles a veto within the lexicon of legal jurisdiction and the United Nations' Charter.* The Charter should protect justice and lies:

> The Organization and its Members, in pursuit of the Purposes stated in Article 1, shall act in accordance with the following Principles.
> 1. The Organization is based on the principle of the sovereign equality of all its Members.
> 2. All Members, in order to ensure to all of them the rights and benefits resulting from membership, shall fulfill in good faith the obligations assumed by them in accordance with the present Charter.
> 3. All Members shall settle their international disputes by peaceful means in such a manner that international peace and security, and justice, are not endangered.
> 4. All Members shall refrain in their international relations from the threat or use of force against the territorial integrity or political independence of any state, or in any other manner inconsistent with the Purposes of the United Nations.
> 5. All Members shall give the United Nations every assistance in any action it takes in accordance with the present Charter, and shall refrain from giving assistance to any state against which the United Nations is taking preventive or enforcement action.
> 6. The Organization shall ensure that states which are not Members of the United Nations act in accordance with these Principles so far as may be necessary for the maintenance of international peace and security.
> 7. Nothing contained in the present Charter shall authorize the United Nations to intervene in matters which are essentially within the domestic jurisdiction of any state or shall require the Members to submit such matters to settlement under the present Charter; but this principle shall

not prejudice the application of enforcement measures under Chapter VII.[16]

In order to address the issue of justice, the discussion surrounding its scope and principles remains open to new perspectives from readers. However, it is evident that there are no positive outcomes that warrant our concern. Logically speaking, there should be a response to the opinions of victims or those who are severely targeted by discrimination. Yet, for reasons unrelated to the social conditions of these victims, their opinions are neither validated nor respected. Every significant question is overlooked, buried beneath the suffering of the victims. We find ourselves in a situation that is not unpredictable, given the immeasurable military and political power wielded by those in the highest positions within the United Nations. Thus, the fundamental rights of nations are disregarded, and the obstacles to achieving these rights are politically, legally, and morally nonsensical. As a result, the pain felt within the homes and hearts of the victims becomes a permanent affliction. This persists despite the universal aversion to suffering and the widespread desire to attain rights. *In this context, no moral framework is offered to the victims, while political and military pressure on them intensifies daily, with the singular aim of displacing them from their lands and annihilating entire populations.*[17]

5. Games Rooted in the Reasoning of Injustice

The philosophy of justice has been examined in various contexts, particularly evident during the meetings of different organs within the United Nations. Indeed, every issue brought before these gatherings pertains to determining the appropriate decision, thereby engaging with the concept of justice consistently. Consequently, a significant criticism of the discourse surrounding justice, widely acknowledged by many, is its failure to uphold the fundamental rights of victims. This shortcoming has repeatedly manifested not only in the actions of major powers but also in the voting procedures of the Security Council. By prioritising a collective sense of satisfaction regarding

[16] Article 2 of the United Nations Organisation.

[17] Examine Antonio Cassese, (ed.), *The New Humanitarian Law of Armed Conflict* (Naples: Editoriale Scientifica, 1979); Thomas G. Weiss, *Military-Civilian Interactions: Humanitarian Crises and the Responsibility to Protect* (2nd ed., Rowman & Littlefield Publishers Inc, Lanham (MD), 2005).

international human rights declarations or conventions, the theoretical framework of justice within this organisation can often both overlook and undermine victims' rights.

Although individual rights have been emphatically articulated in human rights declarations and subsequent instruments, they are frequently regarded as valid only when those who are vulnerable are subjected to the will of more powerful entities that disregard their entitlements. This assertion is substantiated by observable patterns in conflicts instigated by dominant powers. It suggests that whenever instances of injustice are obscured, one should examine them through the lens of power politics and observe how authoritarian regimes impose sanctions on weaker victims with apparent impunity of their political association.[18]

Similar arguments can be observed in the current global context, where the victims are subjected to the whims of powerful entities and their political, economic, and moral machinations. This observation does not imply that these dominant powers lack an understanding of right and wrong or are unaware of what constitutes a crime. Rather, the issue lies in their subjective interpretations of justice, which inherently conflict with the rights of the victims. This suggests that significant political powers have already predetermined their expansionist agendas, rendering them indifferent to acknowledging the legitimate and evident rights of those victimised. Moreover, these influential governments, which construe justice within their own frameworks and impose it upon the world, do not merely infringe upon

[18] "But what is a 'political' association from the sociological point of view? What is a 'state'? Sociologically, the state cannot be defined in terms of its ends. There is scarcely any task that some political association has not taken in hand, and there is no task that one could say has always been exclusive and peculiar to those associations which are designated as political ones: today the state, or historically, those associations which have been the predecessors of the modern state. Ultimately, one can define the modern state sociologically only in terms of the specific means peculiar to it, as to every political association, namely, the use of physical force. 'Every state is founded on force,' said Trotsky at Brest Litovsk. That is indeed right. If no social institutions existed which knew the use of violence, then the concept of 'state' would be eliminated, and a condition would emerge that could be designated as 'anarchy,' in the specific sense of this word. Of course, force is certainly not the normal or the only means of the state nobody says that but force is a means specific to the state. Today the relation between the state and violence is an especially intimate one. In the past, the most varied institutions beginning with the sib –have known the use of physical force as quite normal. Today, however, we have to say that a state is a human community that (successfully) claims the monopoly of the legitimate use of physical force within a given territory. Note that 'territory' is one of the characteristics of the state. Specifically, at the present time, the right to use physical force is ascribed to other institutions or to individuals only to the extent to which the state permits it." Max Weber, *Politics as a Vocation* (1948), pp. 77-78.

victim rights; they also engage in actions that are morally reprehensible as well as legally indefensible under both domestic and international law. Specifically, they orchestrate scenarios of torture designed to humiliate victims - scenarios so extensive and pervasive that they aim to obliterate any future aspirations among victims to seek justice.[19] Consequently, international criminal justice is redefined as a mechanism for preserving humanity and ensuring equality among diverse groups or nations.[20]

Through the implementation of torture and the extraction of false information and accusations, these authorities believe they are eliciting intelligence from alleged terrorists. It is at this juncture that justice devolves into a mere game or becomes a pretext for egregious violations of international criminal law - serving instead the self-serving interests of authoritarian regimes.[21] Therefore, the actions of powerful criminals not only lack justice, but they also violate the moral imperative surrounding the issue of justice, particularly in relation to the torture of innocent individuals and victims. This violation is perpetrated by those who purport to be representatives of justice while simultaneously engaging in efforts to establish peace among nations. Substituting scenarios involving torture with those involving terrorists can attain a clearer understanding of this situation. In this context, it becomes evident that the negotiators of justice or representatives of humanity often label groups, nations, or self-defence entities acting on behalf of victims as terrorists. It is evidently unrealistic for the constructs of justice to suggest that every grievance presented by victims is erroneous while deeming all actions

[19] Neil Sammonds, War on Gaza: How Israeli Torture Methods Resemble Islamic State Horrors, https://www.middleeasteye.net/opinion/gaza-war-israeli-torture-methods-resemble-islamic-state-horrors. Examine also Michael Otterman, *American Torture: From the Cold War to Abu Ghraib and Beyond* (Pluto Press, 2007); Kristine Huskey with Aleigh Acerni, Justice at Guantanamo: One Woman's Odyssey and Her Crusade for Human Rights (2009).

[20] "My depiction of the system of international criminal justice is not about finding a way to cure it, since the system is so ill and damaged that it cannot be treated with the expression of rules or theories. The only alternative to the reestablishment and application of a healthy system of international criminal justice is to achieve an understanding of its sickness and to place weight on ethical and moral values, which in turn could potentially affect the respect of its intentions. As we know, the system is a large and complex piece of legislation that consists of different parts and expresses a broad variety of philosophical issues that should not be treated generally by argumentation, but rather by the *theory of wisdom and tolerance*." Farhad Malekian, *Barrels of Justifications Violating International Criminal Responsibility* (New York: Nova Science Publishers, 2025), p.xiii.

[21] Farhad Malekian, *Conundrums of Paternalism in International Criminal Justice* (New York: Nova Science Publishers, 2024). See also Farhad Malekian, I*mperative Philosophy of International Criminal Justice: Visible Power – Invisible Essence* (New York: Nova Science Publishers, 2022); Farhad Malekian, *Tour de force of Moral Virtue in International Criminal Justice* (New York: Nova Science Publishers, 2022).

taken by criminals as justified. This observation underscores the fact that the concept and definition of "justice," along with its application, are manipulated and monopolised by unjust governmental mechanisms.

Those who believe that the system of international criminal justice remains unviolated are not only mistaken but also complicit in the ongoing genocide in Gaza.[22] To address this objection regarding genocide, we do not need to resort to violence; it is sufficient to acknowledge the criminal decisions made through the use of vetoes, whether directly or indirectly. This implies that it is impossible to consolidate all moral interpretations of justice into a singular value for our decisions or practical policies. Consequently, our significant decisions regarding the perpetration of genocide against victims are validated and allowed by criminal states, which continue to drag innocent individuals into the abyss of injustice.

Undoubtedly, we tend to overlook the principles and definitions associated with appropriate justice in favour of acknowledging others' rights while disregarding those rights for our own private interests. In simpler terms, if we assert that a government, which supports genocide in Gaza through various means, is just and equitable, we undermine the foundations of fair justice and insult the concept of human dignity itself. *There is no doubt that anyone who claims that the acts of genocide in Gaza do not constitute genocide or fail to contravene international criminal justice fundamentally ignores the universal nature of human rights. The moral integrity of the justice system, particularly in the realm of international human rights, is increasingly compromised by criminal elements.*

[22] For the crime of genocide, see J. Duffett, Against the Crime of Silence (New York, London, 1968). W. Michael Reisman, 'Legal Responses to Genocide and Other Massive Violations of Human Rights,' 59 Law and Contemporary Problems (1996), p.75; William L. Hurlock, 'The International Court of Justice: Effectively Providing a Long Overdue Remedy for Ending State-Sponsored Genocide (Bosnia-Herzegovina v. Yugoslavia),' 12 American University Journal of International Law and Policy (1997), p.299; Beth van Schaack, 'The Crime of Political Genocide: Repairing the Genocide Convention's Blind Spot,' 106 Yale Law Journal (1997), p.2259; John D. van der Vyver, 'Prosecution and Punishment of the Crime of Genocide,' 25 Fordham International Law Journal (1999), p.286; Mary Robinson, Genocide, War Crimes, Crimes Against Humanity, 25 Fordham International Law Journal (1999), p.275.

6. Deteriorating Justice

Let us revisit the question of whether all values of justice can be defined within the framework of legislation. Specifically, how can we legislate the moral principles connected to humanity in legal terms, particularly in the constitutions of states that advocate for democracy and uphold international human rights standards, yet whose actions often contradict these ideals? Some legislative frameworks may attempt to analyse the interplay between morality and justice. It is even posited that Kantian philosophy has influenced constitutional systems regarding the role of imperative morality.[23] However, it is fundamentally impossible to encapsulate the essence of morality within the language of a constitution.[24]

Even if we strive to do so, the language of the law often lacks the trustworthiness necessary to convey the true essence of morality without potential misinterpretation. One of the issues with judgements passed by various judges is that they are all reading the same passages but coming away with an individual understanding of what the words mean in practice. Legal provisions in a manner that ensures its protection cannot adequately or effectively regulate the value of human life. Since the adoption of the Universal Declaration of Human Rights, and even extending back to the codifications of international humanitarian law nearly two hundred years ago, we have witnessed the deaths of millions, often justified under the guise of implementing human rights norms. These tragic losses underscore the moral shortcomings of legislation and, more profoundly, the vacuous rhetoric of the United Nations Charter.

However, powerful governments, including those that profess to uphold human rights and democracy, often act in ways that undermine the effectiveness of our legislation and reveal their inability to enforce the law. Simultaneously, they may protect injustices. This indicates that no legislation or treaty provisions can embody the essence of morality or yield positive outcomes. It is pertinent to note that the value of humanity diminishes progressively due to our individual interests that lead to the infringement of humanitarian principles and the portrayal of injustices as if they were just. This assertion is substantiated by practical evidence. Powerful governments tend

---

[23] Farhad Malekian, The Mirage of International Criminal Law: Kant Metaphysics of *Mens Rea* (Cambridge: Cambridge Scholars Publishing, 2018), pp. 60-61.

[24] Read also views of Nietzsche Friedrich, Beyond Good and Evil (2014); Nietzsche Friedrich, On the Genealogy of Morality: A Polemic (19998); Clark, Maudemarie Nietzsche on Truth and Philosophy (1991).

not to perceive the plight of victims as a consequence of their own actions, a stance that is directly or indirectly corroborated by the behaviour of numerous Western governments.

The challenge lies in addressing the arguments put forth by these powerful entities and their allies, given that their ethical, legal, and moral foundations are so tenuous that they cannot be effectively countered through systematic references to the crimes committed by their military forces or the violation of victims' rights. A perspective that is unable or unwilling to acknowledge reality cannot be swayed by additional arguments; hence, our efforts in articulating any commentary become increasingly futile. This issue has reached epidemic proportions and poses significant challenges for both current and future generations.[25]

A recurring inquiry pertains to how the international human rights system can maintain strength and efficacy within legal circles and courts when it is evident that justice-related questions are compelled to align with the agendas of major political factions. Traditionally, most legal practitioners tend to align themselves with a particular party they deem favourable. This practice of selecting allegiance based on prevailing authority not only undermines the integrity of the international human rights framework but also severely isolates the theory underpinning international criminal justice. While we acknowledge that lawyers possess the autonomy to endorse specific legal policies, they also bear responsibility for perpetuating misunderstandings regarding the role of law. This becomes especially critical in contexts where foundational principles of international law are called into question by dubious arguments propagated by dominant powers, which often seek to monopolise legal frameworks at the expense of weaker nations. Thus, we find ourselves confronting a scenario devoid of any moral foundation beyond the pernicious tenets of inequality and injustice espoused by authoritarian regimes under the guise of upholding democratic norms.

It is imperative to recognise that the liberties afforded to lawyers and the freedom to express opinions do not inherently grant them the right to undermine the lives of individuals by endorsing the immoral and inhumane

[25] Rawls interprets this by saying that "The veil of ignorance is so natural a condition that something like it must have occurred to many. The formulation in the text is implicit, I believe, in Kant's doctrine of the categorical imperative, both in the way this procedural criterion is defined and the use Kant makes of it. Thus when Kant tells us to test our maxim by considering what would be the case were it a universal law of nature, he must suppose that we do not know our place within this imagined system of nature." John Rawls, *A Theory of Justice* (1999), p.118.

actions perpetrated by governments. This limitation becomes particularly evident when the policies of authoritarian regimes entail the unlawful killing of innocent individuals, alongside the occupation and appropriation of their resources. Such actions exemplify a utilitarian philosophy that prioritises self-interest, personal satisfaction, and sovereign development at the expense of other groups, nations, or governmental rights.

The aforementioned instances prompt a critical examination as to why we should accept that colonial or imperialist governments can continue to uphold enforced and appropriated rights belonging to others. Our assertions regarding the criminal activities conducted by dominant states against the principles underpinning international human rights and criminal justice are substantiated; therefore, they cannot be dismissed as mere conjecture. These violations persistently manifest themselves in observable ways. Consequently, any dissenting opinion from any international lawyer cannot be deemed accurate or partially accurate. The crimes of genocide and crimes against humanity cannot be trivialised by legal writings or through passive complicity with those who perpetrate such offenses.[26]

Ultimately, through an unwavering focus on self-gain, authoritarian governments engage in international crimes and infringe upon the rights of victims to such an extent that it could lead to the systematic extermination of entire groups or nations; a salient illustration of this is found in the experience of Indigenous peoples of North America, whose rights were completely obliterated by British colonial powers. A similar fate befell Australia's Aboriginal population, which was almost entirely eradicated by British imperialist forces. Analogous conclusions can be drawn regarding various regions worldwide, including, notably, the Palestinian people, whose rights were initially usurped by agents of British colonial governance.

7. Spirit of Authoritarian Injustice Infringing Justice

The paramount issue in the realm of justice is its intrinsic relationship with truth. In its absence, the concepts of justice and injustice may lead a nation to

---

[26] See even Schabas his own previous statements. William A. Schabas, Genocide in International Law, the Crime of Crimes (2000); Matthew Lippman, 'Genocide,' in International Criminal Law, Vol. I (M. Cherif Bassiouni, ed., 2008) pp. 405-455. In particular, see the statements of Bertrand Russell and the Russell International War Tribunal held in Stockholm, Sweden, May 2-10, 1967 and Roskilde, Denmark from November 20 to December 1, 1967. The Tribunal was essentially created as a result of different meetings in London in 1966.

a state of insignificance, indicative of its non-existence. It is not merely important to consider what justice accomplishes or how it administers and distributes the concept of justice; rather, it is crucial to examine the manner in which justice qualifies as just. This implies that any definition ascribed to justice must be devoid of any form of monopolisation, whether overt or covert. Overt monopolisation can be likened to the provisions outlined in Chapter VII of the United Nations Charter and the dominance exerted by certain member states over global international norms. An illustration of overt injustice occurs when a permanent member explicitly invokes its veto power to obstruct decisions it deems necessary, irrespective of potential violations against others' rights.

Conversely, covert monopolisation manifests through powerful criminal governments that impose their interests while employing direct or indirect means via other states, all while asserting they are safeguarding the enforcement of international human rights law norms.[27] This suggests that such a criminal government not only subtly undermines the framework of international criminal justice but also audaciously claims adherence to international human rights standards.[28] The clandestine violations stemming from this monopolisation are clear indicators of the frailty within international law and reflect an imposed system constructed under conventional or customary international law aimed at ostensibly protecting individuals from further suffering.

Both visible and invisible monopolisations within the frameworks of international criminal justice and human rights law are predicated on the speculations and interests of powerful governments, which constitute the true essence of existing legal frameworks.[29] Given that justice embodies the moral

---

[27] Some instruments of international law implying the right to justice, equality and peace are Charter of the United Nations, 1945; Universal Declaration of Human Rights, 1948; The Four Geneva Conventions of 12 August 1949; The 1977 Protocols Additional to the Geneva Conventions of 12 August 1949; International Covenant on Civil and Political Rights, 1966; International Covenant on Economic, Social and Cultural Rights, 1966; International Convention on the Elimination of All Forms of Racial Discrimination, 1965; Convention on the Elimination of All Forms of Discrimination against Women, 1979; Declaration on the Elimination of All Forms of Intolerance and of Discrimination based on Religion or Belief, 1981; Convention on the Rights of the Child, 1989; Statute of the International Tribunal for the Former Yugoslavia, 1993; Statute of the International Tribunal for Rwanda, 1994; Rome Statute of the International Criminal Court, 1998; Declaration on the Rights of Persons Belonging to National or Ethnic, Religious and Linguistic Minorities, 1992.

[28] *Id.*

[29] "One of the essential and fundamental arguments in the system of criminal justice concerns the relevance of the virtue of certain provisions regarding the proof of a guilty mind. This

foundation of norms, it ought to manifest this substance practically and refrain from favouring any elements that disregard the core principles of justice. Consequently, the standards of justice are not evaluated based on those who oversee the process of attaining justice but rather by the degree of equitable distribution of justice that is afforded. The failure to recognise the rights of victims - whether through overt or covert monopolisation - essentially represents a manifestation of the powerful imposing their will upon the vulnerable. This phenomenon has been particularly evident in the political and economic practices of the paternalistic governments that infringe upon the rights of other nations under the guise of upholding human rights law.[30] Such

---

is what I call the value of the philosophy of the system of international criminal justice, and it searches for and examines the elementary reasons for the existence or codification of certain laws. Thus, the invisible philosophy of the system is based on wisdom and not necessarily on the interests of the accused or their lawyers. As a result, we initiate a search for a common understanding of values that have been harmed or damaged during the commission of certain international crimes. Thus, the term "philosophy" in the system of international criminal justice not only has strong academic, abstract, and theoretical values, it also has preventive, defensive, precautionary, and demanding values concerning the realisation of the value of the virtue of certain provisions of core international crimes. In sum, the anatomy of the philosophy of the system of international criminal justice presents an analysis of the basis of, and concepts expressing, major beliefs in the structure of the relevant criminal legal discipline. In this way, the invisible legal philosophy of international criminal justice attempts to strengthen the visible parts of the legal discipline. With visible part, I refer here again to the observable, perceptible, evident, detectable, demonstrable, calculable, and obvious part of the system of international criminal justice which is normally referred to by international criminal lawyers, judges, and the prosecutors of international criminal courts. This means the system of philosophy within the international criminal justice is the same as that which is based on its invisible part and benefits from basic understandings of the law and is under philosophical pressure not to stray from the main understanding of the law. Thus, I am referring here to the original philosophy of the system of international criminal justice in combination with its original source. This does not necessary mean that I am separating the visible and invisible parts of the system of international criminal justice from each other. However, I would argue that no opinions or expressions, or judgments of any court, tribunals, or lawyers should be treated in isolation from the original/invisible parts of the system of international criminal law which aid in the interpretation of the legal system and refer to its framework. The philosophy of the system of international criminal justice here can therefore be considered a theory which underlies and contains a sphere of activity and thus underscores the development of the entire discipline. This means that the reasons behind such theories or dogma should not be mistreated or reduced through our actions which promote our personal interests. I therefore reject the influence of the theories of "criminalvisibilism," "criminalinvisibilism" and "powertionism." Farhad Malekian, I*mperative Philosophy of International Criminal Justice: Visible Power – Invisible Essence* (New York: Nova Science Publishers, 2022), pp. 26-27.

[30] Farhad Malekian, *Conundrums of Paternalism in International Criminal Justice* (New York: Nova Science Publishers, 2024). See also Farhad Malekian, I*mperative Philosophy of International Criminal Justice: Visible Power – Invisible Essence* (New York: Nova

actions exemplify a characteristic lack of impartiality inherent in authoritarian justice.

Authoritarian regimes invariably perceive their circumstances as both just and reliable within the framework of international criminal justice, often issuing directives to the International Criminal Court to adhere to their interpretations and fully respect their decisions. This situation raises serious questions regarding the integrity of international justice and subsequently engenders considerable debate concerning its quality, specifically whether it truly embodies essential justice and equality for its constituents. The resulting discourse challenges the very essence of justice, calling into question its authenticity with respect to victims' rights. This suggests that an obsession with power and wealth accumulation undermines the credibility of justice, thereby necessitating heightened scrutiny regarding its presentation.

When justice is predicated on upholding one party's claims while disregarding another's rights, the theoretical foundation for true justice erodes, rendering discussions about equality, fairness, and peace increasingly hollow. Consequently, it becomes imperative to address and rectify violations perpetrated by oppressive powers against other groups, nations, or governments. This task is essential yet complex, as the political policies of those in power function like an unyielding adhesive that cannot be extricated, leading to the death and isolation of its victims. Consequently, rectifying the destruction wrought by these policies is often rendered permanently unattainable due to the ongoing occupation of properties or territories belonging to victimised nations.[31] This reflects a harsh reality, despite our possession of appropriate tools aimed at alleviating the detrimental effects imposed upon other nations.

A pertinent illustration is found in the provisions of Chapter VII of the United Nations Charter, which have been formulated and adopted since 1944 against the inherent rights of other nations and remain fully applicable in all circumstances affecting victims of international crimes. This indicates that their impact has become even more detrimental since their inception. As a result, governments wielding power exploit their positions to impose their

---

Science Publishers, 2022); Farhad Malekian, *Tour de force of Moral Virtue in International Criminal Justice* (New York: Nova Science Publishers, 2022).

[31] Human Rights Council resolution 31/36 recalls reports of the UN Secretary-General, resolutions of the UN General Assembly and Security Council, an advisory opinion of the International Court of Justice and the opinions of several human rights bodies reaffirming the illegality of the Israeli settlements in the Occupied Palestinian Territory, including in East Jerusalem.

interpretations and dictate notions of justice. Thus, we lack a definitive standard of justice within the framework of international criminal law; any semblance of such justice is unattainable under the existing stipulations outlined in Chapter VII of the Charter. Consequently, attempts to compare justice levels across various international instruments with those dictated by Security Council provisions are futile and fail to uphold the rights of victims. This situation holds true even concerning the existence of the International Criminal Court (ICC) and its assertions regarding the promotion of justice.[32]

A court that fails to apprehend all criminals or initiate proceedings against influential offenders is not deemed fair, but rather completely unfair. How can we assert that judgments rendered by this court regarding African leaders are just and authoritative when it selectively targets certain criminals? This raises significant and legitimate concerns about the international criminal justice system and highlights serious infringements on victims' rights, resulting in millions suffering globally. A glaring example includes severe violations within international human rights frameworks and the deaths of countless

[32] M. Koskenniemi 'Solidarity Measures: State Responsibility as a New International Order?' 72 *BYIL*, (2001), pp. 337–56 ; Farhad Malekian, '*International Criminal Responsibility,*' in *International Criminal Law* (M. Cherif Bassiouni, 2[ed], ed., 1999); Gracia-Amador, 'The Crime of Apartheid: Responsibility and Reparations,' *Review of Contemporary Law* (1981), pp. 31-38 ; Jørgensen, *The Responsibility of States for International Crimes* (OUP Oxford 2000) ; A. de Hoogh *Obligations Erga Omnes and International Crimes: A Theoretical Inquiry into the Implementation and Enforcement of the International Responsibility of States* (Kluwer The Hague, 1996) ; A. Bellamy, *Responsibility to Protect: the Global Effort to End Mass Atrocities* (Polity Press, Cambridge, 2009) ; R. Bellamy (ed.), *C Beccaria, On Crimes and Punishments*. (1995) ; J. Crawford, S. Olleson, 'The Continuing Debate on a UN Convention on State Responsibility,' 54 *ICLQ*, (2005), 959–71 ; J. Hoover *Moral Practices: Assigning Responsibility in the International Criminal Court*, 76 *Law and Contemporary Problems* (2014), pp. 263-86 ; F. Malekian, 'Armenian Genocide and the Questions of Responsibility of the Turkish Government,' *House of Commons Conference on the Armenian Genocide, Armenian Solidarity, British-Armenian All-Party Parliamentary Group, No Security Publication* (2007), pp. 31-9. T. G. Weiss, *Military-Civilian Interactions: Humanitarian Crises and the Responsibility to Protect* (2nd ed., Rowman & Littlefield Publishers Inc., Lanham (MD), 2005) ; N. Roht-Arriaza, State Responsibility to Investigate and Prosecute Grave Human Rights Violations in International Law, 78 *California Law Review* 451 (1990) ; R. Rosenstock, 'An International Criminal Responsibility of States?,' in United Nations/International Law Commission (ed.), *International Law on the Eve of the Twenty-First Century: Views from the International Law Commission* (United Nations New York, 1997), pp. 265–85; Farhad Malekian, *International Criminal Responsibility of States: A Study on the Evolution of International Responsibility of States with particular Emphasis on the Concept of Crime and Criminal Responsibility* (Stockholm, 1985); Farhad Malekian, *System of International Law: Formation, Treaties, Responsibility* (Uppsala, 1987); Farhad Malekian, 'International Criminal Responsibility: International Criminal Responsibility of Individuals' in M. Cherif Bassiouni, *International Criminal Law,* Vol. *Crimes* (2[ed], ed., New York: Transnational Publishers, 1999).

innocent individuals under directives from the United States government. This is the way in which the lies of powerful governments empower all international criminal justice reasoning, with the intention of imposing the use of force and infringing on all forms of international criminal justice, including universal jurisdiction, upon international criminals. Universal jurisdiction does not follow the system of international criminal justice in the ICC, but is the traditional or classic international criminal jurisdiction, which has been exercised upon pirates or other war criminals.[33]

---

[33] *Id.*

Chapter 3

A Legacy of Shame: The Disgrace of International Justice

1. Marginalised Lifeboat of Justice

It is imperative to acknowledge that justice serves as a lifeboat, rescuing all individuals who have fallen victim to the unjust actions of others. This principle is especially pertinent when considering the frameworks established by the United Nations and the International Criminal Court, both of which are intended to uphold justice and protect those who subjected to unlawful treatment by powerful criminal governments. This protective role is particularly vital for states, nations, or governments that are vulnerable and fighting for their fundamental right to independence. Consequently, the United Nations bears the responsibility of maintaining an impartial framework of justice while safeguarding these entities within the international arena, ensuring that their rights remain inviolate through all available means. Thus, both the UN and the ICC bear not only a legal obligation but also a practical duty to uphold equitable justice and advocate for victims' rights.[1] They must

---

[1] The Preamble of the Statute of International Criminal Court in The Hague clearly states that "the States Parties to this Statute

Conscious that all peoples are united by common bonds, their cultures pieced together in a shared heritage, and concerned that this delicate mosaic may be shattered at any time,

Mindful that during this century millions of children, women and men have been victims of unimaginable atrocities that deeply shock the conscience of humanity,

Recognizing that such grave crimes threaten the peace, security and well-being of the world,

Affirming that the most serious crimes of concern to the international community as a whole must not go unpunished and that their effective prosecution must be ensured by taking measures at the national level and by enhancing international cooperation,

Determined to put an end to impunity for the perpetrators of these crimes and thus to contribute to the prevention of such crimes,

Recalling that it is the duty of every State to exercise its criminal jurisdiction over those responsible for international crimes,

Reaffirming the Purposes and Principles of the Charter of the United Nations, and in particular that all States shall refrain from the threat or use of force against the territorial integrity or political independence of any State, or in any other manner inconsistent with the Purposes of the United Nations,

neither evade their responsibilities nor selectively choose between perpetrators and victims. In this sense, they serve as guardians of justice's lifeboat.

A compelling argument posits that under current circumstances and evidence, members of the General Assembly should possess significantly greater voting authority than those of the Security Council if the genuine intent of achieving justice is to be realised. The absence of achieved justice renders its very existence meaningless. This assertion holds particular weight in relation to the ICC or claims presented under Chapter VII of the United Nations Charter.

The function of justice as a lifeboat is to advance its own cause and guide individuals toward the intended objectives outlined in numerous international conventions concerning human rights and justice. For any nation dismayed by the decisions of the Security Council and its unwarranted resolutions, the concept of justice appears to have already been diminished, rendering discussions about its existence futile. This suggests a relentless struggle to attain justice, which often seems elusive.

It can be asserted that justice has regrettably been undermined on multiple occasions, with arguments both for and against victims' rights severely compromised.[2] Consequently, all moral considerations have been reduced to

---

Emphasizing in this connection that nothing in this Statute shall be taken as authorizing any State Party to intervene in an armed conflict or in the internal affairs of any State,

Determined to these ends and for the sake of present and future generations, to establish an independent permanent International Criminal Court in relationship with the United Nations system, with jurisdiction over the most serious crimes of concern to the international community as a whole,

Emphasizing that the International Criminal Court established under this Statute shall be complementary to national criminal jurisdictions,

Resolved to guarantee lasting respect for and the enforcement of international justice.."

[2] It is significant to note that Article 68 of the Statute concerning Protection of the victims and witnesses and their participation in the proceedings

1. The Court shall take appropriate measures to protect the safety, physical and psychological well-being, dignity and privacy of victims and witnesses. In so doing, the Court shall have regard to all relevant factors, including age, gender as defined in article 7, paragraph 3, and health, and the nature of the crime, in particular, but not limited to, where the crime involves sexual or gender violence or violence against children. The Prosecutor shall take such measures particularly during the investigation and prosecution of such crimes. These measures shall not be prejudicial to or inconsistent with the rights of the accused and a fair and impartial trial.
2. As an exception to the principle of public hearings provided for in article 67, the Chambers of the Court may, to protect victims and witnesses or an accused, conduct any part of the proceedings in camera or allow the presentation of evidence by electronic or other special means. In particular, such measures shall be implemented in the case of a victim of sexual violence or a child who is a victim or a witness, unless otherwise ordered by the Court, having regard to all the circumstances, particularly the views of the victim or witness.

disregarded norms, and the principles of morality regarding victims' rights have been overlooked and appropriated by those who self-righteously claim legitimacy in their actions.

This situation demonstrates that while human rights principles are codified within our constitutions, they are readily transgressed. Moreover, those wielding legal authority often pursue self-serving interests at the expense of victims' rights, perpetually placing them in jeopardy.

Certainly, as long as justice is administered equitably and does not inflict harm upon any individual, all such analyses will ultimately fade away and fail to attract public interest. However, when the foundational rules or principles of justice are compromised, the very essence of fair justice is overlooked, leading to the marginalisation of victims' rights due to the gravity of violations perpetrated by an oppressive government. Consequently, one must consider the true extent of these violations. In other words, the discourse surrounding justice has not been adequately aligned with the magnitude of these violations.

Thus, our focus is often diverted towards comparing situations involving powerful entities rather than examining the inherent nature or substantive essence of the violations and their resultant harm. This implies that we fail to ascribe appropriate significance to both the extent and impact of these violations on their victims. Furthermore, it suggests that human dignity is not accorded paramount importance, and our flawed and circumscribed definition of appropriate justice ultimately erodes any potential for achieving moral rectitude. In effect, we dismantle both moral and legal principles while

---

3. Where the personal interests of the victims are affected, the Court shall permit their views and concerns to be presented and considered at stages of the proceedings determined to be appropriate by the Court and in a manner which is not prejudicial to or inconsistent with the rights of the accused and a fair and impartial trial. Such views and concerns may be presented by the legal representatives of the victims where the Court considers it appropriate, in accordance with the Rules of Procedure and Evidence.
4. The Victims and Witnesses Unit may advise the Prosecutor and the Court on appropriate protective measures, security arrangements, counselling and assistance as referred to in article 43, paragraph 6.
5. Where the disclosure of evidence or information pursuant to this Statute may lead to the grave endangerment of the security of a witness or his or her family, the Prosecutor may, for the purposes of any proceedings conducted prior to the commencement of the trial, withhold such evidence or information and instead submit a summary thereof. Such measures shall be exercised in a manner which is not prejudicial to or inconsistent with the rights of the accused and a fair and impartial trial.
6. A State may make an application for necessary measures to be taken in respect of the protection of its servants or agents and the protection of confidential or sensitive information."

obstructing any possibility of attaining justice for those who have suffered egregious injustices.

Our actions or responses may arise either from intentionality or inadvertence, stemming from our divergent interpretations of justice and varying levels of awareness among individuals. It remains true that each one of us endures the consequences resulting from unjust actions or decisions. This matter is particularly crucial in the context of international crimes perpetrated by powerful governments against weaker nations. Evidently, no nation or government globally condones the commission of international crimes against its own people, which underscores the suffering and frustration experienced by the marginalised majority of weaker nations due to violations of their rights. However, when a significant bloc of dominant governments aligns its perspective with that of their most influential counterparts, discussions on equitable justice and the representation of victims' rights become ineffective and virtually stagnant.

To clarify the debate surrounding justice, both the Security Council (SC) and the ICC must ensure that the concept and essence of equal justice are not compromised. This includes addressing whether acts resulting in mass killings can ever be deemed legally, morally, or professionally acceptable.

If this situation were merely hypothetical and not feasible, one must question why millions continue to suffer as a result of genocides committed against their nations or generations. This raises concerns about the tenability of international criminal justice and human rights law, which appear to rest precariously on unreliable principles concerning human dignity, equality among individuals, and most notably, the sovereign equality of all nations within the monopolised framework established by the United Nations Charter.[3] Consequently, it is imperative that the system governing international criminal justice and human rights law is reinforced with a more robust moral foundation. However, a fundamental ethical norm appears conspicuously absent from the current structure of international laws. Naturally, hegemonic governments and their allies may dispute this assertion.

---

[3] Consult Application of the Convention on the Prevention and Punishment of the Crime of Genocide (Bosnia and Herzegovina v. Serbia and Montenegro). Separate Opinion of Judge Weeramantry, http://www.icj-cij.org/docket/files/91/7361.pdf, 55.

2. Dissenting Toward True Forms of Justice

The central inquiry remains: why should we accept that maintaining justice under the jurisdiction of powerful or authoritarian governments - and allowing them to exercise legal authority - will effectively enhance the welfare of international society as a whole? The international human rights system and the framework of international criminal justice cannot sustainably operate in the long term if their interpretation and authority are subject to monopolisation. I do not intend to convey a dissenting perspective regarding the power of law or the enforcement mechanisms of international human rights and criminal justice out of personal inclination; rather, I wish to emphasise that both systems have demonstrated pathways to achieving justice and upholding humanity while ensuring that the principle of equality among all nations is preserved. The rationale is straightforward: the entire human rights framework underpins the structure of international criminal justice, and reciprocally, international criminal justice sustains the enforcement of human rights. This interdependence suggests that permitting these systems of international law to be monopolised, with varying definitions of justice dictated by dominant powers wielding authority through coercive means, diminishes the rights of individuals, groups, and nations.

Furthermore, it is essential to recognise that even when we express dissenting views contrary to those held by authoritarian governments - often misrepresented as democratic discourse - such dissent may indeed reflect valid truths. If articulated not from a standpoint of antagonism but with the genuine aim of fostering equality among all nations and acknowledging the shared dignity of all humanity across diverse geopolitical contexts, these dissenting perspectives can serve not only as affirmations of truth but also as corrective mechanisms for existing provisions within international criminal justice and human rights law that may be failing in their intended purposes. They can also propose alternatives for addressing the entrenched monopolisation of these legal frameworks under paternalistic regimes.[4] Moreover, should we assume that such dissenting viewpoints offer legally sound interpretations that counter those advanced by oppressive governments - subjecting their positions to rigorous scrutiny within an overarching commitment to international equality as enshrined in United Nations Statute? This approach would undoubtedly mitigate further suffering endured by individuals or nations resulting from

---

[4] Farhad Malekian, *Conundrums of Paternalism in International Criminal Justice* (New York: Nova Science Publishers, 2024).

unjust decisions and actions perpetrated by powerful criminal states. It would also protect against the entrenchment of monopolised reasoning and bias.

We refer here to the troubling justification provided by both political and legal authority vested in the Security Council, which consistently reflects a philosophy rooted in monopolisation rather than one grounded in equality or defence of individual, group, or national rights.[5] Therefore, it is crucial to determine whether dissenting opinions against powerful governments should be perceived as adversarial forces opposing justice or recognised as legitimate avenues through which principles of justice might be realised. The fundamental principle asserts that justice must be free from any external constraints and influences. If this essential requirement for justice is not considered necessary and vital, then the acceptance of a theory of justice - whether it is claimed to have been achieved or purported to be achievable - is not merely indicative of a prudential theory but, regrettably, suggests a fundamentally flawed premise. It is indeed true that attempting to circumscribe the principles of justice and aligning its norms with the daily outcomes derived from the interpretations of certain permanent members is both impractical and unwise, ultimately resulting in manifest injustice.

Without reservation, a system such as the United Nations, which imposes legal and official obligations on its members through the threat of military force and the arbitrary exercise of veto power, adheres to a flawed interpretation of international human rights law. This situation results in many nations succumbing to a detrimental conformity that undermines their independence and ultimately their integrity as a collective entity. Consequently, the provisions outlined in Chapter VII of the United Nations Charter strip nations of their sovereign capacity to advance international human rights law and support victims suffering from the criminal actions of governments whose conduct constitutes international crimes, reflecting a state

---

[5] "Thus, such states must ignore the truth while within the United Nations Security Council or anywhere else if their government wants to survive. This is obviously how the truth ought to be upheld by a rational government within an impartial international human rights jurisdiction. However, the fact is that the will and wishes of the Zionist government have targeted the rights of both Palestinians and of the Jews who oppose their actions. It then follows those opinions must be merely parroted from the Zionist government within all national, regional, or international economic, military, and political contexts. This is because they are never opposed to by any Western powers or powertionist governments in the Security Council. This is the core of the philosophy of the Zionist government which believes that their views should be given priority, particularly as it concerns the belief that the land of the Palestinians are on rightfully belongs to them." Consult Farhad Malekian, *International Crime of Blackboard-Barbarism* ((New York: Nova Science Publishers, 2025), p.160.

of barbarity. It is evident, without exaggeration, that the current framework for international human rights is reaching an alarming state that threatens the fundamental philosophy of these rights and erodes its validity and credibility. The imperative to respect the rights of nations to promote the rights of victims has become an essential aspect of the international criminal justice system - an unavoidable norm that must be upheld by all states, including permanent members of the Security Council and their allied regimes. This unwavering pursuit of justice creates not only perilous conditions for victims but also renders the realisation of their rights nearly unattainable within the context of international criminal justice history. This indicates that conceptions of justice may necessitate a more robust power base than currently exists.

The reality is that human faculties of perception are predominantly theoretical rather than empirical, which complicates the attainment of an accurate understanding of justice and fosters pessimism regarding its realisation. Consequently, the most significant acknowledgment within the concept of justice pertains to the theory of equality, which may also be perceived as heretical or unconventional. This implies that we are striving to establish moral equality as a foundational principle within the definition of justice, questioning whether justice truly embodies the ideal paradigm for human welfare or if it serves merely as a construct designed to satisfy and promote principles favourable to hegemonic powers. The foundation for discerning right from wrong rests upon justified circumstances; thus, since the prevailing conditions for presenting justice are inadequate, all forms of injustice are detrimental to the foundational theories of humanity and impede efforts to protect victims' rights from harm.

3. Logic of Injustice

In our discussions, the primary focus is not solely on the plight of victims but rather on the principles and scope of justice. If justice is not upheld, any efforts to assist victims become futile and lack substantive support. This implies that we must prioritise the preservation of justice principles if we are to advocate for the rights of victims and ensure that those entrusted with the administration of justice do not simultaneously undermine its foundational philosophy through various means and tactics. Our unwillingness to distinguish between justice and injustice, as articulated in Security Council resolutions or government declarations, places victims in a precarious position and denies them their inherent rights. Such an approach diminishes the significance of "justice" itself, rendering it a concept manipulated by powerful governments according to their preferences and strategic interests. A pertinent illustration of this is evident in Gaza, where culturally and traditionally established nations face egregious violations through acts characterised as genocide, crimes against humanity, and war crimes - all aimed at usurping territories and undermining sovereignty.

To put it differently, if acknowledging the traditional rights of a nation is deemed inappropriate due to conflicting interests with a criminal regime, how can victims hope to attain justice when it appears merely as a mechanism through which authoritarian governments enforce their sanctions and perpetrate criminal actions? When experiences of observing both justice being served and violated yield similar outcomes for victims, we risk trivialising the concept of justice itself, manipulating its definition through various political agendas that may be deemed unethical.[6] The pertinent question at hand is which approach is both just and rational: the malevolent justice practiced by criminal governments, or the equitable and wise recognition of the rights of all nations on an equal footing?[7] It is essential to clarify that our focus does not lie in evaluating the quality of justice or determining who supports it; these considerations are beyond our purview, nor do we engage with questions pertaining to justice as a contingent construct. Justice transcends the identification of parties that either uphold or oppose it. Rather, such a perspective transforms justice into a contest among various factions pursuing their individual interests. Consequently, this ceases to be justice and instead devolves into an assessment of power dynamics between groups, accompanied by diverse political and individualistic interpretations.

Justice does not require categorisation among individuals nor does it necessitate competing theories that undermine one another's foundational reasoning. It remains a neutral concept, impartial to external influences or vested interests. Justice neither serves as an arbiter of rights nor interests; rather, it embodies equality. When there exists equality of arms - where every individual is regarded with complete personal integrity, equivalent to that of others - justice prevails. This principle signifies that justice should not be distributed as if it were a commodity; rather, it must be perceived collectively

---

[6] Consult also Martti Koskenniemi, *The Politics of International Law* (Hart, 2011); Martti Koskenniemi, *The Gentle Civilizer of Nations: the Rise and Fall of International Law*, 1870-1960 (Cambridge University Press 2002);

[7] Examine Farhad Malekian, *Gravity of Wisdom in International Criminal Law* (New York: Nova Science Publishers, 2021); Farhad Malekian, *Powertionism in International Criminal Justice* (New York: Nova Science Publishers, 2022).

and individually as a singular entity grounded in equity across all dimensions - whether concerning voice, treatment variation among nations, ethnic diversity, or the status of individuals before courts established to uphold justice. Thus, neither national nor international courts should selectively designate certain individuals as criminals while exonerating others who contribute significantly to inequality and perpetuate various forms of systemic violations.

It is evident that the domain of justice faces substantial challenges in achieving accurate judgments and articulating truths with complete objectivity. Absent such objectivity, numerous criticisms arise regarding the philosophy of justice itself; one must question why we would label it 'justice' when it embodies elements of injustice. In essence, employing the coercive power of law to advance and entrench the desires of authoritative figures amounts to disregarding the rights of others while masquerading this conduct as moral convictions held by a majority within powerful governments. Such conduct is unequivocally morally objectionable when measured against the fundamental philosophy advocating for universal equality among all individuals and raises serious doubts about the true function underlying both national and international judicial theories.

These expressions reflect a profound faith in the appeal of the higher faculties of human reasoning, particularly concerning universal moral law and the natural rights of all individuals to be treated equitably. This implies that, in matters pertaining to justice and its interpretations, every issue of equality is fundamentally significant and not merely a lesser aspect of existence. As previously articulated, justice should not be viewed as a matter for negotiation; rather, it concerns how to attain its intrinsic values. Indeed, justice ought to eschew modesty and assert the rights of all individuals, affording them the opportunity to defend those rights. Should justice fail to recognise its purpose in relation to rights and equality, it risks leading to division and the monopolisation of others' rights.[8]

4. Resisting Against the Barbarity of Disingenuous Justice

Initially, it is often challenging to ascertain whether the foundational question of justice primarily serves profit or provocation. This is precisely the dilemma confronting the international community today. When the United Nations and

---

[8] *Id.*

the Universal Declaration of Human Rights were established, they were intended to comprehensively empower justice and its promotion. However, it soon became evident that both entities had evolved into mechanisms for consolidating the rights of weaker nations, resulting in an increasing number of victims subjected to unlawful justifications. The organisation's practical policies have demonstrated that contemporary notions of justice are predominantly aligned with the exercise of coercive power rather than genuine rights. As previously articulated, this represents a significant challenge facing international criminal justice today. Assisting others should not be mandated; nor should individuals be compelled to relinquish their possessions and territories.

The nation, group, or individual whose protective apparatus of "being" of *somebodiness* is destroyed by the system of inequality within the United Nations Charter will, of course, function differently than others because they have lost their existence.[9] The reason for this is that the visible system of the United Nations goes against the invisibility of its good formulations and intentions. This means that with our visible philosophy of international criminal justice, international human rights law, international organisations, the United Nations Charter, and a number of other bodies protecting human rights law, we deliberately disregard the very basic philosophy of the invisibility of the system and pretend that we have done nothing of the sort. However, these very strong governments and their very aggressive military powers feign ignorance regarding all matters which relate to the essence of humanity, justice, and the establishment of permanent peace.[10]

Nevertheless, under the influence of powerful governments, the system governing international criminal justice fails to uphold these principles and instead egregiously violates the sovereignty and inherent rights of other

---

[9] "W*e are obliged to respect the provisions of the law of somebodiness. In other words, the law of somebodiness is precisely what the law is and should be. This is because, as we have mentioned elsewhere, the law of somebodiness was the first primary law, and contains all laws within it-- even including traces of international peremptory law. Let us put the question of law so: if the objective of the laws that we have codified, such as those which address the protection of human rights, international criminal law, or the international humanitarian law of armed conflict, do not contain the law of somebodiness, then they must be flawed. This means that there must be some misunderstanding of the nature of law. Alternatively, if the intention of all these laws is to violate the law of somebodiness, then we do not have the law of somebodiness but the non-existence of all laws.* Farhad Malekian, *International Criminal Law, the Law of Somebodiness, the Law of Nobodiness* (New York, Nova Science Publishers, 2021).

[10] Farhad Malekian, I*mperative Philosophy of International Criminal Justice: Visible Power – Invisible Essence* (Nova Sciences Publishers, 2022), p.55.

nations. Setting aside any further discussion regarding the nature of justice or morality's paramount importance, let us consider whether justice can truly be equated with that which is imposed by aggressive Western governments upon other nations worldwide. Does such a definition of justice foster peace and respect for vulnerable victims? Would similar treatment be meted out to more powerful entities without inciting protest?

This line of reasoning leads us to the moral core of governmental power dynamics, which have long relied on a skewed interpretation of justice rather than honouring the rights of other nations. Numerous examples exist, too extensive to enumerate here, ranging from the egregious international crimes committed in Vietnam to the contemporary aggressive military strategies employed by the governments of the United States, Britain, Germany, and Turkey in Syria. If nations hold sovereignty over their territories and cultures, then why should they be subjected to domination - particularly by oppressive regimes - as history has often illustrated?

Given that nations are deemed equal under the principles outlined in the United Nations Charter and various international human rights treaties, they ought to have the right to govern themselves freely within their own territories without external coercion, let alone conditions akin to slavery. The tenets of the United Nations Charter and relevant international agreements assert that nations are entitled to determine their own futures and manage their sovereign resources; however, in a misguided attempt to prevent future violations vis-à-vis upholding international order, these powers engage in acts amounting to international crimes - including territorial annexation and policies constituting as genocide against entire populations.

In an effort to persuade other nations and provide reasoning that transcends mere logic, powerful governments, such as the United States, impose severe sanctions on countries that resist their unjust demands. Subsequently, any attempt to raise concerns regarding justice is met with the assertion that their interpretation constitutes the true essence of justice, thereby monopolising its definition. They further claim to embody civilised nations tasked with imparting lessons on justice to developing states.[11] This flawed and irrational line of reasoning reconfigures the understanding of justice - particularly international criminal justice - within the global political and legal

---

[11] Read also Baum L. M., 'Pursuing Justice in a Climate of Moral Outrage: An Evaluation of the Rights of the Accused in the Rome Statute of the International Criminal Court,' 19 *Wisconsin International Law Journal* (2001), 197; Hoover Joseph, 'Moral Practices: Assigning Responsibility in the International Criminal Court', 76 *Law and Contemporary Problems* (2014), pp. 263-86.

arenas. Consequently, institutions like the United Nations become instruments for enforcing the will and interests of certain dominant powers, including Israel, the United States, Britain, France, Australia, Canada, and Germany.

Consider an analogy wherein authoritarian governments strip individuals of their rights and property, justifying such actions as counterterrorism measures. What recourse do individuals have in such circumstances? Should we acquiesce to their claims over our lands, possessions, and natural resources, including gold and oil, or should we resist? When resistance is voiced through protest - expressing dissent - we are branded as terrorists. Western-imposed sanctions further vilify us as barbaric or uncivilised nations. While we may hope for a change in this oppressive conduct, such hopes often prove futile; thus, resistance becomes our only viable option.

This situation is precisely what those in power desire - they can easily label us as terrorists. Notably, these same Western governments are among the leading manufacturer of weapons for warfare and violence against civilians. When oppressive regimes plunder the resources of other nations, they leave victims with no alternative but to oppose the brutality inflicted upon them. Clearly, these authoritarian governments are not merely thieves; they also perpetrate terrorism themselves. This conclusion holds true irrespective of any rationalisations we attempt to employ or adjustments made regarding our actions - as seen in conflict zones such as Syria, Gaza, Afghanistan, Iraq, Libya, Lebanon, and elsewhere.

In articulating these interpretations and assertions, I do not infringe upon any government's rights; rather, I seek to uphold them. Regardless of how vigorously my views are contested, it is paramount that I advocate for the rights of all - both strong and weak. Our discourse on justice should not revolve around governmental power exerted over other states but must focus on ensuring that the concept of justice remains free from monopolisation. This principle is particularly relevant to the Charter of the United Nations, which ought to represent a commitment to righteousness and equity but often fails in this regard.[12] It is essential that our understanding of fair justice and just

---

[12] The United Nations Charter Chapter VI on the *Pacific Settlement of Disputes* reveals the existence of colonialism, fascism, and a dictatorship of powertionism government, which is responsible for controlling international peace. The irony of this situation is that the Security Council has brought equality, peace, and justice to the current contemporary situation in the world. United Nations Charter, Chapter VI:

Pacific Settlement of Disputes

Article 33

The parties to any dispute, the continuance of which is likely to endanger the maintenance of international peace and security, shall, first of all, seek a solution by negotiation, enquiry,

governance contributes to preserving its inherent purity without distortion or domination by powerful governments dictating its definition. Failure to do so renders any claim of justice within powerful governments not only perilous but also a catalyst for grave international crimes. The same holds true for unfortunate victims who serve as mere tools for aggressive powers and authoritarian regimes at home.

5. Metaphorical Consumption of Justice

The concept of justice resembles a fish - a vibrant and living entity while it remains within its aquatic environment; however, once it is removed from

---

mediation, conciliation, arbitration, judicial settlement, resort to regional agencies or arrangements, or other peaceful means of their own choice.

The Security Council shall, when it deems necessary, call upon the parties to settle their dispute by such means.

Article 34

The Security Council may investigate any dispute, or any situation which might lead to international friction or give rise to a dispute, in order to determine whether the continuance of the dispute or situation is likely to endanger the maintenance of international peace and security.

Article 35

Any Member of the United Nations may bring any dispute, or any situation of the nature referred to in Article 34, to the attention of the Security Council or of the General Assembly.

A state which is not a Member of the United Nations may bring to the attention of the Security Council or of the General Assembly any dispute to which it is a party if it accepts in advance, for the purposes of the dispute, the obligations of pacific settlement provided in the present Charter. The proceedings of the General Assembly in respect of matters brought to its attention under this Article will be subject to the provisions of Articles 11 and 12.

Article 36

The Security Council may, at any stage of a dispute of the nature referred to in Article 33 or of a situation of like nature, recommend appropriate procedures or methods of adjustment. The Security Council should take into consideration any procedures for the settlement of the dispute which have already been adopted by the parties. In making recommendations under this Article the Security Council should also take into consideration that legal disputes should as a general rule be referred by the parties to the International Court of Justice in accordance with the provisions of the Statute of the Court.

Article 37

Should the parties to a dispute of the nature referred to in Article 33 fail to settle it by the means indicated in that Article, they shall refer it to the Security Council. If the Security Council deems that the continuance of the dispute is in fact likely to endanger the maintenance of international peace and security, it shall decide whether to take action under Article 36 or to recommend such terms of settlement as it may consider appropriate.

Article 38

Without prejudice to the provisions of Articles 33 to 37, the Security Council may, if all the parties to any dispute so request, make recommendations to the parties with a view to a pacific settlement of the dispute.

water and captured by fishing means, it transforms into a metaphorical representation of others' rights under false pretences - that it willingly entered our nets. This illustrates how international criminals articulate their interpretation of justice and their belief in the right to exploit any fishing grounds. Authoritarian criminal governments and major criminal regimes subsequently allocate their fishing apparatus among various factions that they deem suitable for executing their intentions, thereby facilitating the implementation of their covert agendas. This ultimately culminates in a widespread deployment of their fishing nets.

While this analogy may appear unrealistically figurative, it is crucial to acknowledge that the overarching policies adopted by those intent on undermining the structure of international criminal justice and advancing their illicit objectives are themselves often unrealistic. They are themselves often unrealistic yet frequently succeed in claiming the lives of millions of innocent individuals who remain oblivious to being ensnared by the might of authoritarian or paternalistic governments.[13] Such governments operate under the delusion that the system of international law and the framework of international criminal justice are inherently theirs to manipulate.[14]

In truth, this notion not only is valid but has also become an established reality permeating the entire framework of international human rights law. It can be asserted that both the systems of international criminal justice and international humanitarian law governing armed conflicts function as two interconnected platforms, each grounded in a theoretical construct derived from international human rights law. *However, this legal framework does not genuinely uphold human rights as intended; instead, it serves to guide individuals toward goals while fostering illusions of prosperity and perpetually favourable conditions throughout their existence. When one is seduced by principles related to material gain or monetary justice, justice itself becomes analogous to a predatory fishing expedition. This occurs because there are fish that possess greater strength than others do; thus, for personal gain or lucrative opportunities, certain fish find themselves at risk from formidable predators such as sharks, whales, and saltwater crocodiles. This represents a stark reality of how justice is administered for the majority within this metaphorical context, rendering them victims of unlawful schemes orchestrated by powerful governments.*

---

[13] Farhad Malekian, *Conundrums of Paternalism in International Criminal Justice* (New York: Nova Science Publishers, 2024).

[14] *Id.*

A pertinent example can be seen in the administration of justice under NATO's auspices - particularly involving the United States, British, Israeli, and Turkish governments in Syria. These entities have sought to disarm a dictator while concurrently imposing their own form of dictatorship and partitioning Syria, along with its resources, among themselves. This underscores a manifestation of international dictatorship superseding national sovereignty. The majority of individuals who have suffered injustices at the hands of their governing authorities, with the expectation of attaining freedom and equitable treatment, often align themselves with the criminal ideologies perpetuated by dominant powers - represented metaphorically as killer whales and saltwater crocodiles. They believe they are engaged in a struggle against the sustained injustices imposed by their dictators, even as the military apparatuses of the aforementioned governments undermine their efforts.

The true nature of justice and the ways in which major offenders manipulate its theoretical frameworks are exemplified by this situation. Their manipulation is carried out under the pretence of promoting and reinforcing international human rights principles. Consequently, many advocates for justice, particularly within the realm of international criminal justice, define this concept in a manner that aligns with the priorities and elevated interpretations of justice theory held by their adversaries. They also endorse the establishment of international criminal courts, but only when such courts direct their scrutiny toward victims or those whom powerful entities label as terrorists.[15] The fundamental issue lies not in the intended purpose behind the creation of the International Criminal Court but rather in the monopolisation of rights wielded by influential governments on the Security Council, whose demands must be satisfied.

In essence, there exists a form of judicial cannibalism orchestrated by dominant criminal governments; this phenomenon signifies a profound

---

[15] Consult also Farhad Malekian, *Corpus Juris of Islamic International Criminal Justice* (Cambridge Scholars Publishing, 2017), p. 17; M Abdel Haleem (ed.), *Criminal Justice in Islam: Judicial Procedure in the Sharīah* (2000); Abdelkader, Deina, *Social Justice in Islam* (Herndon, VA: IIIT, 2000); Mohamed Elewa Badar, 'Islamic Criminal Justice in the 21st Century,' *International Criminal Law Review*, Vol. 9, Number 4, 2009, pp. 591-595; M. Cherif Bassiouni, *The Islamic Criminal Justice System* (London: Oceana Publications, 1982); M. Cherif Bassiouni, 'Protection of Diplomats under Islamic Law,' *74 American Journal of International Law* (1980), pp. 609-655;, M. Cherif Bassiouni, '*Islam: Concept, Law and Word Habeas Corpus*,' 2 *Rutgers Camden Law Journal* (1970); M. Cherif Bassiouni, *Sources of Islamic Law, and the Protection of Human Rights in the Islamic Criminal Justice System*, see Bassiouni, pp. 5-55;, M. Cherif Bassiouni, *Studies in Early Hadith Literature* (Indianapolis, 1978); Richard Bell, *Introduction to the Quran*, (Edinburgh University Press, 1955).

examination and characterisation of justice itself. In this context, it is these criminal regimes that effectively dictate notions of justice and identify who qualifies as a criminal. Notably, they consistently portray themselves as innocent while casting their opponents as wrongdoers. Thus, all manifestations of this judicial cannibalism remain acceptable so long as they serve the objectives of authoritarian states - evident in cases such as Syria's conflict, mass genocidal actions in Gaza, and genocide committed against Vietnamese communities.

However, if we were to adopt these perspectives, they would only be deemed valid when judgments from the International Criminal Court target those who do not adhere to an established definition of justice predetermined by representatives of oppressive regimes. It is conceivable that powerful criminal governments may acknowledge rulings from this court when such decisions condemn other nations opposing their aggressive human rights policies - illustrated by instances like Ukraine's situation involving U.S. and NATO intervention.[16] This case demonstrates that Western or NATO governments critical of Russian policies are perceived as correct in their interpretation, while those denouncing NATO actions or U.S. aggression are deemed misguided.

6. Desperate Justice

The question regarding the issue of justice is: why do we consistently prioritise our own interests, which often infringe upon the significant rights of victims? This reflects a form of exploitation of the rights of weaker nations, which we control through various means, particularly through the power of our military forces. This is precisely what NATO countries do to appease their dominant leadership. Consequently, the principles of international human rights and international criminal justice have become increasingly disregarded within the global criminal justice system. Perhaps this is due to our concern for our own lives, which leads us to overlook the destruction of others' lives, preventing

---

[16] Farhad Malekian, *Powertionism in International Criminal Justice* (Nova Sciences Publishers, 2022); Farhad Malekian, 'Conundrums of *Jus cogens:* In Case Law' (Part II), No. 13 *Вісник Південного регіонального центру Національної академії правових наук України,* [No. 13 *Journal of the South regional Center of National Academy of Legal Sciences of Ukraine*] (2017), pp. 12-21; Farhad Malekian, 'Conundrums of *Jus cogens*: in International Criminal Law' (Part I), *Вісник Південного регіонального центру Національної академії правових наук України* [*No.12 Journal of the South regional Center of National Academy of Legal Sciences of Ukraine*] (2017), pp. 8-16.

us from responding to the aggressive and brutal actions of powerful governments and their heinous crimes against humanity.

Many governments that comply with the harsh directives of the United States, for instance, fear sanctions and restrictions on their activities. For example, Sweden follows the United States' lead to ensure its survival and maintain its right to produce and sell weapons. This indicates that the threat of coercion influences its decisions regarding international policy, shaping its choices between right and wrong.[17] We assert that the system of international human rights and international criminal justice is significantly undermined by the Swedish government's diplomatic actions aimed at survival.[18] This country's government bases its arguments on the principle of democracy and particularly emphasises the importance of international human rights law in all matters.[19]

Therefore, there is no reason to assume that the affluent will relinquish the benefits derived from the trade of weapons. Consequently, human rights are violated, and the international criminal justice system does not function properly. When it does function, it is primarily directed at the leaders of governments with African backgrounds. This is not merely a statement; it is an attempt to highlight false and unlawful accusations. A brief examination of the history of the establishment of the United Nations reveals that all accused individuals have been Africans. Strangely enough, there has not been a single Western leader who has been accused and condemned by the International Criminal Court. This situation is evidently untenable, as the justice system appears to be defined and applied in ways that are acceptable to powerful criminal government regimes.

Furthermore, judges are often, directly or indirectly, influenced by the interests of powerful governments. This implies that judges are, in one way or another, compelled to align the court's decisions with the agendas of these powerful governments to safeguard the fruits of justice in favour of oppressive regimes. This assertion is supported by evidence and should not be dismissed as an exaggeration of the injustices associated with the term.

This is true even though none of these criminal government regimes are parties to the Statute of the Court; nevertheless, they act as the primary arbiters of the Court, determining who falls under its jurisdiction. The duty of the International Criminal Court extends beyond the prosecution of criminals; it

---

[17] Consult Farhad Malekian, *International Crime of Blackboard-Barbarism* ((New York: Nova Science Publishers, 2025).

[18] *Id.*

[19] *Id.*

also involves articulating the truth about justice and its definition. However, none of the judges or prosecutors of the Court have taken significant action against any major terrorist criminal governments in the world. We must remember that in defining justice and its scope, we should not focus solely on accusations but rather on who can be accused and brought under the jurisdiction of the Court. In simple terms, accusations lose their significance when the power of law does not lie in the act of accusation itself, but in the principle that all judges are required to adhere to the reasoning of the Security Council.

Although the duty of the prosecutor of the International Criminal Court is to educate and inform the international community about the commission of international crimes by any individual, group, or government, it appears, and has been demonstrated, that the prosecutor often remains silent. The prosecutor is silent regarding crimes perpetrated by oppressive governments or their close allies, such as the United States and Israel. [20]

7. Scrutiny of the Values of Justice

Although we recognise that it is the official responsibility of prosecutors and judges not to overlook international crimes, they unfortunately do so for several reasons.[21] These reasons often depend on whether the perpetrators of such crimes are politicians from their own governments, whom they may protect through various rationalisations, or whether they fear losing their positions.[22] In the meantime, they perform their relevant duties in a cursory and superficial manner to avoid scrutiny in legal matters.[23] This reflects the current state of the international criminal justice system and raises concerns about how effectively justice can be served for the victims. Tragically, many victims find themselves without judges, prosecutors, or legal representation.

Most supporters of the current international justice system, particularly in light of the Security Council's position and the perceived legitimacy of NATO's power, are not advocating for universal human rights law. Instead,

---

[20] Farhad Malekian, *Conscience of Prosecutors in International Criminal Law, the Heart of the Matter* (New York: Nova Science Publishers, 2021).

[21] Farhad Malekian, *Conscience of Judges in International Criminal Law, the Heart of Judgements* (New York: Nova Science Publishers, 2021); Farhad Malekian, *Conscience of Prosecutors in International Criminal Law, the Heart of the Matter* (New York: Nova Science Publishers, 2021).

[22] *Id.*

[23] *Id.*

they endorse a system of human rights that serves the interests of those who wield power in warfare and legislation. Consequently, when a serious international issue arises, they turn to the laws of the powerful rather than adhering to the fundamental principles of morality and equality among nations. Whenever the topic of morality is raised, it is often subjected to numerous interpretations and distortions, leading to a perception that morality is synonymous with aggressive warfare or brutality. This leaves little room for meaningful discourse, suggesting that discussions about the foundational principles of natural law or morality are dismissed as irrelevant. This situation implies that we should refrain from discussing morality and instead accept the definitions of justice and human rights as dictated by the leaders of NATO, as well as the governments of the United States, the United Kingdom, and Israel. This is the framework through which we are compelled to confront justice, and failure to comply results in being labelled as terrorists or aggressors.

Paradoxically, a significant number of international lawyers, when discussing justice, refer to their own interpretation of justice, which prioritises securing full compensation. This perspective often leads them to neglect the political and legal complexities surrounding justice, which are manipulated by powerful governments. In reality, they inadvertently condemn the victims by ignoring the truth and perpetuating the narratives of oppressive regimes, which are responsible for the atrocities and the international crime of genocide. The reasoning behind this is quite straightforward: lawyers are motivated by substantial financial gain, and as long as that income is assured, they remain indifferent to the victims' lost rights. This highlights the troubling reality that moral considerations are not reflected in the earnings of lawyers, but rather in the financial settlements that significantly influence the outcomes of cases. [24]

A clear example of this is the manner in which the major powers' political policies and human rights agendas operated during the Iraq War, ostensibly with the sole intention of delivering justice and removing a dictator. These messages were not only propagated by the interventionist government of the United States but also by NATO. The outcome was stark: the pursuit of justice - or the lack thereof - resulted in the deaths of over one million people, including more than half a million children. The architects of war referred to

[24] Consult much closely Farhad Malekian, *Conscience of Judges in International Criminal Law, the Heart of Judgements* (New York: Nova Science Publishers, 2021); Farhad Malekian, *Conscience of Lawyers in International Criminal Law, the Burden of Doppelgängers* (New York: Nova Science Publishers, 2021); Farhad Malekian, *Conscience of Prosecutors in International Criminal Law, the Heart of the Matter* (New York: Nova Science Publishers, 2021).

this as justice, framing the killings as necessary for achieving a so-called victory for justice.[25]

To address the question of justice and its appropriate definition, we must first examine the underlying causes of the massacres and the ongoing injustices in the region. It is particularly noteworthy that those who participated in the killing of innocent individuals and actively contributed to the civilian massacres, such as Tony Blair, are now expressing regret and revealing the truth about past and present criminal activities of governments, especially the United States and its nefarious plans worldwide.[26] However, Tony Blair has returned to his aggressive and brutal criminal position, and is now aiding the American criminal government in genocide of the entire population of Gaza. Western political powers tend to lie, regret, and then lie again. Blair is one of the most perilous criminals in human history.[27] Consequently, the use of coercive legal force and the claim to enforce international human rights justice serve as tools for these powerful political entities.

---

[25] Farhad Malekian and Kerstin Nordlöf, *Confessing the International Rights of Children: The Basic documents with Analysis (*Cambridge: Cambridge Scholars Publishing, 2012); Farhad Malekian and Kerstin Nordlöf,'International Legal Status of Children' in Jay S. Albanese (ed.), *The Encyclopaedia of Criminology & Criminal Justice* (United States: Wiley-Blackwell (5 volumes, 2013), vol. III, pp. 1173-1178; Farhad Malekian, Kerstin Nordlöf, *Prohibition of Sexual Exploitation of Children Constituting Obligation Erga Omnes* (Cambridge: Cambridge Scholars Publishing, 2013); Farhad Malekian, Kerstin Nordlöf, *The Sovereignty of Children in Law* (Cambridge: Cambridge Scholars Publishing, 2012).

[26] By accepting guilt, these individuals confuse the public and simultaneously demonstrate their full sincerity to their political masters.

[27] Of course, this is not surprising since the British government's political strategy is basically based on lies.

Chapter 4

Lying with Precedent: Distorting International Criminal Justice

1. Selective Observation in the Imposition of Justice

Many of our most intense debates regarding justice revolve around the complete safeguarding of the powerful and an outright dismissal of victims' rights. This raises a critical question about the fairness of our reasoning.[1] Do legal professionals make the assertions deliberately provocative, or do they serve to uphold the tenets of international human rights law?[2] If they are indeed protective, then where can we identify their roles in safeguarding humanity, and how may we uncover these roles?[3] These inquiries highlight the delicate nature of justice and underscore pressing expectations from human rights law theories, which aim to protect individuals in highly contentious circumstances. Consequently, when criminals are summoned for trial, they often find themselves entangled in judicial provisions and decisions that ought not to tolerate impunity.

Some writers and international lawyers may object to our statements, believing that justice and human rights law are imposed by powerful entities, even if, in certain situations, their words are disregarded. However, they often perceive such violations as minimal and not detrimental to the overall system of international human rights law. This perspective suggests that many individuals value the legal provisions of a system characterised by one-sided

---

[1] For the notion of justice and its serious violations see Farhad Malekian, 'Mutilating the Philosophy of Justice in the Time of Armed Conflicts,' *Contemporary Journal of International Criminal Law* (2007); Farhad Malekian, *The Concept of Islamic International Criminal Law, A Comparative Study* (1994); Farhad Malekian, 'The Miserable Wedding of Naturalism into Positivism,' 2 *ID EST Journal* (2009). Immanuel Kant, *Religion within the Limits of Bare Reason* (1795), p. 87. Launched by Jonathan Bennett, Available online at http://www.earlymoderntexts.com/pdfs/kant1795part4.pdf; Alf Ross, *On Law and Justice* (London: Stevens & Sons Limited, 1958); Vagn Greve, 'Sheep or Wolves' 4 *European Journal of Crime, Criminal Law and Criminal Justice* (2005), 515-552; Hans Kelsen, 'What is Justice?' *Justice, Law and Politics in the Mirror of Science* (1957); Farhad Malekian, 'The Functions of International Criminal Law and the Problem of Positivism and Neutralism Philosophy,' *Contemporary Journal of International Criminal Law* (2007).

[2] *Id.*

[3] *Id.*

justice while ignoring the extreme violations and large-scale massacres of populations in other nations. Consequently, many of these writers and international lawyers selectively observe what aligns with their views and disregard what does not. This indicates a lack of moral integrity in their judgments; they do not genuinely protect people or victims but rather serve their own interests.

Thus, this reductionist approach to law and human rights is underpinned by a rationale that distances itself from the reality of events and the killing of individuals. Furthermore, some lawyers support the actions and decisions of powertionist criminal governments, maintaining that justice has been upheld and equality achieved.[4] For instance, there are lawyers who endorse Israeli military actions and the displacement of a nation to seize their land and property. This defensive stance has also been reflected in the statements of other lawyers worldwide.[5]

Typically, issues of justice become increasingly challenging to realise due to the influence wielded by offenders. This suggests that no legal framework effectively safeguards victims' rights as long as victims are essentially positioned akin to judges and prosecutors as mere tools within the courts - serving as instruments for advancing the interests of major offenders. This scenario is particularly evident in relation to Gaza, where both the prosecutor and Pre-Trial Chamber I of the Court showed reluctance to issue arrest warrants owing to various political considerations initially. Such hesitance has exacerbated victim casualties to alarming levels and has now become an integral aspect of modern genocide's historical narrative.[6]

Recently, it has been asserted and demonstrated that the concept of genocide is not only rejected by powerful states but is also used to undermine the rights of democratic nations. However, these states fail to provide a comprehensive justification for their arguments, as their statements are rooted in falsehoods, which form the foundation of their international human rights and criminal justice frameworks. Politicians and their legal advisors often discuss rights, including their governments' claims to territories that rightfully belong to the victims. The reason these arguments lack fundamental principles

---

[4] Farhad Malekian, *Powertionism in International Criminal Justice* (Nova Sciences Publishers, 2022).

[5] Farhad Malekian, *Conscience of Lawyers in International Criminal Law, the Burden of Doppelgängers* (New York: Nova Science Publishers, 2021); Farhad Malekian, *Powertionism in International Criminal Justice* (Nova Sciences Publishers, 2022).

[6] Consult also Otto Kirchheimer, Political Justice: The Use of Legal Procedure for Political Ends (Princeton University Press, 1961).

is that they are built upon lies, which perpetuate further deception, ultimately leading to the construction of more lies. This reflects the policy of the United States government, which is characterised by a combination of warfare and deceit. The perpetuation of lies does not absolve these powers of responsibility; by the time the truth is revealed, it is often too late to protect the rights of victims or support their existence. Moreover, the most significant lies hinder clear thinking and provide no support, as lies become the very essence of justice. It is important to note that the impact of the falsehoods propagated by major political powers on judicial relationships and the jurisprudence of the International Criminal Court creates a disheartening situation for the value of justice, reducing it to a mere illusion for those who celebrate their deceit and victories built on lies.

The issue at hand is that there exists no alternative solution to the problem of justice. As the rationale for ultimate justice is consistently articulated by those who also hold authority over judges and court decisions. In such circumstances, various opposing responses emerge; however, individuals who endeavour to advocate for the rights of victims often face threats or hostility from adversaries. The principal competing response to these intricate issues aligns with and intersects with the perspectives of dominant political governments and their strategies for addressing the international community as a whole.

Nevertheless, even in this context, justice remains unsupported since the foremost members of the international community, according to United Nations provisions, are the powerful permanent members. On one hand, the rights of victims across all forms are not protected by established norms of justice. Furthermore, when discussing international human rights and international criminal justice provisions, it becomes evident that both serve instrumental purposes while simultaneously embodying theories that condemn weaker nations rather than stronger ones. Consequently, the pursuit of an accurate definition of justice may indeed be regarded as a futile utopian aspiration rather than a tangible reality. This assertion underscores that overlooking independent principles of justice and thereby disregarding the unifying characteristics inherent to rules of justice is entirely impractical. Thus, the concept of rights corresponding to obligations within the framework of international human rights fails to confront its objective reality.[7]

---

[7] Examine also E. Cannizzaro, 'A Higher Law for Treaties?' in E. Cannizzaro (ed.),The Law of Treaties Beyond the Vienna Convention (2011); Emerson DeAnna, Mars/Earth Enigma: A Sacred Message to Mankind (1996), 238Danilenko G. M., 'International *Jus cogens*: Issues of Law Making,' *European Journal of International Law* (1991).

2. Elevating Lies Over Victims

As with many aspects of the international criminal justice system, there is no straightforward answer or solution to the challenges posed by authoritarian governments against the fundamental principles of justice. Consequently, any definition of justice must navigate a complex and arduous landscape. The precise role of the International Criminal Court and numerous international conventions remains ambiguous, particularly considering that during the formation of international norms pertaining to justice and its safeguarding, governments typically focus on drafting, approving, and adopting these norms rather than enforcing them. Thus, governments retain considerable latitude in interpreting the concept of justice on a case-by-case basis, depending on the specific circumstances under investigation.[8]

The authoritarian government, as highlighted in this situation, ultimately determines the outcome of enforcing justice to prevent international crimes. It follows that no aspect of the international human rights framework or resolutions from the General Assembly can be enforced when justice lacks substantive expression and instead embodies a distorted model. Therefore, whether resolutions passed by the General Assembly or conventions ratified during governmental meetings possess binding authority is contingent upon governmental policies at any given time.

An even more complex scenario may arise when governmental claims lead to an increase in international crimes and consequently elevate the number of victims. A poignant illustration of this phenomenon is the ongoing genocide in Gaza, which appears aimed at eradicating the entire Palestinian population.[9] Although both international courts - the International Court of

---

[8] Examine also Mario Jori (ed.), Legal Positivism (1992); C Sypnowich, The Concept of Socialist Law (1990); C. Perelman, The Idea of Justice and the Problem of Argument (1963); Douzinas Costas, Peter Goodrich and Yifat Hachamovitch, Politics, Post modernity and Critical Legal Studies (1994); David Sugarman, ed., Legality, Ideology and the State (1983); James D.A. Boyle, ed., Critical Legal Studies (1992); Peter Goodrich, Languages of Law (1990); D. Kennedy, Law and Ideology' 3 Tikkun (1988); R. Unger, 'The Critical Legal Studies Movement,' 96 Harvard Law Review 561 (1983); J. Derrida, 'Force of Law: Mystical Foundation of Authority,' 11 Cardozo Law Review 919 (1990); James Boyle, 'Is Subjectivity Possible? The Postmodern Subject in Legal Theory,' 62 University of Colorado Law Review 489 (1991); Dangerous Supplements: Resistance and Renewal in Jurisprudence (P. Fitzpatrick, ed., 1991); S. Fuller, 'Playing Without a Full Deck: Scientific Realism and the Cognitive Limits of Legal Theory,' 97 Yale Law Journal 549 (1988); Alasdair MacIntyre, After Virtue: A Study in Moral Theory (1982); Dennis Patterson, ed., Postmodernism and Law (1994).

[9] Human Rights in Palestine and Other Occupied Arab Territories: Report of the United Nations Fact-Finding Mission on the Gaza Conflict, GA. A/HRC/12/48 (25 September 2009).

Justice and the International Criminal Court - located in The Hague have unequivocally stated through their rulings that the Israeli government is perpetrating international crimes, specifically crimes against humanity and genocide, there has been little significant action taken regarding this issue. [10]As a result, the system of international law, which is intended to serve as a guiding framework for all nations, has become effectively paralysed.

We should remember that the judgments of both Courts, including those of the judges of the ICJ and the three-judge panel of Chamber I of the ICC, were issued after a clear analysis of the given case and massacres of civilians. As we know, the provisions incorporated into a treaty context are binding on the parties to it; however, the judgments of both Courts have been declared by the powertionist as unjust and not binding. This clearly implies the monopolisation of justice which is not only unlawful but a crime against the natural law of all nations.

In its Wall Advisory Opinion, the Court found that Israel's settlement policy was in breach of the sixth paragraph of Article 49 of the Fourth Geneva Convention, which provides that "[t]he Occupying Power shall not deport or transfer parts of its own civilian population into the territory it occupies." In the Court's view, there is nothing in the terms or the context of the provision, or in the object and purpose or the drafting history of the Fourth Geneva Convention, to suggest that that provision prohibits only the forcible transfer of parts of the occupying Power's civilian population into the occupied territory. In the present case, there is extensive evidence of Israel's policy of providing incentives for the relocation of Israeli individuals and businesses into the West Bank, as well as for its industrial and agricultural development by settlers. There is also evidence that Israel regularly legalizes outposts that have been established in contravention of domestic Israeli legislation and that Israel's construction of settlements is accompanied by specially designed civilian infrastructure in the West Bank and East Jerusalem, which integrates the settlements into the territory of Israel.[11]

The Court further notes that Israel's settlement policy has given rise to violence by settlers and security forces against Palestinians. Having examined the evidence before it in light of the relevant provisions of international law, the Court considers that the violence by settlers against Palestinians, Israel's failure to prevent or to punish it effectively and its excessive use of force against Palestinians contribute to the creation and maintenance of a coercive

[10] *Id.*
[11] https://www.icj-cij.org/node/204176.

environment against Palestinians. In the present case, on the basis of the evidence before it, the Court is of the view that Israel's systematic failure to prevent or to punish attacks by settlers against the life or bodily integrity of Palestinians, as well as Israel's excessive use of force against Palestinians, is inconsistent with its obligations. 8. Conclusion on Israel's settlement policy (paras. 155-156). In light of the above, the Court reaffirms (see Wall Advisory Opinion) that the Israeli settlements in the West Bank and East Jerusalem, and the régime associated with them, have been established and are being maintained in violation of international law. The Court notes with grave concern reports that Israel's settlement policy has been expanding since the Court's Wall Advisory Opinion.[12]

What it seems to boil down to is that the obligations of the system of international human rights and international criminal justice, and even the decisions of the ICJ and ICC, are lawless and thusly rendered ineffective, albeit they express the practical imposition of the system of international law

---

[12] https://www.icj-cij.org/node/204176. Moreover, the International Court of Justice in The Hague expresses that the "*Legal consequences of the violation by Israel of its obligations.*

Israel's international responsibility Israel obliged to comply with the international obligations it has breached by the construction of the wall Israel obliged to put an end to the violation of its international obligations Obligation to cease forthwith the works of construction of the wall, to dismantle it forthwith and to repeal or render ineffective forthwith the legislative and regulatory acts relating to its construction, save where relevant for compliance by Israel with its obligation to make reparation for the damage caused Israel obliged to make reparation for the damage caused to all natural or legal persons affected by construction of the wall.

Legal consequences for States other than Israel Erga omnes character of certain obligations violated by Israel Obligation for all States not to recognize the illegal situation resulting from construction of the wall and not to render aid or assistance in maintaining the situation created by such construction Obligation for all States, while respecting the Charter and international law, to see to it that any impediment, resulting from the construction of the wall, to the exercise by the Palestinian people of its right to self-determination is brought to an end Obligation for all States parties to the Fourth Geneva Convention, while respecting the Charter and international law, to ensure compliance by Israel with international humanitarian law as embodied in that Convention Need for the United Nations, and especially the General Assembly and the Security Council, to consider what further action is required to bring to an end the illegal situation resulting from the construction of the wall and its associated régime, taking due account of the Advisory Opinion.

Construction of the wall must be placed in a more general context Obligation of Israel and Palestine scrupulously to observe international humanitarian law Implementation in good faith of all relevant Security Council resolutions, in particular resolutions 242 (1967) and 338 (1973) "Roadmap" Need for efforts to be encouraged with a view to achieving as soon as possible, on the basis of international law, a negotiated solution to the outstanding problems and the establishment of a Palestinian State, with peace and security for all in the region." https://www.un.org/unispal/document/auto-insert-178825/.

and international criminal justice. This means that they are not truly law in reality or practice.

In this context, the United Nations Special Rapporteur, Francesca Albanese, has explicitly stated in her report that the definition of justice has been violated and the value of justice has become the value of genocide, not only in terms of its commission but also as a necessary condition enforced by the dominant powers.[13]

I may summarise my explanations concerning the different systems of international law by stating that they are all based on sources and obligations but with the distinction being which governments we are dealing with when speaking about justice, equality, and peace.

Thus, the real question is: do we need the systems of international laws if they cannot operate when necessary? Although the academic discourse on international human rights and international criminal justice assumes that their existence is a necessary and imperative requirement, the practical conditions of these systems remain more ambiguous and unreliable up to this day. Therefore, I was led to the foregoing conclusions, whilst many renowned lawyers of corrupt integrity may not accept them. That is their problem.

3. Justice Encouraging the Superiority of Lies

For many writers and lawyers, the concept of justice is often viewed as the means by which we adhere to the principles of equal treatment. This expectation aligns with the theory of justice, where we ultimately anticipate that violators will be punished and victims will be protected throughout the

[13] Albanese is on the right track, but Palestinians have been subjected to blatant violations of their rights for years. The International Court of Justice accurately states that "Given the character and the importance of the rights and obligations involved, the Court is of the view that all States are under an obligation not to recognize the illegal situation resulting from the construction of the wall in the Occupied Palestinian Territory, including in and around East Jerusalem. They are also under an obligation not to render aid or assistance in maintaining the situation created by such construction. It is also for all States, while respecting the United Nations Charter and international law, to see to it that any impediment, resulting from the construction of the wall, to the exercise by the Palestinian people of its right to self-determination is brought to an end. In addition, all the States parties to the Geneva Convention relative to the Protection of Civilian Persons in Time of War of 12 August 1949 are under an obligation, while respecting the United Nations Charter and international law, to ensure compliance by Israel with international humanitarian law as embodied in that Convention." Legal Consequences of the Construction of a Wall in the Occupied Palestinian Territory (I.C.J. Reports 2004), Para. 159.

judicial process. This defines a well-ordered criminal justice system, whether at the national or international level, which aims to fulfil the core intentions of justice and administer it without discrimination among individuals or within society. If this ideal is achieved, there would be no need to discuss the stability of criminal justice, particularly regarding the rights of victims. The rationale is that justice functions as it should, fulfilling its purposes without external interference.

The framework for presenting justice is not shaped by individual power or social privileges, but rather by the intrinsic purpose of justice itself and how it should be perceived and applied. In other words, the evolution of our understanding of justice, as it ideally should develop, is firmly established and predictable in its fairness. This is why any notion of legal and moral psychology is treated with equal consideration. This approach respects the inherent dignity of individuals and underscores the natural basis for the equality of all people in a civilised international society. However, this raises the question of whether such a civilised international society truly exists, given that the ultimate aim of human power often seems to be conflict and warfare.

At the outset of our pursuit of justice, particularly in the realm of international criminal justice, we may mistakenly believe that waging wars is essential for the advancement of international society. This perspective has led us to characterise a well-ordered military force within our territories, which we continue to promote and develop through advanced military technology. We perceive this as a means to achieve justice, and we believe that for the system of international criminal justice to succeed, it requires the enhancement of military power. This military strength, we argue, can foster peace, equality, and justice on a global scale. However, this notion implies that the advancement of military technology and the arming of our military forces serve the greater good of the world's population, as we claim to be combating terrorist groups.

In reality, the true terrorists may be those whose military technologies are effectively regulated by a political interpretation of justice. This situation often results in the violation of the rights of others under the guise of fighting terrorism and delivering justice both domestically and globally. Consequently, the concept of justice imposed by powerful governments does not reflect a genuine theory of justice and its protection; rather, it perpetuates a hierarchy of power. It is imperative to acknowledge that no victims of our injustices can be deceived by our theories of justice or the technological advancements of military powers, particularly in relation to the principles of justice. This indicates that the fundamental social institutions associated with the concept of justice cannot be satisfied in any manner that leads to a stable and enduring peace.

Through such misinterpretations, we ultimately distort the theory of justice and fairness, which ought to align with the ideals of international criminal justice or universal international criminal justice. This framework should be grounded in a mutual understanding of human rights and the necessity for justice to be administered appropriately and free from political influence. The foundational premise of justice assumes that it is selected and implemented with comprehensive assessments of its conceptions, which embody a balance among its core principles without denying their existence. We refer to those conceptions of justice that sufficiently serve their own principles and safeguard them, as these principles constitute the primary purpose behind establishing justice and are fundamental to discussions surrounding its notions and tenets. Furthermore, it must be emphasised that since such principles of international criminal justice are agreed upon based on genuine collective beliefs held by all nations regarding their authentic nature, these beliefs should not be employed detrimentally nor undermine original theories of justice.[14] In fact, there is no requirement to invoke theological or metaphysical doctrines to uphold the principles of international criminal justice or justify their necessity for safeguarding international human rights law.[15]

In strictly practical terms, we should refrain from conceiving an alternative notion of national or international criminal justice that diverges significantly from the original definitions of justice principles and fails to address or rectify inequalities arising from advancements in technology. Such disparities have resulted in countless victims due to wars waged under the pretext of combating terrorism and preventing its proliferation, while it remains evident that we ourselves contribute to these terrorist activities through our strategies aimed at fostering insecurity in various regions for our political, economic, and military interests.[16] The appropriate frameworks for

---

[14] Michael J. Perry, A Global Political Morality: Human Rights, Democracy, and Constitutionalism (Cambridge University Press, 2017); Farhad Malekian, *Tour de force of Moral Virtue in International Criminal Justice* (New York: Nova Science Publishers, 2022), p. 103. Consult also Farhad Malekian, *The Mirage of International Criminal Law, Kant Metaphysics of Mens Rea* (Cambridge Scholars Publishing, 2018).

[15] *Id.*

[16] "Although I believe that there are certain objections to my statements, it is also true that those objections may be exaggerated in certain instances because nothing indicates that the entire system of international criminal justice is not playing a game under the full protection of those powertionist governments. This *means that the system of international criminal justice is the institution of powertionism in international criminal justice, and its provisions*

international criminal justice must be validated by considering the conditions faced by victims and recognising what has been extracted from them under the guise of counter-terrorism efforts. This reality suggests that victims affected by our unfounded theories of justice have endured significant suffering because of our plans and future intentions regarding their existence - including their lands, resources, and territories. The rationale behind this argument is that a well-structured international society, exemplified by esteemed organisations such as the United Nations and the International Criminal Court, should endure through time. Their interpretation of justice is not only equitable and valid but also presumably rests on a stable foundation of universal morality that serves the interests of all humanity.

4. Institutional Framework for Distorting International Justice

Engaging in these frameworks of justice principles established within international organisations necessitates an understanding of international criminal justice that aspires to provide meaningful support for victims of unlawful and immoral actions perpetrated by powerful political entities. This explains why we observe insufficient stability in the conception of justice. If the notion of international criminal justice, which aims to foster equality and comprehensive understanding of victims' positions, is undermined by disruptive tendencies, and if the institutions involved promote weaker impulses and temptations regarding appropriate notions of justice and equality among individuals and nations, then the stability of international criminal justice relies on balancing victims' rights with the fundamental essence of justice. The proper realisation of victims' rights can thus illuminate pathways toward justice while countering tendencies toward injustice from dominant political powers.

---

have been colonised by authoritarian terrorist governments. This indicates that the contrary view concerning the system of international criminal justice and its preliminary intentions is now considered common. It seems absurd to many international criminal lawyers and international human rights supporters to speak about the fake face of international criminal justice on the platforms created by terrorist governments, and their interpretations are seen as normal. This is very natural and a common sickness of the system of justice, based on the fact that many lawyers of international criminal justice and human rights are the vassal lawyers of certain governments." Farhad Malekian, *Barrels of Justifications Violating International Criminal Responsibility* (New York: Nova Science Publishers, 2025), p.25.

To eradicate injustice, it becomes imperative to scrutinise and reassess the oppressive power over rights wielded by major political factions against their victims through various means. It is essential to reject any conceptions of international criminal justice that suggest its stability derives from military might be exercised by powerful political entities. In essence, a coherent framework for international criminal justice, along with adherence to human rights, should not be predicated on mere numbers - such as lawyers or conventions - or advanced warfare tools; rather, it must involve an examination of the relative strength inherent in existing notions of justice as they manifest in practical applications.

By asserting that the theory of justice constitutes an institution in itself, we acknowledge that a world devoid of justice cannot thrive; it will never experience true peace. Consequently, the foundational structure of international society is built upon impressions and rules reflecting individuals, groups, and nations. We posit that a public system comprising international rules ought to have similar foundational principles. This implies that the fundamental understanding of justice must be universally consistent across nations while developing according to comparable standards; although variations may exist within individual systems, ultimately, their conclusions regarding justice should align with established roots of authentic and practicable principles. Hence, we contend that the core objectives of justice resemble an institution designed to safeguard all humanity.

Furthermore, it underscores the necessity for individuals to comprehend what international human rights norms or principles governing international criminal justice require from themselves and others. It is widely acknowledged within the international community that all parties are aware of the established rules and principles, and there exists an expectation that individuals from various regions around the world possess a similar understanding of human rights norms. Consequently, it is reasonable for all nations to uphold these protective measures, which are likewise expected to be safeguarded by all authorities and governments.

The principles governing international criminal justice apply universally to all governments, irrespective of their military capabilities within the international framework. While it is plausible that differing interpretations exist regarding the system of international criminal justice and its institutions, as long as these interpretations adhere to the foundational principles of justice and its inherent objectives, variations in understanding do not pose a significant issue. However, should such interpretations exceed the boundaries set by justice norms or contravene fundamental tenets of international criminal law - resulting in the perpetration of international crimes - these understandings would clearly lack support and serve as evidence against the perpetrators' accountability. Achieving justice and adhering to its provisions does not stem from infringing upon their essence but rather from respecting them through universally accepted institutions that do not undermine the principles of international human rights or their legal, political, and intrinsic values.

The philosophy underpinning international criminal justice delineates which actions are permissible and encouraged under legal provisions, while categorically prohibiting certain acts. There exists a common foundation for cultivating an international consensus on justice principles and associated expectations. Furthermore, within a well-structured institution such as the International Criminal Court, it is reasonable to assume that all regulated principles reflect a shared conception of justice held by the global legal and political community on behalf of humanity without supporting lies or falsehoods. This collective understanding enhances effectiveness compared to national definitions of justice institutions.

As a result, there emerges a general consensus regarding what constitutes justice versus injustice - a notion that resonates philosophically, ethically, and even theologically. It is imperative to underscore that distinctions among varying interpretations of justice are largely superficial and lack practical significance when they infringe upon fundamental justifications for protecting universal justice principles. In essence, strategies and maxims aimed at defining and defending these principles must remain impartial; crimes must be recognised unequivocally as crimes without alternative definitions. This holds particular importance in cases involving international crimes and assigning criminal responsibility for such offenses. Ultimately, these strategies often reflect self-interest on the part of specific entities, posing potential harm to the integrity of the entire system of international criminal justice while exacerbating conflicts.

5. Determining Who Wields Authority Over Justice

Ideally, both the framework governing international criminal justice and governmental policies should align with foundational principles of justice rather than being driven by self-serving interests that further infringe upon established rules. This necessitates that not only individual conduct within a state but also governmental actions be harmonised as much as possible to yield outcomes consistent with general principles of justice. This principle is particularly significant in relation to customary law, conventional law, and *jus cogens* within international criminal jurisprudence, all of which demand strict adherence to their legal statutes.[17] Although governments may not intend to undermine the justice system - and may even be unaware of potential violations - they nonetheless breach fundamental tenets of international criminal law when pursuing their political, military, or economic agendas.

We assert that any alterations or reinterpretations of the principles governing international human rights law and international criminal justice must be grounded in rationality and should not contravene fundamental notions of justice; otherwise, they may lead to injustice and an increase in victimisation. Consequently, an analysis of the schemes and tactics employed by powerful entities undermines the definition of justice while demonstrating that their unlawful actions violate societal expectations for authentic justice. This misinterpretation and personal politicised interpretation of international criminal justice tend to foster conflict, violations, and warfare.

It is therefore imperative to clarify that the strategies and maxims in question do not constitute a component of international criminal justice, nor are they integral to the institution of justice itself. Instead, they reflect the personal or political interests of certain parties, revealing a propensity to undermine the principles of just governance. For instance, various governments and their affiliates offer definitions of justice that are purely theoretical rather than practical, contradicting the widely accepted understanding of justice and its applicability. Any proposals aimed at achieving a fair and comprehensive articulation of justice norms - wherein the power associated with justice is equitably distributed - may prove redundant if international crimes perpetrated by individuals, groups, or governments are shielded under such definitions.

These assertions arise alongside various provisions within international human rights frameworks and commitments articulated through international

---

[17] E. de Wet, '*Jus Cogens* and Obligations Erga Omnes' in, E de Wet and Vidmar (eds.), J *Hierarchy in International Law: The Place of Human Rights*, (2012). A. J. J. de Hoog, 'The Relationship between *Jus Cogens*, *Obligations Erga Omnes* and International Crimes: Peremptory Norms in Perspective' 42 *Österreichische Zeitschrift für öffentliches Recht und Völkerrecht* (1991); A. de Hoogh, *Obligations erga omnes and International Crimes: A Theoretical Inquiry into the Implementation and Enforcement of the International Responsibility of States* (Kluwer The Hague, 1996). See also Erika de Wet, 'The Prohibition of Torture as an International Norm of *Jus Cogens* and its Implementation for National and Customary Law,' 15 (1) *European Journal of International Law* (2014), Vol. 15, No. 1, 97-121.

conventions designed to protect victims in specific contexts. Consequently, discussions concerning principles of justice and their efficacy based on prevailing definitions are not evaluated through philosophical considerations regarding strength or perfection but rather through their ultimate applicability governed by state power dynamics - essentially determining who wields authority over whom. Thus, compliance with directives issued by powerful states becomes imperative; failure to adhere may result in severe consequences such as violence or displacement from positions of authority.

One significant issue is how to characterise these conceptions of violations and justice across various systems without compromising the original position of justice and its reliable definition. The reality is that there is no guarantee that the arguments presented by political parties and their lawyers are true and authentic. This is largely due to the fact that the rhetoric of many lawyers is often intertwined with the misleading statements propagated by powerful entities or determining who yields authority over whom. [18] For instance, it would be absurd to believe that the descriptions of international crimes or the definitions of international justice put forth by powerful governments have any genuine connection to the truth or present real evidence. As a result, the policies that might be most beneficial could be repeatedly overlooked. There may be no definitive alternative to the definition of justice because of the pervasive mixture of lies and truths, which intentionally obscures each conception of international criminal justice with entirely new falsehoods. Since these lies are not grounded in truth, the policy of deception can be modified at any time. This implies that there is always another lie that may seem better than the previous one, and this cycle continues indefinitely, reinforcing the malicious principle of determining who wields authority over whom.

6. Subservience of Justice to Political Lies

Discrepancies in defining justice emerge when individuals, groups, or governments privatise questions surrounding its nature and scope. This issue becomes especially critical when matters related to international justice fall

---

[18] Farhad Malekian, *Conscience of Judges in International Criminal Law, the Heart of Judgements* (New York: Nova Science Publishers, 2021); Farhad Malekian, *Conscience of Lawyers in International Criminal Law, the Burden of Doppelgängers* (New York: Nova Science Publishers, 2021); Farhad Malekian, *Conscience of Prosecutors in International Criminal Law, the Heart of the Matter* (New York: Nova Science Publishers, 2021).

under the dominion of specific powers; consequently, this leads to a dismissal of the international criminal justice system while violations against human rights principles become entrenched as political norms. In such contexts, there is often a lack of constructive alignment with foundational tenets of justice; thus, objectives associated with achieving true justice become distorted over time - resulting in an increased number of victims suffering from breaches of international criminal law.

Nevertheless, the most detrimental outcome is that the victims are not only defenceless but also subjected to sexual violence, and yet these immoral actions, which contravene the principles of international criminal justice, are justified through the moral justifications provided by the perpetrators. This suggests that the strategies and tactics employed by governments regarding the conceptualisation of justice primarily address the matter of self-interest representation. For example, Israeli criminal military power currently renowned for its brutality is called "the most moral army in the world."

Furthermore, a distinction can be made between justice as defined by those who commit serious crimes and justice as perceived by their victims. The interpretation of justice articulated by perpetrators of international crimes legitimises acts such as genocide, crimes against humanity, war crimes, aggression, torture, and rape, among others. This indicates that institutions of justice are influenced by theories of injustice and that these offenders have compromised the fundamental framework of the system.[19] A significant factor contributing to this situation is that numerous provisions within international criminal law are construed in a manner that serves the interests of powerful criminals; for instance, genocide may be framed as self-defence or a means of safeguarding justice. When interpretations of justice devolve into such explanations, genuine justice collapses, leading to a scenario where criminal activities are regarded as morally acceptable while lawful and ethical behaviours are depicted as criminal offences deserving punishment.[20]

---

[19] William A. Schabas, 'The Banality of International Justice,' 11 *Journal of International Criminal Justice* (2013), pp. 545–551; William A. Schabas, 'Justice, Democracy and Impunity in Post Genocide Rwanda: Searching for Solutions to Impossible Problems,' 7 *Criminal Law Forum* (1996); William A. Schabas, 'Sentencing by International Tribunals: For a Human Rights Approach,' 7:2 *Duke Journal of Comparative & International Law* (1997), pp. 461-518.

[20] "It seems implausible to me that we can reach a convincing ethical explanation in the case of accepting and remaining silent concerning the wrongful decisions made by big governments. We must be strict about what is really being carried out - whether it is morally right or not - and not try to avoid engagement since we are not parties to the war. An example of this is the killing of innocent Jews during the Second World War, wherein a number of European governments chose an objective position at the start of the war despite

This illustrates how the system of justice - particularly under the auspices of the United Nations - is imposed upon weaker entities or governments. The underlying theory is straightforward: both the social and legal frameworks for implementing and defining justice - especially within international criminal law - are constrained by the political lexicon utilised by dominant governments. I refer to these entities as "powertionist" governments. This designation highlights those regimes that possess their own legal systems or forms of international criminal jurisdiction that supersede established norms within international criminal law, thereby monopolising all legal frameworks including those governing national jurisdictions.

It is evident that not only may their directives and institutional decisions lack sufficient authority for enforcing international systems independently, but also that within their national structures or intelligence networks lies substantial influence over global political systems concerning both criminal law and human rights legislation. Consequently, injustice permeates all facets of both national and international legal systems. Thus, it becomes clear that the entire concept of justice and human rights holds significantly greater value than any unjust interpretation of law. In this context, we encounter what can be termed "barbaric justice" - a form predicated on coercive power wherein dissent may lead to fatal consequences for protestors. Furthermore, it is conceivable that this "barbaric justice" within the justice system may exist, even though none of its institutions appear unjust when considered in isolation.

The concept of injustice arises from how we have allowed the entire United Nations Organisation to be dominated by certain member states, particularly the British and United States governments. This implies that a governmental institution may promote and seem to uphold principles that, in reality, are unjust and brutal, yet are perceived as just and fundamental.

The situation has consistently been observed in the actions of the United Nations, particularly under the authority of the Security Council. The distinctions between the legal and political characterisations of authoritarian governments are sufficiently clear to categorise them as barbaric powers. Furthermore, when evaluating the justice systems of such governments, we may not require additional evidence beyond the fact that the system of justice is monopolised. In both broader and narrower contexts, justice becomes

---

being aware of the brutal idea of authoritarian power. This was the same in Palestine, Iraq, Syria, and Afghanistan, where a large number of governments were aware that the situations of those victimised nations are incredibly immoral and unfair, but chose to be silent or neutral about almost all events." Farhad Malekian, *Conundrums of Paternalism in International Criminal Justice* (New York: Nova Science Publishers, 2024), p.172.

subservient to power, and power emerges as the dominant principle of justice. It is important to note that government institutions - whether the entire government or its various branches - cannot allow pure justice to be recognised and applied in a regular and ordinary manner, as outlined in the principles of justice.

The unfortunate reality is that, although governments recognise that the language of justice and its inherent power are often manipulated, they continue to adhere to a system of injustice and remain indifferent to the potential dangers it poses for vulnerable nations around the world. Undoubtedly, many governments are appealing to the masters of barbaric justice in pursuit of their own interests. This is not a hidden phenomenon. It would be inaccurate to judge them by the fundamental principles of justice and claim that they are champions of justice, with intentions focused on peace and the equitable treatment of every individual, nation, or government globally.

The true essence of justice is therefore compromised and intertwined with a broader theory of injustice and barbaric ideologies.[21] When the principles of international criminal justice become shackled and manipulated by criminals, we can no longer expect progress in the development and implementation of justice.[22] Although we may not typically perceive justice as unfair and barbaric, the historical record since the establishment of the United Nations, particularly the Security Council, demonstrates that governments are far more inclined to align with the theory of barbaric justice than with true justice, and even with injustice itself.

---

[21] "Barbaric acts, such as mass murder, aggression, genocide, jailing, rape, or torture, are justified by the authorities of the political opponents of those who do not submit themselves to the philosophy and policy of *international human-snaking rights*, and naturally oppose those rights that are full of fangs and dangerous to their political opponents. This means we contaminate the systems of international human rights law and international criminal justice, and as a result, the venomous fangs of powerful nations go into the system of international criminal jurisprudence, and become the epitome of law and order. My designation, "Paternalism in International Criminal Jurisprudence," implies the power and authority of one or few governments over other governments or their nations, as a result of the former deciding that they are the most capable of understanding socio-political reasoning." Farhad Malekian, *Conundrums of Paternalism in International Criminal Justice* (New York: Nova Science Publishers, 2024), pp. 19-20.

[22] "Additionally, torture constitutes the most severe insult to the dignity of victims. It is the most intense disgrace and is barbaric to the victims' international human rights. Respect for the significance of any personal and group existence prohibits injuring others to gain an advantage, for any reason. That is why, both internationally and historically, we cannot wisely convince the ethical and moral aspect of natural and jurisprudential norms that committing a holocaust of several million Jews in Europe was correct or necessary for any reason." Malekian, *Conundrums of Paternalism in International Criminal Justice*, id., p.33.

7. Standardisation of Barbaric Coercive Force

Presumably, the concept of justice must involve, in some manner, the assumption of certain rights and values that are essential for its existence. However, I will not delve into the various forms of injustice, as doing so would detract from the primary definition of justice. It is important to assert that the concept of justice, which is predicated upon the use or threat of force and aggression, has significantly deviated from its intended path. Such a form of justice, associated with the barbaric political powers within the United Nations, cannot genuinely align itself with true justice. Instead, it operates alongside the fundamental principles of justice while feigning an impartiality that purportedly benefits all nations globally. This approach is fundamentally rooted in a structure characterised by barbarism, humiliation, and the imposition of aggressive force against weaker nations or those not aligned with its interests. The primary objective of this distorted notion of justice is to eradicate governments that assert their rights and oppose major institutions of injustice. Consequently, this redefinition equates the barbaric authorities' concept of justice with a standardised form that claims to be fair and equal for all nations.

Let us then consider a hypothetical basic framework that must be respected by all governments regardless of their legal, military, or political power within the United Nations. Its rules are designed to uphold a certain conception of justice that no government can reasonably contest. Nevertheless, such a framework struggles to endure when subjected to scrutiny by dominant governmental powers. Despite our personal rejection of these interpretations of justice as abhorrent and unjust, this rejection has ultimately proven ineffective. Our reasoned ethical arguments are often undermined through various means - most notably through the exercise of veto power and ultimately through coercive force. The principles underpinning justice - those that delineate fundamental rights and obligations for all governments - fail to achieve their purpose due to the overwhelming influence exerted by veto powers that distort the administration of justice for victims.

Furthermore, let us consider international criminal justice as an established institution responsible for attributing international criminal responsibility under the Statute of the ICC. Here too lies a significant impediment preventing the preservation of genuine criminal justice and subverting all notions thereof; we witness an environment dominated by barbaric practices perpetuated by powerful criminal states worldwide. This situation indicates that authentic justice is largely unrecognised within the framework of international law and remains under the control of imperial powers within the Security Council. That means the lies empowering international criminal reasoning are a fact and reality of the Council's system and its subordinate countries as a whole.

The current situation remains unstable, regardless of the necessity for justice institutions, whether under the auspices of the United Nations or the International Criminal Court, to administer their functions impartially and consistently in accordance with established laws and prevailing circumstances. This instability implies that judges and other officials within these organisations are compelled to adhere to similar legal arguments dictated by superior authorities. Consequently, the pertinent similarities and differences between legal subjects and applicable decisions primarily reflect those already established by powerful governments, which often align artificially with existing norms. The proper frameworks of international justice, human rights, and criminal justice - defined by various institutional regulations - are therefore frequently overlooked. This is also applicable to companies that operate under national legislation and aid in the commission of international crimes such as genocide.[23]

---

[23] "2.3. When responsibility may entail criminal liability

Failure to act responsibly in line with international law may implicate corporate entities in more serious violations giving rise to criminal liability, for the corporate entity and/or for its executives.

Drawn from the legacy of the Industrialists' trials at Nuremberg, corporate accountability for international crimes is based on a recognition of the critical role the economy plays in times of war and conflict, and the fact that corporate entities may be involved in heinous violations of international law constituting international

Individual executives can be held criminally liable for the actions of their corporate entities, including before the International Criminal Court. While, increasingly, corporate entities themselves, could also face criminal liability as a result of the emerging crystallization of customary international legal principles. This includes some domestic jurisdictions which attribute criminal liability to corporations, and a growing body of treaties enshrine criminal liability of legal persons, which means that under international law corporations can be criminally liable for specific crimes, including genocide, apartheid, financing terrorism, organized crime[361] and corruption.

The conduct of corporations and their executives may entail direct criminal liability but more commonly constitutes complicity or aiding and abetting liability. This may involve instigating, moral support, or abetting, furnishing aid or assistance for or procuring the means for the commission of a crime or the creation of conditions necessary for atrocity crimes to occur. International tribunals have generally found that criminal liability for such forms of complicity: (a) can be established where the aid or assistance has a material effect on the commission of the crime, and (b) depends on the knowledge possessed by the entity/executive of how its services or activities will be utilised, and the effect on the commission of the crime.

In other words, it is not necessary to show that the entity or individual intended the particular harm; it is sufficient that in providing logistical, financial or operational support, they had actual or constructive knowledge that the principal perpetrators were engaged in a given

As a result, advocates of justice fail to accurately interpret these systems and inadvertently bolster the authority of authoritarian entities within the Security Council. This leads to a decline in the impartial and consistent application of legal principles, ultimately resulting in an outcome contrary to the intended fairness that these institutions should promote. The contemporary state of international justice is marked by the devastation experienced by vulnerable nations and their populations. Regardless of how substantive principles of justice may be characterised within international criminal law, we continue to confront insecurity and significant violations despite formal legal provisions. This predicament illustrates why international criminal justice struggles to function effectively against unlawful actions imposed by historical colonial powers or those exercising paternalistic control.[24] If we regard international human rights and criminal justice as articulating a form of equality, substantial evidence is required to support our assertions regarding their implementation.

It is essential to recognise that the potential efficacy of any justice system, particularly international criminal justice, necessitates robust principles and enforceable provisions at its core rather than merely ornamental regulations. Therefore, it is imperative that the laws governing institutions such as the United Nations and ICC apply uniformly across all subjects without discrimination based on social status or national classification - such as developed versus developing nations - which has historically persisted under political policies enacted by many Western governments while superficially aligning with international human rights standards.[25] It is evident that both the

---

crime, or, in the case of prosecutions before the ICC, acted "for the purpose of facilitating the commission of such a crime". Financial and managerial control over a corporate entity engaged in the crime is sufficient to establish the basis for individual criminal responsibility. Jurisprudence has confirmed that corporate actors cannot avoid accountability by claiming that they were merely fulfilling commercial contracts." Francesca Albanese, From Economy of Settler-Colonial Occupation to the Economy of Genocide, Report of the Special Rapporteur on the situation of human rights in the Palestinian territories occupied since 1967; https://www.un.org/unispal/document/a-hrc-59-23-from-economy-of-occupation-to-economy-of-genocide-report-special-rapporteur-francesca-albanese-palestine-2025/.

[24] Farhad Malekian, *Conundrums of Paternalism in International Criminal Justice* (New York: Nova Science Publishers, 2024).

[25] "The right to refuse to endure injustices perpetrated by Western governments against the Palestinian population is indisputable. *Nevertheless, it is evident that this population lacks the means to resist and, moreover, they possess no intention of opposing malevolent governments that contravene fundamental principles of international criminal justice while committing grave violations of the United Nations Charter. This assertion is not an exaggeration; rather, it reflects a reality in which the provisions of the Charter demand unwavering respect. However, what remains unfulfilled is the adherence to these rights. The reality is that Western*

conceptualisation of justice institutions and international criminal justice are conceived as frameworks aimed at fostering equal access to justice while simultaneously striving to eliminate injustices perpetuated through power politics and enforcement mechanisms.[26]

governments, primarily with support from the United States, infringe upon the rights of other nations whenever opportunities arise. This has been starkly illustrated by the ongoing genocide against the Palestinian people, who face a dire existential crisis. Consequently, we have sought dialogue regarding ICC—an entity currently stifled or rendered ineffective under immense pressure from Western powers, particularly from the United States and the United Kingdom. What is the legal justification for the U.S. to direct another country when it is the primary and largest nuclear possessor?" Farhad Malekian, *Empires of Genocide* (New York: Nova Science Publishers, 2025), p.55.

[26] "The attribution of international criminal responsibility to Western heads of states or the permanent members of the Security Council is necessary, but nearly impossible for the prosecutor. This is however, not necessarily the failure of the prosecutor of the ICC. There is a double standard or binary morality which guides Western diplomacy in international criminal court. After the First World War, Western states attempted, to bring British witnesses to the court with the assistance of the Detective Inspector Collins of Scotland Yard, who could testify to criminal atrocities committed by the Germans at the War Guilt Trial in Leipzig, Germany on 1 June 1921.

After the Second World War, the Western government brought the criminals of Germany under criminal prosecution at the International Military Tribunal in Nuremberg which was headed by Robert Jackson, the chief prosecutor of the Tribunal. The holocaust of the Jews could not be tolerated and could not be committed to collective memory without an annotation of justice. Western states were the initiators, leaders, and creators of the *International Criminal Tribunal for the Former Yugoslavia* and the *International Criminal Tribunal* for Rwanda, they were the killers of millions across the globe, and the creators of the conspiracy theories used to launch wars in many nations - nevertheless the ICC has never been able to be held them accountable."

Western crimes all over the world have been tolerated due to their power. This means that although States Parties to the ICC authorise the prosecutor of the ICC, they are actually not powerful enough to bring cases against strong states parties or those in the Security Council. Several European states encourage expanding the power of the prosecutor of the ICC, even though they continue to sell weapons to Saudi Arabia to fuel its full-scale war in Yemen. This policy is still continuing with most weapon-producing European states and is considered legal, although the ICC prosecutor and their office must be against it. This means that certain political control exists in the house of the prosecutor of the ICC and the prosecutor cannot prosecute the politicians of states who have fuelled the war in Yemen." Farhad Malekian, *Conscience of Prosecutors in International Criminal Law, the Heart of the Matter* (New York: Nova Science Publishers, 2021).

Chapter 5

Disequilibrium Empowering International Criminal Reasoning

1. Describing the Equilibrium of Justice

There exists no universally accepted philosophical interpretation of the theory of justice that is acknowledged by all governments globally or upheld by major powers. This absence of a widely recognised definition of justice renders the pursuit of peaceful resolution to justice issues unfeasible and significantly undermines the efficacy of the international criminal justice system. My reference to international criminal justice pertains to the framework established by the Statute of the International Criminal Court, along with the procedures that state parties have agreed upon for its implementation. In this context, I intend to summarize of the characteristics of arguments regarding international criminal justice that are encountered in practice and articulated by both weaker and stronger governments. My objective is to assess the potential of international criminal justice from various perspectives within the framework of international legal and political society, particularly focusing on how authoritarian or powertionist governments formulate their policies regarding this established system of justice. This analysis suggests that specific conditions define the initial context in which justice is applied, conditions deemed acceptable by prevailing power structures and their political mechanisms.

In other words, if barbaric military intervention is deemed necessary by a powerful state and its allies or NATO members, it is against the systems of international human rights law and international criminal justice. As a consequence, we have both explicitly and implicitly imposed the *human-snaking rights* and *snaking justice* of the biggest, most powerful governments into the system of international jurisprudence. For criminal acts, not only does the main government have direct criminal responsibility, but other governments cannot escape from their international accountability by attempting to claim ignorance. Their claims that there were unaware of the criminal plans of the nation with the most military power in the world should not save them from being held accountable. A clear example of this is the

British Prime Minister who claimed ignorance and naively accepted and participated in NATO attacks in Iraq and still received high recognition from the royal family. All of this indicates that the venomous fangs of international criminal jurisprudence are authorised and controlled through a paternalist system imposed by a powerful government, or as I have explained in my earlier work, *Powertionism in International Criminal Justice*, by a powertionist government.[1]

To elucidate the distinctions among various conceptions of justice, it is imperative to recognise both the common intentions held by governments and the intuitive notion of fairness associated with international criminal justice as advocated by most states in an effort to prevent violations. However, there exists a significant disparity between the idealised notions of justice promised by the ICC and the realities observed in practice among dominant nations, where breaches of international criminal justice norms appear almost inevitable for those in power.[2] To comprehend this divergence between conventional interpretations of just principles and their political applications, one must acknowledge that perceptions of justice fluctuate depending on the context; consequently, knowledge concerning law adapts according to how powerful entities influence legal terminology.[3] This indicates that governmental interests often supersede those aligned with true judicial fairness. Reaching an agreement on this understanding becomes unnecessary, since when international criminal justice is put into practice, viable alternatives for achieving peaceful prosecution become obscured.[4]

Evidently, victims are unable to realise their rights or see them fulfilled while authoritarian regimes obstruct meaningful progress toward just

---

[1] Farhad Malekian, *Conundrums of Paternalism in International Criminal Justice* (New York: Nova Science Publishers, 2024), pp. 35-36. Consult also Farhad Malekian, *International Criminal Law, the Law of Somebodiness, the Law of Nobodiness* (New York: Nova Science Publishers, 2021); Farhad Malekian, *International Criminal Law: The Legal and Critical Analysis of International Crimes* (2 vols. 1991); Farhad Malekian, *The Monopolization of International Criminal Law in the United Nations, A Jurisprudential Approach* (Stockholm: Almqvist Wiksell International, 1st ed., 1993); Farhad Malekian, *Jurisprudence of International Criminal Justice* (Introduction by Professor Benjamin B. Ferencz, the former Prosecutor of the Nuremberg Tribunal (Cambridge: Cambridge Scholars Publishing, 2014); Farhad Malekian, *The Monopolization of International Criminal Law in the United Nations, A Jurisprudential Approach* (Stockholm: Almqvist Wiksell International, 2nd ed., 1995); Farhad Malekian, *Paralysing International Criminal Justice* (New York: Nova Science Publishers, 2021); Farhad Malekian, *Orchestrating Diversity in International Criminal Justice* (New York: Nova Science Publishers, 2021).

[2] *Id.*

[3] *Id.*

[4] *Id.*

principles. Consequently, it becomes apparent that every victim's expectation for redress fails when confronted with prevailing injustices. Ultimately, one must conclude that true justice remains elusive, and aspirations for fair treatment diverge significantly from reality. Criminal regimes and powerful governments that exert control over the Council are unlikely to consent to terms of justice that disregard their decisions, thereby positioning themselves as violators of the framework of international criminal justice. Nonetheless, such self-serving attitudes exhibited by influential political entities should be categorically rejected.

However, the fundamental role of international criminal justice principles will remain intact, as the concept of justice serves as a theory governing the use of force, with ongoing manipulation and monopolisation by those advocating for their own interpretations of appropriate justice. That means there is an absence of justice, equality, and love.[5] It is imperative to recognise that these principles of justice are the culmination of long-established rights that advocate for and respond to the rights of all individuals, particularly under the auspices of the ICC aimed at restoring violated rights. Consequently, while there are demands for justice corresponding to victims' rights, it is regrettable that these rights are often granted not to victims but rather to offenders who are members of the United Nations Security Council. Thus, it can be asserted that justice within ICC procedures fundamentally represents an enforcement mechanism for perpetuating injustice.

As a result, choosing this conception of justice - rooted in the interests of powerful political entities - is not a genuine choice but rather an imposition exercised by those who possess control over what constitutes justice. Therefore, no singular solution exists regarding the challenges posed by certain members' original positions within the Security Council concerning structures and principles of justice. Engaging in disputes over these principles inevitably leads us to address the monopolisation of victims' rights. This situation reflects a broader procedural context within international criminal justice institutions in general and specifically within the Security Council's jurisdiction. It underscores why discussions surrounding the terminology

---

[5] S Mendus., 'The Importance of Love in Rawls's Theory of Justice' 29 (1) *British Journal of Political Science* (1999), pp. 57-75 ; Examine Farhad Malekian, 'The Canon of Love against the Use of Force in Islamic and Public International Law: Part II: The Anatomy of Love Against Violations,' 15 *International Criminal Law Review*, 2015), pp. 861-895; Farhad Malekian, 'The Canon of Love against the Use of Force in Islamic and Public International Law: Part I: The Chamber of Love within Legal Discipline,' 15 *International Criminal Law Review*, 2015), pp. 591-628.

associated with justice remain subjects of human debate - not due to an inability to define it or a paralysis in philosophical discourse - but because ultimately, in moments requiring adaptability or acceptance, notions of justice become defined through frameworks dominated by militarily powerful nations.

Consequently, we may conceptualise various perspectives on justice and establish connections among them based on choices made by major governmental powers regarding its nature. These portrayals do not necessarily stem from foundational legal knowledge or international criminal law; rather, they generally reflect patterns employed by authoritarian regimes seeking to persuade other governments regarding specific interpretations related to their theories surrounding justice. What is particularly significant in this context is that the principles of justice are governed and enforced by powertionist governments, even when the justice system and its definitions are compromised due to the personal interests of certain government officials aiming to extend national policies into the territories of other nations or governments. The actions of these politicians stem from their individual interpretations of international human rights and how they perceive the relationship between international criminal law and their own beliefs and agendas. Consequently, their circumstances and available options enable them to present a portrayal of the international criminal justice system that aligns with their desires and interests. Thus, it is through this lens that both the concept of justice and the overarching structure of international criminal justice are defined and implemented.

2. Presenting Unattainable Views of Justice

The framework of international criminal justice, which purports to embody fairness in addressing the rights of victims, essentially represents a legal farce. This observation equally applies to our moral sentiments as articulated through our judgments, which serve as a thoughtful equilibrium rooted in the foundational principles of justice.[6] These sentiments regarding both philosophy and particularly international criminal justice significantly influence our thoughts, decisions, and actions.[7] Although the

[6] Farhad Malekian, 'Judging International Criminal Justice in the Occupied Territories,' 12 *International Criminal Law Review* (2012), pp. 827–869.

[7] *Id.*

conceptualisation of international criminal justice presents an ostensibly independent model of justice, it raises serious concerns about who wields substantial influence within this system and who does not. Therefore, it becomes less significant whether the original position of justice and its comprehensiveness constitutes a genuine achievement in defending justice or distributing equitable norms since its effectiveness hinges on the timely enforcement of its principles.[8]

As a result, within their skewed depiction of justice and its norms, nations or governments find themselves entrenched in a profound abyss that reflects solely the decisions made by oppressive regimes, devoid of any adherence to international human rights or standards of international criminal justice. When numerous Western governments each pursue their own agendas, they facilitate one another's political, military, and economic ambitions. This often results in an appropriation of resources from weaker nations in exchange for what they most covet - the presentation of falsehoods and a distortion of truth. For these governments, this state represents an equilibrium of justice achieved through cooperation among various nations or governmental entities worldwide.

A clear illustration can be found in the European Union, which operates by undermining the rights of other nations while endorsing U.S. governance as a legitimate expression of justice in the Middle East. Each member state within the European Union perceives this arrangement as optimal due to its complicity with fellow member states and alignment with U.S. policy objectives. All these notions are articulated and embraced as being consistent with governmental rights and freedoms under public international law provisions aimed at furthering similar interests. It is upon these foundations that the political framework governing international law - including institutions such as the United Nations - views itself as achieving a balance among rights, justice, and national interests. Should there be any deviation from this established state of justice orchestrated by powertionist governments, then such equilibrium regarding justice and interest divisions would become precarious.

It is imperative that the prescribed notion of justice, which embodies the equilibrium of equality, remains unviolated and is upheld at all times. Failure to do so undermines the stability of justice purportedly provided and enforced by the dominant political and criminal authorities, thereby distorting the true definition of justice as understood by powerful governments. This implies that a balance characterised by aggression and hostility may be introduced as a

[8] Farhad Malekian, *Allegations by Political Laundering* (Cambridge Scholars Publishing, 2019).

supposed stable equilibrium. Consequently, there exists no moral evaluation of the rules governing this equilibrium of justice; rather, circumstances are contingent upon the prevailing interests of the authoritarian government that dictates what is deemed right or wrong. It is at this juncture that the initial conception of injustice masquerading as justice reveals its authentic nature and aligns with certain moral theories. While theories of justice advocate for equal treatment among subjects, such ideals remain largely unattained.[9]

3. Shaping the Shifted Moral Reasoning of the ICC

The principles agreed upon within the framework of international criminal justice play an essential role in shaping our moral reasoning and conduct during their application while demonstrating their capability and desirability in delivering equal justice. Furthermore, it should be emphasised that acceptance of these principles within the Statute of the International Criminal Court should not be construed merely as a psychological reflection concerning victims or their prospects for redress. Ideally, international criminal justice encapsulates one overarching concept: rights - specifically, the right to attain justice. This interpretation transcends personal opinion; rather, it reflects a collective endorsement through codification, signature, and ratification processes associated with the Court's Statute - signifying victims' rightful expectation that justice will be duly rendered without neglect or oversight.

The concept of attaining rights is fundamentally a pursuit of justice rather than a reflection of reality. This issue transcends mere national political concerns, as individuals face accusations and are subjected to incarceration by various political authorities through diverse means. Notably, the entire

---

[9] Although the United Nations Charter demands right to justice, equality, and peace, all these have been violated. Right to justice *inter alia* can be seen in the Charter of the United Nations, 1945; Universal Declaration of Human Rights, 1948; The Four Geneva Conventions of 12 August 1949; The 1977 Protocols Additional to the Geneva Conventions of 12 August 1949; International Covenant on Civil and Political Rights, 1966; International Covenant on Economic, Social and Cultural Rights, 1966; International Convention on the Elimination of All Forms of Racial Discrimination, 1965; Convention on the Elimination of All Forms of Discrimination against Women, 1979; Declaration on the Elimination of All Forms of Intolerance and of Discrimination based on Religion or Belief, 1981; Convention on the Rights of the Child, 1989; Statute of the International Tribunal for the Former Yugoslavia, 1993; Statute of the International Tribunal for Rwanda, 1994; Rome Statute of the International Criminal Court, 1998; Declaration on the Rights of Persons Belonging to National or Ethnic, Religious and Linguistic Minorities, 1992.

framework of international criminal justice operates as an extension of powerful nations. The assertion that colonialism has ended and that the principles of justice are accurately articulated exists merely in rhetoric and does not align with the actual state of international social dynamics. It is essential to highlight that the acknowledgment of justice principles by superpowers or colonial entities represents only a selective vocabulary concerning crime and its associated tenets, failing to correspond with a comprehensive understanding of the original theoretical framework concealed behind closed doors. *My argument appears to be strictly deductive, grounded in both historical and contemporary practices enacted by colonial powers. The crux of my position lies in the observation that colonialism has not truly ended; rather, it has transformed its appearance while adopting new guises.*

It is undeniable that the principles of justice, when viewed from their original context, exert certain psychological effects; however, these principles have been rearticulated under various conventions or agreements pertaining to international human rights law, leading us to believe we have entered a new era of justice. In reality, the harsh realities associated with colonialism or authoritarian regimes have been obscured by ostensibly noble norms surrounding human rights. Given the multitude of expectations surrounding the genuine characteristics attributed to major criminal powers - including their ideologies and interests - the foundational function and definition of authentic justice have been compromised. Consequently, interpretations favoured legally and philosophically regarding the initial premise of international criminal justice have found themselves beholden to new authorities, resulting in conditions deemed reasonable for imposing established principles on notions of justice that ultimately lack significance.

This unjust state implies that even those principles deemed beneficial may diverge from their true purpose from both a legal and moral perspective. As such, the original premise surrounding justice - particularly within international criminal justice - is defined in such a manner that injustice becomes an entrenched aspect of law whereby any victim seeking redress for international crimes must comply; noncompliance often results in further suffering. Therefore, definitions and applications of justice as construed by oppressive governments are presented as equitable. A poignant illustration of this predicament can be seen in the current plight faced by the Palestinian nation, which finds itself ensnared within a web woven by terrorist actions orchestrated by Western governmental powers.[10]

The systems governing international criminal justice and human rights operate under assumptions wherein all governments are equally represented as subjects possessing legal and moral rights unless proven otherwise. Nevertheless, the actual circumstances surrounding these governments are significantly different from their moral or legal standing as defined by both legal systems, primarily due to the exercise of their practical powers. Consequently, influenced by arbitrary factors related to their military capabilities, the interpretation of justice varies greatly, rendering the concept of justice as fairness for victims virtually unattainable. The notion of pure procedural justice aimed at safeguarding victims' rights from the onset of crimes to the present is similarly elusive. It becomes evident that the foundational understanding of justice in establishing the ICC and its Statute serves merely a decorative and symbolic purpose, existing in a purely hypothetical context intended to mislead the public. In this complex scenario regarding definitions of justice, there is little relevance in discussing any semblance of it.

Thus, comprehending definitions of justice, rights, and the realisation thereof within the corridors of the ICC proves to be exceedingly difficult. The Court essentially functions as a façade representing colonial power over other states in both legal and official capacities. This dynamic explains why cases brought before the Court predominantly involve African nations engaged in conflicts with one another based on divisions imposed by colonial powers or due to leaders supported or opposed by Western governments. Therefore, what is termed 'justice' at the ICC reflects a systematic adherence to constraints established by dominant global powers. This suggests that the original conception of criminal justice under the auspices of both the Court and even the United Nations does not genuinely address the dire conditions faced by victims; rather, it seeks only to acknowledge that victims possess legal rights - albeit only nominally within legal discourse. This implies that avenues for legal or moral adjudication remain firmly closed, failing to facilitate a genuine transition from injustice to practical justice.

---

[10] "Israel has behaved like a mafia, attempting to bully Gaza into a different deal altogether." In David Hearst, Israel's Ramadan massacre obliterates any remaining western claims of moral leadership (19 March 2025), https://www.middleeasteye.net/opinion/ramadan-massacre-obliterates-wests-claim-moral-leadership; https://www.middleeasteye.net/news/tributes-pour-slain-journalists-hossam-shabat-mohammad-mansour.

4. Lobbies of Characteristic Lies

The issue at hand is not merely an exaggeration in the definition of justice, but rather the underlying realities associated with various definitions of justice that are periodically incorporated into our international treaties for diverse reasons and under differing circumstances. It is evident that arguments stemming from significant political powers, which do not genuinely engage in or ratify the content of a treaty or international convention addressing their criminal actions, do not support justice nor serve the interests of victims. We ought to pursue a form of moral geometry that aligns with the strict standards of international criminal justice and reinforces its foundational principles. Regrettably, few governments undertake this responsibility; predominantly, Western governments perceive other nations as the source of all issues.

Unfortunately, the reasoning I present here may fail to meet the expectations of justice theorists operating within criminal government lobbies and their legal representatives. This concern is not mine; when justice is commodified, lawyers become similarly commodified, leading to an erosion of victims' rights. [11] Consequently, when victims' rights are compromised, the entire framework of international criminal law - including human rights - collapses. In instances where we fall significantly short of addressing these critical aspects of justice, it becomes increasingly apparent that what remains is profoundly deficient. If I am permitted to repeat myself, *despondently the reasoning that I present here may not satisfy the expectations of justice theorists in the lobbies of the criminal governments and in the office of their lawyers. That is surely not my problem. When justice is sold, then lawyers, too, are sold, and when the lawyers are sold, then the rights of the victims are sold, and when the victims'* rights *are sold, then the whole system of international criminal laws, including human rights, collapses.*[12]

---

[11] Farhad Malekian, *Conscience of Lawyers in International Criminal Law, the Burden of Doppelgängers* (New York: Nova Science Publishers, 2021).

[12] "Lawyers who promote one-eyed justice are not truly lawyers but people of business. They deal with the lives of those who have been killed or are going to be killed. Clear examples of this are how we truly protested the commissions of genocide committed during the Second World War in Europe, but we ignore the same crimes with similar victims in other parts of the world, such as in Palestine, which is a nation that has been suffering for hundreds of years as a result of Western governments' crimes.

Am I wrong? In what sense? If you are a lawyer and cannot see all the occupations and devastations of civilization in other countries and their nations, then you believe that you should protect violations. Eventually, you will even embrace and share and the idea of the commission of genocide, crimes against humanity, and war crimes.

It is imperative for every reader engaged in studying justice to keep in mind the ideal of equitable justice - one that encompasses not only the needs of victims but also upholds justice for all individuals on an equal footing. This underscores why we cannot arrive at definitive conclusions regarding the definitions or interpretations of justice under current circumstances. Consequently, various definitions exist within systems of justice, particularly in relation to international criminal justice; this suggests that numerous interpretations concerning principles of justice may emerge solely for the purpose of achieving appropriate outcomes. The conceptions surrounding justice may differ depending on how relevant authorities or their agents perceive the value inherent in true justice, or whether regard it as a legacy steeped in falsehoods and injustice. *Thus, there exists a substantial array of theories regarding the parameters defining justice - wherein terms like "justice as injustice," "justice as humiliation," "justice as violations," "justice as aggression," and "justice as fairness" represent varying legal definitions influenced by who articulates them and for what purposes they are proposed.*

The fundamental focus of the principles governing international criminal justice is to evaluate all evidence while discarding any that is founded on deceit and the complete degradation of victims. This underscores the necessity for an international criminal justice system, which unfortunately struggles to operate effectively. The core issue lies in the presentation of fabricated facts and evidence that lack veracity, all rooted in falsehoods. In essence, entire nations are subjected to destruction through various means and definitions based on untruths, which are then introduced into the processes of international criminal justice with the expectation that the Court and its judges will be persuaded by these presentations, resulting in a determination of guilt for the victims while exonerating those who have perpetrated crimes.

This has been the trajectory of justice over decades within a framework governed by the Court's independent international legal personality, which

All these actions mean that you are aiding, assisting, protecting, and supporting the criminal conduct of other nations. Nations whose existence is not essential for your existence, and therefore must be taken out of their own traditional countries. This is precisely the situation that the United States government created in Latin America with its full-scale terrorist aggression. *What principle of international criminal justice or of the United Nations permits the US to call most governments terrorists but not itself?* Consult the brilliant works of Professor Richard Falk from Princeton University, or the works of Professors John Mearsheimer, Richard Wolff, Douglas Macgregor, Avram Noam Chomsky, and Professor Jeffrey Sachs if my word alone is not sufficient." Farhad Malekian, *Concreting Righteousness in International Criminal Justice* (New York: Nova publishers, 2024), pp. 26-27.

seeks to assign concepts of international criminal responsibility to individuals suspected of committing genocide, war crimes, aggression, torture, or sexual violations.[13]

5. Manufacturing False Evidence

The foundational structure of the international criminal justice system should ideally rest upon principles of truthfulness and trust regarding the evidence submitted by involved parties. Nevertheless, the International Criminal Court frequently encounters various claims questioning the authenticity of such evidence. This situation does not arise from any inadequacy on the part of the Court in discerning between accurate and false evidence; rather, it stems from the overwhelming influence wielded by significant political powers or authoritarian governments capable of manufacturing false evidence without limitation. Consequently, this renders control over misleading evidence elusive for the Court for various reasons. Although major global institutions appear to operate under a cohesive framework for international criminal justice procedures, their capacity to present credible evidence is ultimately subjugated to prevailing superpower interests. It has become apparent that these principles, which were intended to govern rights and responsibilities within these institutions the protection of victims, often produce contrary effects.

It is essential not to conflate genuine principles underlying international criminal justice with those artificial principles promulgated by superpowers as legitimate norms. Through legal and political stratagems employed in particular circumstances by their representatives, these entities can obfuscate the entire framework of international criminal justice and advance their

---

[13] Miranda Cleland, Why Israel can Torture Detained Palestinian Children with Impunity (2023), https://www.middleeasteye.net/opinion/israel-palestine-war-torture-detained-palestinian-children-impunity; Fayha Shalash,' I was crying': The plight of wounded Palestinian children in Israeli custody (2023), https://www.middleeasteye.net/news/israel-palestine-children-wounded-plight-jails; Neil Sammonds, War on Gaza: How Israeli Torture Methods Resemble Islamic State Horrors, https://www.middleeasteye.net/opinion/gaza-war-israeli-torture-methods-resemble-islamic-state-horrors; Examine also Michael Otterman, *American Torture: From the Cold War to Abu Ghraib and Beyond* (Pluto Press, 2007); Kristine Huskey with Aleigh Acerni, Justice at Guantanamo: One Woman's Odyssey and Her Crusade for Human Rights (2009); Katherine Hearst, Israel-Palestine war: The Palestinian children detained by Israel (2023), https://www.middleeasteye.net/news/israel-palestine-war-children-detained-explained; https://www.middleeasteye.net/live/gaza-war-hamas-israel-ceasefire-negotiations-doha-resume.

multifaceted criminal agendas. Consequently, it becomes increasingly challenging for the Court to apply its mandates uniformly across different subjects. Indeed, discussions surrounding plans aimed at securing political victories for both established and emerging colonial powers often occur behind closed doors, away from public scrutiny.

The establishment of the International Criminal Court does not necessarily indicate that we have modernised the system of international law or established a system of equality of arms. We must recognise the power and positions that arise with the creation of any norm of equality. It is important to note that the entire Charter of the United Nations emphasises the equality of all states, their protection under the rule of law, and the universal application of United Nations regulations. However, the reality is that behind each principle of equality in the Charter lies a force, often referred to as the power of guns. That means the principle of state equality is safeguarded by an underlying power, both within and beyond the Charter, which is not explicitly stated but is influenced by powerful governments.

The authority of the International Criminal Court, influenced by the superpowers, similarly governs these rules, norms, and principles. The underlying philosophy is straightforward: if the Court accepts the interpretations provided by these dominant nations, it may relax its standards; conversely, if the Court rejects their interpretations, it faces various forms of criticism. Consequently, certain actions committed by powerful criminals may be deemed permissible rather than forbidden. One should consider this a game of deception rather than a game of law. While this may sound peculiar, it reflects a harsh reality. Indeed, there is ambiguity surrounding many matters and decisions; however, the reality of power remains unchanged. This dynamic has persisted since the establishment of the League of Nations, the Nuremberg Tribunal, the International Court in The Hague, and the International Criminal Court in the same region. It is best to assert that these institutions represent the interests of Western authorities, who have historically been the primary architects of colonialism.[14] Thus, legal institutions, including those pertaining to criminal law, serve as representations of justice that discuss concepts of right and wrong. Nevertheless, the definitions of justice within these institutions do not

[14] Jonathan Cook, The new fascism: Israel is the template for Trump and Europe's war on freedom (24 March 2025), https://www.middleeasteye.net/opinion/israel-new-fascism-lockstep-trump-waging-war-terror-home; Jonathan Cook, How the West hides its Gaza genocide guilt behind Holocaust Day remembrance (31 January 2025), https://www.middleeasteye.net/opinion/west-hides-gaza-genocide-guilt-holocaust-day-how.

significantly alter the interpretations of justice as articulated by contemporary colonial powers.

Therefore, the questions surrounding the justification of rights and equality among different subjects of law remain unresolved. It appears that asserting a singular interpretation of the entire system of international criminal justice, which is governed by a sole power of control, is merely a façade. This façade is nothing more than the false narratives propagated by the United States, which are further elaborated and supported in the international arena by its allies. The current state of international criminal justice reflects the conditions that are broadly considered reasonable for imposition upon all governments and states, including individuals who are already acknowledged as unequal under the United Nations Charter's principles of equality. Furthermore, there is a lack of choice regarding the principles within the justice system - particularly as experienced by those occupying legal positions that, in reality, hold no substantial authority. It is not my intent to present a favoured or standard interpretation; rather, I aim to convey a fact that should have been recognised long ago by those genuinely pursuing justice - not as a means to empower the principles of injustice dictated by modern colonial powers within the United Nations organisation.

It is certainly plausible to suggest that each principle of international criminal justice corresponds to a specific conception of justice that may resonate with our writings and their audience. This possibility has been demonstrated in our discussions. Consequently, there may exist an interpretation of the justice system, specifically international criminal justice, which presents itself as an acceptable and preferred solution for defining the contentious issue surrounding the acknowledgment of international crimes committed under military commands. This suggests that we can justify actions resulting in the deaths of millions, including countless children, while still labelling such acts as justifiable and necessary. Such reasoning exemplifies how politicians from powerful governments operate and guide societal perceptions with respect to justice.[15]

---

[15] Examine Farhad Malekian, *International Criminal Law of Children* (New York: Nova Science Publishers, 2021); Farhad Malekian, *Prohibition Governing Child Soldiers Constituting an Integral Part of Jus cogens and Obligatio Erga Omnes*, XVII *World Congress of the International Association of Youth and Family Judges and Magistrates*, Belfast, Northern Ireland, 27 August – 2 September (2006); Farhad Malekian, 'Conundrums of *Jus cogens:* In Case Law' (Part II), No. 13 *Вісник Південного регіонального центру Національної академії правових наук України,* [No. 13 *Journal of the South regional Center of National Academy of Legal Sciences of Ukraine*] (2017), pp. 12-21; Farhad Malekian, 'Conundrums of *Jus cogens*: in International Criminal Law' (Part I), *Вісник Південного регіонального*

Thus, the average utility principle associated with definitions of justice tends to expand, reflecting how we perceive and evaluate interpretations of international criminal justice as presented by these political leaders. This implies that fundamental truths regarding definitions of justice often fall prey to political influence, with authority over legal matters reverting to their hands. Therefore, it is asserted that the framework governing international criminal justice operates under the dominion of coercive power rather than lawful governance. The absence of limits upon various definitions of justice illustrates its subordination to dominant political forces and their strategic interests. These variations in definitions are not confined merely to initial conceptualisations but persist throughout all processes observed during diverse global events.

6. Privatised Definition of International Crimes

In the presentation of justice by the powertionist governments, we delineate the various underlying assumptions inherent in the justice system upon which these conceptions of international criminal justice appear to rely.[16] Nonetheless, it is essential to recognise that the definition of justice articulated today may not hold value tomorrow under the same neo-colonial regime within the United Nations. This fluctuation arises because powertionist governments continuously alter their stance, often prioritising the evolution of

---

центру Національної академії правових наук України [*No.12 Journal of the South regional Center of National Academy of Legal Sciences of Ukraine*] (2017), pp. 8-16.

[16] "Consequently, powertionism can be defined as the use of political and military power in order to accuse others of crimes committed by the accusers themselves. Powertionism may therefore be considered a negative theory of law that does not have rules, provisions or principles and instead uses the established codifications of the systems of international human rights law and international criminal justice for its own intentions Thus, powertionism is understood entirely in terms of the consequential meanings of phrases which are supposed to offer protection but only cause harm in practice. The theory of powertionism is centred on a logical philosophy which adapts the interests of other theories of the law and presents a new form of implementation and a new result. What distinguishes powertionism from utilitarianism or egoism mostly has to do with the choice of the applicable consequences, although one cannot deny the fact that sometimes powertionism cannot only create egoist power, but it can also lead to genocide as seen during the Second World War as well as in Rwanda and Cambodia. From the perspective of powertionism, one may conclude that there may be good, however that good is contingent upon the respect of powerful states and their interests. This is because fundamentally, powertionism is a theory that pits certain groups against others by utilising all possibilities under their power." Farhad Malekian, *Powertionism in International Criminal Justice* (New York: Nova Science Publishers, 2022), pp. 45-46.

the definition of justice based on their influence in different global regions. Consequently, the principles of international criminal justice that inform our judgments are not stable; thus, the processes for justifying the criminal actions of significant offenders transform into a mere game within the corridors of the International Criminal Court.

The fundamental purpose of international criminal reasoning is primarily to attain restitution for victims or targets of aggression. This implies that representatives from major political powers refrain from fabricating falsehoods. However, these representatives not only contravene basic tenets of international criminal justice but also infringe upon natural human rights regarding fundamental liberties. They do not hesitate to deceive themselves, their constituents, innocent individuals, victims, deceased children, and patients in hospitals.[17] Their deceptions extend beyond these groups; they do not hesitate to mislead those who suffer from various epidemics. Furthermore, these representatives persist in deceiving those who lack access to food or clean water. This scenario exemplifies the intentions behind definitions of justice and underscores the imposition of an international criminal justice framework worldwide. It suggests that both just and unjust actions will be tolerated with reservations: what is deemed just is allocated to criminals while injustice is perpetuated against victims for a myriad of reasons rooted in falsehoods.

Thus, although we assert that institutions within the framework of international criminal justice exist at specific times and places to prevent violations against established legal provisions - particularly concerning human rights - these institutions remain incapacitated by a predominant culture of permissible deceit sanctioned under Chapter VII of the United Nations Charter. Therefore, we can characterise these pervasive falsehoods in international reasoning as artificial instruments within international criminal justice wielded by representatives from powertionist regimes who exploit these tools as if they were truths while treating legal norms as fabrications. Such characteristic deceptions are propagated not only by government representatives but also by influential figures such as heads of state, ministers, monarchs, and others holding significant authority.

The objective here is not to inflict harm or assign blame to any state; rather, it is imperative to articulate the truth. Failing to do so leaves us with no

[17] *Id.* See also David William Pear, 'The US-Led Genocide and Destruction of Yemen,' https://www.unz.com/article/the-us-led-genocide-and-destruction-of-yemen/ (October 12, 2019).

alternative but to characterise the situation as a falsehood. In essence, when the commission of international crimes defines actions, we consistently engage in deceit under a covert diplomacy that presents lies as truth and legal principles as falsehoods. In all such circumstances, we undermine the diplomacy of facts and the presentation of truth - not only for the victims but also for the global public. Consequently, the boundary between truth and deception widens significantly, leading even our military entities and those of other governments to propagate falsehoods along with their ethically questionable or immoral assertions. Nevertheless, these deceptions are framed within narratives purporting to be factual concerning victims and justice principles, which fundamentally rely on characteristic fabrications associated with international criminal reasoning. These deceptive rationales ultimately receive endorsement during meetings of the Security Council, which continues to operate under these untruths.

It is indeed accurate to assert that since its inception, the entire framework of the international Security Council has persisted based on *foundational lies inherent in international criminal reasoning*. It would not be an exaggeration to claim that the broader system of enforcement for international human rights by major political powers arises from these fundamental misrepresentations concerning human rights rationale. Such fabrications disseminated by government representatives permeate various parliamentary institutions, fostering misconceptions based on flawed interpretations of international criminal justice systems and misattributing roles of victims as offenders or terrorists.

This scenario engenders disparate interpretations of human rights norms and culminates in significant breaches of international criminal justice frameworks, inevitably resulting in heightened conflicts among nations and diverse ethnic groups - manipulated anew by representatives of powerful governments seeking to ignite discord for territorial and resource acquisition purposes. Thus, the system governing international criminal justice perpetually confronts emerging conflicts in diplomatic relations, encompassing actions ranging from orchestrating deceptive parliamentary sessions aimed at persuading populations that their endeavours are justified and meaningful. A salient illustration can be found in statements made by leaders of the British government regarding their transgressions in various regions worldwide; notable examples include India, Iran, Afghanistan, a number of countries in Africa, Iraq, Egypt, Libya, among others.

The leaders of the United Kingdom, both in governmental and state capacities, have not hesitated to employ notable falsehoods within the context of international criminal justice. They have utilised various forms of reasoning to persuade their parliaments, their citizens, and the global community that their actions are exclusively directed at combating terrorism. In actuality, the designation "terrorist" has become interchangeable with all forms of international crimes committed by resistance groups advocating for victims' rights. The question at hand is who the real terrorists are.

Consequently, every vote on proposals introduced by government representatives is perceived not only as critical for preserving the deceptions perpetuated by authoritarian regimes but also as a fundamental necessity. This situation undermines the integrity of justice, which is anticipated to prevail in numerous criminal cases tainted by brutality, atrocities, barbarism, and cruelty. As a result, governmental representatives validate their inherent falsehoods through diverse rationalisations and moral philosophies that manipulate various overarching principles within the justice system. It is noteworthy that significant untruths are frequently employed by these representatives to influence public opinion. A prominent example is found in statements made by Israeli leaders on October 7th regarding alleged mass killings of civilians conducted by members of resistance groups, particularly involving accusations related to the beheading of children; however, they have provided no verifiable evidence to support such claims. Investigations into these allegations by United Nations authorities have been resolutely obstructed and entirely prohibited. As far as the final words go, there were no infant beheadings.

Such deliberate fabrications, left unchallenged, not only undermine the legitimacy of international criminal justice institutions but also further marginalise victims by weaponizing truth itself.

7. Empowering Lies Through the Abandonment of Justice

The definition of justice and its principles are framed in such a way that all subjects of the law ought to achieve their equal rights, ensuring that these rights are not violated due to the political power of one individual over another. This issue extends beyond the realm of international criminal justice and its application to those who have committed international crimes; it is a fundamental consideration in addressing questions of justice from both legal and moral perspectives in cases involving criminal violations.[18] Equality is a foundational element of any investigation. The theory of equality in the context of justice and the equal assessment of all evidence and consequences is not limited to international justice; it is also a crucial principle within the procedures of national criminal jurisdiction. In other words, if the rules and norms of national justice advocate for equality of arms among all parties, then it is imperative that this principle is upheld for both weaker and stronger parties alike.

To determine whether the current formulation of national criminal justice is accurate, we must examine the implementation and enforcement of the relevant systems, as well as the integrity of their leaders and the legitimacy of their elections.[19] This task is inherently challenging, as national justice systems vary significantly from one country to another. Understanding the realities of these systems is not only demanding but often impossible due to corruption and the monopolisation of justice by certain groups. While it may be tempting to simplify our understanding of justice according to subjective preferences, such simplifications do not align with the criteria for genuine, truthful justice, which must respect all its principles. The principles of justice should apply universally to all individuals, as they are intended to be common standards. When a specific aspect of the international criminal justice system fails to function properly or is neglected by those responsible for its implementation - whether in national or international courts - we may

---

[18] For the development of the idea of international criminal justice consult Vespasian V. Pella, *Plan d'un Code Répressif Mondial,* 6 *Rewe International de Droit Pénal* 1948 (1955); United Nations War Crimes Commission, History of the United Nations War Commission and the Development of the Laws of War. 445-450 (1949); Vespasian V. Pella, Towards an International Criminal Court, 44 *American Journal of International Law* 57 (1950); Sowilet A, *The Problem of the Creation of a Permanent International Criminal Court* (Nendeln, Liechtenstein : Kraus reprint, 1951); Yeun-Li Liang, 'The Establishment of an International Criminal Jurisdiction: The First Phase,' 46 *American Journal of International Law* (1952); Quincy Wright, Proposal for an International Criminal Court, 46 *American Journal of International Law* 60 (1952); Bienvenido C. Ambion, '*Organization of a Court of International Criminal Jurisdiction,'* 29 *Philippine Law Journa*l 545 (1954); Fannie Klein & Daniel Wilkes, 'United Nations Draft Statute for an International Criminal Court: An American Evaluation,' in *International Criminal Law* 526 (Gerhard O.W. Mueller & Edward M. Wise, eds, 1965); Stone Julius and Robert Woetzel, *Toward a Feasible International Criminal Court* (1970). William A. Schabas, The International Criminal Court: A Commentary on the Rome Statute (Oxford University Press, 2016); Farhad Malekian, *Jurisprudence of International Criminal Justice* (Introduction by Professor Benjamin B. Ferencz, the former Prosecutor of the Nuremberg Tribunal (Cambridge: Cambridge Scholars Publishing, 2014); Carsten Stahn, *The Law and Practice of the International Criminal Court* (Oxford University Press, 2015).

[19] *Id.*

encounter a hierarchy of confusion regarding the true nature of justice.[20] This confusion can lead to a blurring of the lines between justice and injustice, particularly due to the ulterior motives of those who commit crimes. Individuals or groups seeking to manipulate the administration of justice to serve their own interests often perpetuate such a state of confusion.[21]

Consequently, they may establish regulations for themselves, provided that these regulations aim to achieve their own interpretation of justice, which is frequently predicated on significant falsehoods. This implies that widely accepted standards of justice and principles of human rights, as well as other legal doctrines, are disregarded or receive no recognition whatsoever. The ideology propagated by Western powers and their allied subservient governments ensures that those who adhere to this theory engage in a form of injustice characterised by the deceitful narratives of authoritarian regimes; such actions are not merely tolerated but are considered permissible. Thus, there exists no common foundation for delineating mutual expectations regarding the definition of justice and its potential normative values. Furthermore, within the compromised framework of the United Nations, there is an absence of any robustly binding principle to prohibit such deceptions from infiltrating the well-ordered structure established by the Charter of the United Nations.

It is regrettable that parliamentary deceit perpetrated by governmental representatives has come to shape our understanding of justice for self-serving ends. Even when certain UN officials endeavour to address and take appropriate action concerning governments' criminal assertions, the philosophical underpinnings of justice become hindered in their development, effectively preventing progress towards genuine judicial accountability. The outcome is a detrimental effect on the efficacy of international criminal justice systems in addressing actual offenders. This suggests a failure to logically arrive at essential principles of justice that ought to be respected and enforced consistently - despite violations predominantly occurring at the hands of powerful governments within the Security Council.

In summary, within the sphere of international criminal justice there exists an imbalance between truth and deception where falsehoods consistently overshadow facts in criminal cases. Ultimately, this results in a vacuum devoid of reciprocal acknowledgment or understanding of international criminal justice norms applicable to all victims - including perpetrators themselves.

---

[20] *Id.*

[21] *Id.*

Those who commit crimes dictate the trajectory of justice while it remains ensconced within institutions controlled by those responsible for grave international offenses. The criminals drive the train of justice and the train remains permanently stationed within the institutions governed by the perpetrators of serious international crimes. That is to say understanding the provisions of the Statute of the International Criminal Court with its relevant rules becomes not only complicated but even impossible to demand.[22] It is inaccurate to claim that the institution of international criminal justice in The Hague has a flawless system that effectively addresses the crimes of all offenders.[23] This assertion is akin to suggesting that wolves would be willing to consistently approach the court and willingly submit to the processes of criminal justice.

[22] For example, study how international criminal law was violated by the powertionist governments during the events of September 11th, which they planned and carried out themselves. The purpose of this was to initiate wars against other counties. French book *L'effroyable imposture* which was translated into 28 languages and had a print run of 300,000 copies. Thierry Meyssan, 11 September 2001: L'effroyable imposture (2002); Arthur Naiman, *9/11: The Simple Facts – Why the Official Story can't Possibly be True* (US: Soft Skull Press, 2011). Robert F. Kennedy, Why the Arabs don't want us in Syria: They don't hate 'our freedoms.' They hate that we've betrayed our ideals in their own countries - for oil in http://www.politico.eu/book/why-the-arabs-dont-want-us-in-syria-mideast-conflict-oil-intervention/; Washington's Secret Agendas – Truth is being Disguised to Suit, available online at http://www.oneworldofnations.com/2014/09/washingtons-secret-agendas-truth-is.html; 'Former Liberian dictator Charles Taylor had US spy agency ties' available online at http://www.bostonglobe.com/metro/2012/01/17/mass-escapee-turned-liberian-dictator-had-spy-agency-ties/DGBhSfjxPVrtoo4WT95bBI/story.html; Niels H. Harrit, et al., 'Active Thermitic Material Discovered in Dust from the 9/11 World Trade Center Catastrophe' available online at http://911review.com/evidence/wtc_explosives.html; www.bentham-open.org/pages/content.php?TOCPJ/2009/00000002/00000001/7TOCPJ.SGM; See also U.S. Professor Zarembka's very powerful lecture concerning September 11, available online at https://www.youtube.com/watch?v=PinWplT-4vY; David Ray Griffin – 9/11 Myths and Reality Lecture on https://www.youtube.com/watch?v=hQBsWT1xF0w. See *also* https://www.youtube.com/watch?v=1W6QLfXE3wA; https://www.youtube.com/watch?v=ySAUjvWgnws.

[23] *Id.*

Chapter 6

Empowering the Monopolisation of International Criminal Justice

1. Justice as the Monopoly of Lies

The framework of international criminal justice seeks to promote accountability for perpetrators and deliver justice for victims of international crimes. Ideally, regulations governing international criminal justice should be enforced through the collective authority of all parties involved in the ICC in conjunction with a proper understanding of victims' rights. Consequently, state parties must avoid endorsing definitions of justice that reinforce the interests of dominant authoritarian regimes while neglecting victims' rights; otherwise, international criminal justice will fail to achieve meaningful outcomes for victims.

While it is acknowledged that there exists a shared conception of justice within international law applicable to all nations, alongside a common understanding of justice and its principles in the legal domain, we continue to encounter misrepresentations by superpowers that are legitimised as just, while accurate interpretations of rights are deemed unjust. Moreover, it is presumed that the principles governing justice as integrated into the system of international criminal justice are founded on fundamental righteousness and a commitment to truth; however, we face contrary interpretations not only in judicial decisions but also in their practical application. This prevailing state of justice continues to be presented as a natural phenomenon within an authoritarian ideological framework.

Consequently, it becomes imperative to differentiate between the rules governing authoritarian notions of justice and multilateral legislative norms pertaining to justice. The former addresses how power can be monopolised under its own guise while the latter opposes such criminal conduct. This distinction underscores a critical difference between rights associated with genuine justice and those pertaining to co-opted forms thereof. The right to justice articulates laws grounded in substantive reasoning, whereas appropriated concepts omit and disregard true rights based on rational justification. This indicates that authorities exploit the justice system as their personal asset to fulfil their objectives driven by deception. This situation suggests that various rights and obligations held by those wielding dominant legal power are manipulated according to political strategies aimed at optimising exploitation of international criminal justice bodies and human rights frameworks for specific illicit purposes pursued by authoritarian governments. In essence, a coalition of unscrupulous governments determines their actions based on self-interest, ideologies, and conjectures concerning what should be accepted or rejected in relation to their hegemonic principles.

This indicates that they assist each other's agendas. The strategic falsehoods propagated by authoritarian regimes do not adversely affect them, as they are not part of the victimised institution of deceit but are instead driven by political interests. Rather, these governments subscribe to a theory characterised by deception, violence, appropriation, and evasion. Such practices form the foundation of their conception of justice and are an integral aspect of their parliamentary politics. Ideally, a well-functioning legal justice system should adhere not only to the substantive dimensions of legal justice but also to moral justice, ensuring it does not deviate from the principles of natural justice which uphold the rights of all individuals to equitable treatment under any legal framework.

Evidently, justice must not be treated merely as a game on a golf course where one strikes the ball at any angle deemed favourable to manipulate the outcome for personal political gain. Justice institutions, whether at a national or international level, aim to eradicate injustice and prevent its recurrence. In reforming and strategizing within the international criminal justice system while holding violators of international law accountable, it is essential to possess not only legal knowledge but also the fortitude to advocate for its enforcement. This entails that the institution of international criminal justice should scrutinise structural power dynamics and devise necessary strategies aimed at securing victims' rights.

The unlawful actions perpetrated by contemporary colonial powers - rooted in their calculated malevolence - must be curtailed if we are to accurately define and implement a just system aligned with fundamental principles of international jurisdiction. This necessitates that mechanisms designed for appropriate justice replace those predicated on deception which would otherwise become ineffective. In light of the court's limited capacity, this policy faces critical challenges requiring resolution - most notably the imperative for enforcement measures. Although such measures may not have been anticipated or intended by state parties, they remain crucial within the context of international criminal justice since without specific enforcement actions, notions of justice risk becoming entirely ineffectual or non-existent. The strategies and tactics employed by the governments of powertionist states may encompass various alternatives for enforcing their will, while such options may not be central to the evaluation of criminal justice institutions and their enforcement mechanisms. This implies that the concept of justice is intertwined with numerous factors, discussions, and rationalisations that contribute to the development and perpetuation of falsehoods.

In light of the crucial importance of accurately defining justice, we consistently seek a distinction between valid definitions and those that are erroneous. This highlights the fact that the institution of justice grapples with issues of right versus wrong, good versus evil, or misleading representations that reflect the dishonest political nature of contemporary colonial powers such as the United Nations. This brings to mind an institution of justice that has become integral to both the foundational structure and application of justice, yet does not align with the requirements set forth in the Statute of the International Criminal Court. The underlying reason for this situation is our reliance on implementing a system of appropriate justice based solely on a limited perspective. Through these methods, we have inadvertently opted to enforce malevolent decisions and advance our own agendas. It is generally assumed that one or more principles defining justice may be unjust; however, in practice, the application of international criminal justice frequently manifests as fundamentally unjust due to the domination of international legal systems by powertionist governments.[1]

There exists a possibility that not only are institutions of justice deteriorating for various legal, political, and moral reasons rooted in falsehoods but also they are also losing their functions and roles in establishing adequate justice. Within the framework of an international criminal court - whether permanent or ad hoc - justice and victim compensation often fall short when measured against actions deemed unjust according to established definitions. This further indicates a prioritisation of falsehoods or unjust rulings; even when no institution within international criminal justice appears overtly unjust, it still lacks accountability regarding evidence. The injustices

---

[1] Examine the American representative John Bolton declaration against the ICC https://www.aljazeera.com/news/2018/09/full-text-john-bolton-speech-federalist-society-180910172828633.html. USA hotar Internationella brottmålsdomstolen med sanktioner - om krigsförbrytelser i Afghanistan utreds,' available online at https://svenska.yle.fi/artikel/2019/03/15/usa-hotar-internationella-brottmalsdomstolen-med-sanktioner-om-krigsforbrytelser.

faced by victims of international crimes stem from how we have commodified and manipulated norms related to justice while aligning our interests with those who hold significant influence over injustices - the very roots causing a comprehensive breakdown in international criminal justice systems. We consciously and unconsciously amalgamate victims' suffering into an unacceptable process labelled as "justice," which proves unhelpful for victims while undermining genuine values associated with true justice.

2. Negotiating the Consequences of the Injustices Derived from Lies

The legal framework governing justice comprises norms derived from various negotiations among different legal entities. In this context, we refer specifically to representatives from governments tasked with discussing normative values and agreements. However, it is important to note that negotiation structures involving major governments differ significantly from case to case. The significance of negotiations between governments varies considerably. The discussions and terms established at the negotiation table aim to identify solutions and prevent future conflicts; however, this fundamental principle is often not adhered to. Frequently, the language used allows for multiple interpretations, resulting in diverse definitions of justice derived from the stipulated norms. This indicates that the concept of justice, from its inception, has been fragmented into various interpretations that align with the interests of specific governments. Consequently, a universally accepted definition of justice remains elusive among nations. Although voting processes may occur on specific matters, these do not necessarily apply to all parties involved in the pursuit of justice.

One might argue that a comprehensive theory of justice should encompass allocations widely recognised within the framework of justice as negotiated by involved parties. Such allocations imply certain rights and values essential for upholding equitable justice in accordance with what has been mutually agreed upon. However, I will refrain from delving into matters regarding treaties and disproportionate agreements forged after numerous negotiation sessions. Our focus here is solely on the foundational structure of international criminal justice and how reasoning presented before, during, and after negotiation meetings fundamentally alters the accurate definition of justice, ultimately leading to catastrophic consequences, including extensive harm and loss of civilian lives in occupied territories.[2]

When circumstances permit, we adjust our stance and dismiss assertions made during negotiations using various justifications and falsehoods that are intricately linked to prior deceptions. A pertinent illustration of this is the dishonesty displayed by representatives of the United States during negotiations with Russia, specifically regarding NATO's proximity to Russian borders. The current situation reveals that these were blatant falsehoods, as evidenced by recent attempts by the United States to establish bases near Russian territories within NATO's military framework, resulting in the tragic loss of over half a million innocent Ukrainian lives.[3]

Let us consider that a basic structure is necessary for the effective application of international criminal justice; however, when we examine its practical implementation, we encounter approximately eight hundred American military bases worldwide. These installations signify that the United States government exerts control over the operational definition of justice while engaging in egregious international crimes under the guise of imposing its own conception of justice aligned with superpower interests. This results in millions losing their lives under political and legal frameworks dictated by these superpowers. It is evident that this legal definition does not represent an appropriate understanding but rather reflects interpretations crafted by those governments employing the force of arms rather than wisdom to assert their dominance. We may refrain from adhering to the principles of justice dictated by the use or threat of force; however, it is evident that our acceptance or rejection does not influence the means by which justice is implemented. This is particularly true given that deceitful strategies employed at negotiation tables to manipulate the perceptions of other parties have proven effective for a considerable duration.

In discussions concerning international criminal justice and its invaluable provisions - particularly those pertaining to international human rights - it is

---

[2] Consult Farhad Malekian, 'Judging International Criminal Justice in the Occupied Territories,' 12 *International Criminal Law Review* (2012), pp. 827–869.

[3] See the earlier statement of Professor Jeffrey Sachs to President Trump: Please Get U.S. out of Syria, "We've Done Enough Damage" (13th April, 2018); Available online at https://www.realclearpolitics.com/video/2018/04/13/jeffrey_sachs_to_president_trump_please_get_us_out_of_syria_weve_done_enough_damage.html. The current collaboration between the pro-Israeli and pro-Turkish governments of the United States serves as another example of their involvement in the region. In reality, these oppressive regimes have nearly devastated Syria. They assert that they are combating the former dictator of Syria and while simultaneously seeking to expand own territories. Israel's focus primary interests lie in securing oil resources expanding furthering territories.

crucial to note that refereeing to norms such as *jus cogens*, permanent provisions, customary international criminal law, or the esteemed role of the International Criminal Court and *ad hoc* tribunals carries little weight.[4] This is particularly significant when powertionist governments underpin the foundational principles of international criminal justice. This indicates that international criminal justice often operates within a paradigm shaped by force or threats, interwoven with persistent deceit characteristic of U.S. diplomacy since its inception under colonial British governance. While one may find their human rights policies reprehensible and unjust, these powers dictate the frameworks governing both international law and criminal justice, compelling compliance with their directives while inflicting significant losses on populations - including territorial and resource depletion. Major governments typically assert their commitment to safeguarding fundamental rights and responsibilities while overseeing wealth distribution through legal and moral channels provided by international organisations; however, this assertion is fundamentally flawed and laden with deception.

3. Advocacy of Justice by Colonial Governments

Let us reflect on this constructed narrative surrounding a system of international criminal justice built upon lies - a conception perpetuated in our literature and rhetoric at global meetings and conferences - echoing the hollow

[4] On *jus cogens* examine Czaplinski, Wladyslaw 'Concepts of *Jus Cogens* and Obligations Erga Omnes in International Law in the Light of Recent Developments' 23 *Polish Yearbook of International Law* (1997–1998), p. 87; G. Danilenko, 'International *Jus Cogens*: Issues of Law-Making' 2 (1) *European Journal of International Law* (1991), p. 42; A. D'Amato, 'It's a Bird, It's a Plane, It's *Jus Cogens*' 6 *Connecticut Journal of International Law* (1990), p. 1; AJJ de Hoog, 'The Relationship between *Jus Cogens*, Obligations Erga Omnes and International Crimes: Peremptory Norms in Perspective' 42 *Österreichische Zeitschrift für öffentliches Recht und Völkerrecht* (1991), p. 183; E de Wet, '*Jus Cogens* and Obligations Erga Omnes' in de Wet, E and J. Vidmar (eds.), *Hierarchy in International Law: The Place of Human Rights* (2012); P Dupuy, 'Some Reflections on Contemporary International Law and the Appeal to Universal Values: a Response to Marti Koskenniemi' 16 *European Journal of International Law* (2005), p. 131; C. Focarelli, 'Promotional *Jus Cogens*: A Critical Appraisal of *Jus Cogens*' Legal Effects' 77 *Nordic Journal of International Law* (2008), p. 429; M. J. Glennon, 'De l'Absurdité du Droit Impératif (*Jus Cogens*)' 110 *Revue Générale de Droit International Public* (2006), p. 529; Robledo Gómez, A El Ius Cogens Internacional (Estudio Histórico Crítico) (1982); A. Gómez Robledo 'Le *Jus Cogens* International: Sa Genése, sa Nature, ses Fonctions' 9 *Recueil des Cours de l'Académie de Droit International de la Haye* (1982), p. 172; L. Hannikainen, *Peremptory Norms (Jus Cogens) in International Law: Historical Development, Criteria, Present Status* (1988).

claims of contemporary colonial powers within the United Nations while receiving undue validation as correct and legitimate. What is the purpose of the provisions and conventions of international criminal law if they lack independent legal authority when necessary? The reality is that the justice system, particularly the realm of international criminal justice, does not require an abundance of provisions. Instead, it needs to be administered impartially and consistently, not only by judges but also by other officials within government systems. The unfortunate truth is that our judgments are not impartial. Even though we strive for impartiality, the deceitful narratives of terrorist states often undermine this effort.

That is why similar cases in the realm of criminal justice at the ICC are treated alike, based on their hierarchical classification within the ICC. The major powers often refuse to submit themselves to the court of justice, instead opting for what can be termed a court of injustice, namely the ICC. However, the relevant legal and factual similarities and differences in every case handled by the Office of the Prosecutor are shaped by the prevailing norms of deception and interpretation. Consequently, the purported impartial and consistent administration of rules within the system of international criminal courts is, in reality, a presentation of the institutionalisation of falsehoods across various institutions, irrespective of the substantive principles enshrined in the constitutions of any international criminal court.[5]

In other words, addressing similar instances of violations of international criminal law, such as breaches of international humanitarian law during armed conflicts, does not provide a sufficient guarantee for the enforcement of international criminal justice without the influence of significant falsehoods. This is evident in numerous cases where major political powers or contemporary colonial governments advocate for full respect for international

[5] Examine also Roman Boed, The International Criminal Tribunal for Rwanda, in International Criminal Law, vol iii (M. cherif Bassiouni, ed. 2008) pp. 103-116; Colette Braeckman, Rwanda: Histoire d'un genocide (1994); Colette Braeckman, Terreur africaine. Burundi, Rwanda, Zaïre: Les racines de la violence (1996); Christopher Browning, The path to genocide: Essays on launching the final solution (2002); Genocide in Rwanda, Africa Research & Information Centre, (Napoleon Abdulai, ed., 1994); African Rights, Rwanda: Death, Despair and Defiance (1995); J. E. Ackerman & E. O'Sullivan, Practice and procedure of the International Criminal Tribunal for the Former Yugoslavia; with selected material from the International Criminal Tribunal for Rwanda (2000); Michael N. Barnett, Eyewitness to a Genocide: The United Nations and Rwanda(2002); Laurence Burgorgue, Larsen (ed.), La repression internationale du genocide rwandais, (2003); Jacques Castonguay, Les Casques Bleus au Rwanda,(1998); Jean Pierre Chrétien, Le défi de l'ethnisme: Rwanda et Buruni, 1990 - 1996, (1997);Jean Pierre Chrétien., The Great Lakes of Africa: Two thousand years of history, (2003); Makau Wa Mutua, The Rwanda Tribunal: A critical Assessment, Africa Legal Aid Quarterly, April-June (2001).

humanitarian law and its relationship to justice, while in practice, they fail to acknowledge the binding provisions of humanitarian law during armed conflicts.[6] A clear example is the waging of war by western powers against Palestinian population in Gaza, framed as a war against terrorism. If a government or group were to accuse the Western governments of being terrorists, they would reject such allegations and refuse to recognise that they are violating the system of international humanitarian law of armed conflicts and assisting the criminals. Nevertheless, they unequivocally label resistance groups within the Palestinian territories as terrorists, merely because they refuse to adhere to the dictates of imperialist powers, which position themselves as the law, regardless of the fact that the powertionist government's characterisation of justice is not justice but rather a perversion of justice, an evil one, in service of oppression.[7] That is unfortunately, how the system of international criminal justice is legally and politically manipulated by the dominant terrorist governments of the world that engage in state-sponsored terrorism.

I might label the International Criminal Court system as a formalised justice of lies. This is because prosperity is developed through the corrupt and terroristic political views of governments. Consequently, if we think of the system of international criminal justice as always delivering a kind of equality between victims and perpetrators of international crimes, then we are really lost in a forest of lies, having adherents and custodians. The proper, genuine system of justice prohibits the institutionalisation of lies from entering the formal structures of the justice of truth. I mean those principles of justice that belong to the universal principles of morality or the natural rights of every victim to seek truthful justice - defined and defended with the principles of righteousness. This concept of justice has been explored in the very doctrine of righteous morality. Judges or court authorities have wrongly implemented the objective framework of justice. It is obvious that institutions of criminal justice working and functioning under the power of international criminal courts or governments may be equally unjust, depending on the extent of influence wielded by the forces of lies.[8]

---

[6] Thomas G. Weiss, *Military-Civilian Interactions: Humanitarian Crises and the Responsibility to Protect* (2nd ed., Rowman & Littlefield Publishers Inc, Lanham (MD), 2005).

[7] P. Muchnik, *Kant's Theory of Evil: An Essay on the Dangers of Self-love and the Aperiodicity of History* (Lexington Books, 2010).

[8] The United States government rejects and declares war against the ICC: "The ICC prosecutor has requested to investigate these Americans for alleged detainee abuse, and perhaps more – an utterly unfounded, unjustifiable investigation. Today, on the eve of September 11th, I want to deliver a clear and unambiguous message on behalf of the president of the United

The principles established by governments driven by a desire for power fundamentally shape the characterisation of the international criminal justice system. This implies that the foundational framework of human rights and criminal justice is constructed within the confines of international criminal courts, influencing how this system is perceived in the realm of contemporary

---

States. The United States will use any means necessary to protect our citizens and those of our allies from unjust prosecution by this illegitimate court. We will not cooperate with the ICC. We will provide no assistance to the ICC. We will not join the ICC. We will let the ICC die on its own. After all, for all intents and purposes, the ICC is already dead to us. The United States bases this policy on five principal concerns about the court, its purported authority, and its effectiveness. First, the International Criminal Court unacceptably threatens American sovereignty and US national security interests. The prosecutor in The Hague claims essentially unfettered discretion to investigate, charge, and prosecute individuals, regardless of whether their countries have acceded to the Rome Statute. The court in no way derives these powers from any grant of consent by non-parties to the Rome Statute. Instead, the ICC is an unprecedented effort to vest power in a supranational body without the consent of either nation-states or the individuals over which it purports to exercise jurisdiction. It certainly has no consent whatsoever from the United States. As Americans, we fully understand that consent of the governed is a prerequisite to true legal legitimacy, and we reject such a flagrant violation of our national sovereignty. To make matters worse, the court's structure is contrary to fundamental American principles, including checks and balances on authority and the separation of powers. Our founders believed that a division of authority among three separate branches of government would provide the maximum level of protection for individual liberty. The International Criminal Court, however, melds two of these branches together: the judicial and the executive. In the ICC structure, the executive branch – the Office of the Prosecutor – is an organ of the court. The framers of our constitution considered such a melding of powers unacceptable for our own government, and we should certainly not accept it in the ICC. Other governments may choose systems which reject the separation of powers, but not the United States. There are no adequate mechanisms to hold the court and its personnel accountable or curtail its unchecked powers when required. ICC proponents argue that corrupt or ineffective judges can be removed by a two-thirds vote of parties to the Rome Statute and that a prosecutor can be removed by a majority vote. However, I ask everyone in the room today: would you consign the fate of American citizens to a committee of other nations, including Venezuela and the Democratic Republic of the Congo, and entities that are not even states, like the Palestinian Authority? You would not. I would not. And this Administration will not. The ICC's Assembly of States Parties cannot supervise the court any more than the United Nations General Assembly can supervise the UN bureaucracy." https://www.aljazeera.com/news/2018/09/full-text-john-bolton-speech-federalist-society-180910172828633.html. "The declaration of the President of the United States not only contained inclinations towards criminal evil, but also violated the United Nations Security Council resolutions concerning the creation of Israel. If the United States rejects one part of the imposed resolutions of the Security Council, it also simultaneously, *ipso facto,* denounces the part of the same resolution concerning the creation of the State of Israel. This is because Chapter VII of the United Nations Charter emphasises the obligations and duties of the permanent members to maintain justice, peace, and equality between members. Overall, they are responsible for preventing any violations of the system of international criminal law." Farhad Malekian, *Paralysing International Criminal Justice* (New York: Nova Science Publishers, 2021), p. 168.

politics. Notably, there exists a lack of recognition regarding the rights of populations in occupied territories, who are often labelled as terrorists, in complete disregard of the pronouncements and resolutions of dominant modern colonial powers represented in the United Nations Security Council. Consequently, to assert that occupied territories are completely devoid of the right to defend their own traditional and inherent identities constitutes a redefinition of justice that not only misrepresents reality but also amounts to serious violations of international law. This is how we empower international criminal reasoning based on a foundation of lies.

This situation effectively permits egregious forms of discrimination against the recognised rights of individuals in occupied regions while simultaneously facilitating crimes against human rights. Ultimately, the promised formal justice under the auspices of international law, as articulated in the Statute of the International Criminal Court, is frequently undermined by significant injustices perpetrated by oppressive governments and their allied nations. If it is assumed that institutions within the international criminal justice system operate with reasonable fairness, we risk diminishing justice to a level that becomes detrimental rather than beneficial to its theoretical framework.

4. Precarious Positioning of Justice

The handling of specific cases within the framework of international criminal justice is crucial not only for ensuring the protection and survival of victims but also for fostering trust in its ethical foundations, thereby affirming victims' entitlements to their legally established rights. The pursuit of equitable justice within legal frameworks governing international criminal law represents an essential component of upholding the rule of law and ensuring its legitimate enforcement.[9] This expectation should be regarded as inherent rather than

[9] Consult Quincy Wright, Proposal for an International Criminal Court, 46 American Journal of International Law 60 (1952); Bienvenido C. Ambion, Organization of a Court of International Criminal Jurisdiction, 29 Philippine Law Journal 345 (1954); Fannie Klein & Daniel Wilkes, United Nations Draft Statute for an International Criminal Court: An American Evaluation, in International Criminal Law 526 (Gerhard O.W. Mueller & Edward M. Wise eds., 1965); Stone Julius and Robert Woetzel, Toward a Feasible International Criminal Court (1970); Jean Dautricourt, The Concept of International Criminal Court Jurisdiction-Definition and Limitations of the Subject, in1 A Treatise on International Criminal Law 636 (M.C. Bassiouni & V.P. Nanda eds., 1973); Louis Kos-Rabcewicz-Zubrowski, The Creation of an International Criminal Court, in International Terrorism and

merely aspirational. It must be acknowledged that various failures can impede effective administration of justice; one prominent failure involves perpetuating false narratives concerning certain incidents and violations affecting victims' rights. Therefore, adherence to appropriate judicial functions and regulations is imperative, this responsibility rests squarely with both prosecutors and judges at the ICC. Furthermore, even when faced with unjust agreements or decisions imposed by powerful entities, it remains incumbent upon institutions dedicated to international criminal justice to uphold fairness rather than succumbing - whether directly or indirectly - to paths laid out by global perpetrators engaged in terrorism.

In this context, the actors within the international criminal justice system may find themselves in a precarious position due to mechanisms of deception orchestrated by prominent political entities within the United Nations and their allies. It is evident that victims are consistently at a disadvantage within this system, particularly when examining the distribution of power. As previously noted, Western powers, guided by the United States government, perceive themselves as victims of rights violations perpetrated by those who oppose their hegemony. They fail to acknowledge that it is these Western powers and the U.S. government that encroach upon the territories of victims, rather than the reverse. Furthermore, they overlook the fact that it is the United States government, in collusion with various Western governments through their tacit political support that has established over eight hundred military bases across different regions worldwide. The questions and challenges surrounding justice are therefore not difficult to discern or address. However, theories rooted in deception, misrepresented narratives of mistreatment, and the portrayal of victims as criminals while depicting actual criminals as victims complicate and jeopardise the entire framework of international criminal justice; consequently, our understanding of justice becomes obscured. In presenting their arguments, these entities seek to shield themselves from accountability while perpetuating even greater injustices against those who assert victimhood or experience arbitrary treatment.

Political Crimes 519 (M. Cherif Bassiouni ed., 1975); Benjamin Ferencz, International Criminal Court (2 vols. 1980); M. Cherif Bassiouni, Principles of Legality in International and Comparative Criminal Law, in International Criminal Law, vol. I (M. cherif Bassiouni, ed. 2008) pp. 73-105; M. Cherif Bassiouni, The Ratione Materiae of International Criminal Law, in International Criminal Law, vol i (M. cherif Bassiouni, ed. 2008) pp. 129- 203; Consult Morten Bergsmo, Emiliano J Buis, Philosophical Foundations of International Criminal Law (2018).

This distortion undermines the potential role of international criminal justice in safeguarding victims' rights and intertwines them with fabricated narratives that ultimately leave individuals trapped in suffering and despair. On one hand, there may be opportunities within specific cases under this system to alleviate unjust treatment inflicted upon victims and assist them in realising their rights. Nonetheless, even minimal assistance often proves unattainable due to the vested interests held by oppressive governments regarding victim's rights and their classification as uncivilised or inhumane. This situation indicates deliberate deviation from the truth among powerful nations concerning their transgressions against numerous victims of international crimes. *Consequently, one must ponder how far we can justify the moral and legal contradictions in our decisions that impact these victims while simultaneously claiming to combat terrorism. If self-determination and freedom from occupation are labelled as acts of terror, then what terminology should be applied to describe the systematic deceptions and international crimes committed against these fundamental rights?*

In one of my previous works, I have articulated that the actions perpetrated by oppressive governments against certain nations can be characterised as a manifestation of *international crimes akin to blackboard-barbarism.*[10] This term refers to the simultaneous engagement in various international violations under a unified policy framework. It is essential to recognise that these

[10] "The first country that helped Israel with the development of its nuclear program was France, and this cooperation later changed and the United States started making large contributions to Israel. The intention was very clear: no Arab state could really protest the interests of the United States powertionist government, except for the political Zionist government. Therefore, the crime of blackboard-barbarism has been supported and funded by certain Western governments, including the British and French. These crimes have been expanded and deeply empowered as a result of the United States government's close work with the political Zionist government. This thus reflects the obvious monopolization of the terms of the system of international criminal justice by a big powertionist government in order to impose sanctions on the activities of other governments around the world. Despite not partaking in traditional war theory, the Zionist government of Israel, with full support from Western states, is continuing to commit the international crime of *blackboard-barbarism.* This means that Western governments have both directly and indirectly sanctioned the commission of all acts of barbarism to serve their interests and maintain good relations with rich Zionists across the globe. Therefore, certain Western governments, including European governments that have committed genocide, crimes against humanity, war crimes, aggression, medical criminal experiments, including torture, among other crimes, not only in Europe but also in their colonies all over the world, are aiding in the extermination of the population of Palestine." Farhad Malekian, *International Crime of Blackboard-Barbarism* ((New York: Nova Science Publishers, 2025), p.51; Farhad Malekian, *The Monopolization of International Criminal Law in the United Nations, A Jurisprudential Approach* (Stockholm: Almqvist Wiksell International, 1st ed., 1993).

governments commit international crimes on comparable scales, intending that such transgressions remain concealed and unacknowledged as a collective breach of international law.[11]

5. Exceedingly Frangible Inclination of Justice

The reality is that expectations based on good faith regarding existing institutions within the international criminal justice system, including those pertaining to international human rights, are exceedingly fragile and ultimately irreparable. A significant dilemma within the realm of international criminal justice is its profound entanglement with political considerations. To express this succinctly, the entire framework of international criminal justice - and indeed human rights - operates on a foundation of political morality, which implies an alignment with the interests of major powers. Consequently, this indicates that the efficacy of the international criminal justice system is structured in such a manner that adherence to its principles is contingent upon compliance with dictates imposed by oppressive government actions deemed necessary for state security.

As a result, many governments adopt a subordinate stance towards more powerful states, particularly in relation to the United States. This subjugation represents their only means of evading accusations under the framework of international criminal law for committing offenses or supporting groups labelled as terrorists by dominant global powers. It is evident that the

---

[11] "In other words, we confirm all of the statements made by the Israeli government, and thereby succeed in saving our various social positions. *We simply sell justice, we sell humanity, we bargain the right to self-determination, we accept the right to kill children, and we confirm that the occupation of Palestine does not violate international law, international human rights, or international criminal justice, and therefore all killings are in accordance with the principle of proportionality. All of these also mean that the Israeli armed forces are permitted to use Palestinians as human shields. Yet, they kill twenty thousand Palestinian children and accuse the Palestinians of using children as human shields. The accusation is a humiliating experience.* This means that we reject, whether directly or indirectly, the existence of the framework of international peremptory human rights and criminal justice. Therefore, we not only violate, but also prevent, any notion of *jus cogens* norms. The fact is that we claim domination over the immorality, illegality, injustice, and criminal conduct of the Israeli government concerning all aspects of the system of international law.[11] This also indicates that we do not fully accept responsibility for violations of the provisions of human rights. In fact, we do not accept any responsibility for the deaths of fifteen thousand children, and we see all matters as the rights of a criminal government." Farhad Malekian, *International Crime of Blackboard-Barbarism* ((New York: Nova Science Publishers, 2025), p.17.

definition and application of justice are heavily influenced by policies enacted by those governments coalescing around unjust institutions that are inherently immoral and unlawful within jurisprudence. Ultimately, those who challenge or dismiss the political paternalism exerted by these superpowers often find themselves subjected to relentless scrutiny and attacks.[12]

It has been suggested that concerns regarding adherence to the rule of law should not dictate legal frameworks or their implementation; any deviation from definitions imposed by authoritarian powers could potentially jeopardise state interests worldwide. This further underscores how permanent members wield control over mechanisms within international criminal justice through deceptive practices. Such dynamics exacerbate ambiguities surrounding legal definitions and interpretations of international crimes while undermining sound judicial decision-making essential for upholding justice. Therefore, it becomes apparent that well-defined concepts within the purview of international criminal law lack genuine existence in practice.

The inclination to adhere to the principles of international criminal law and the directives of international criminal justice has significantly diminished. Consequently, the inquiry into whether similar cases within international criminal justice are treated impartially and consistently is rendered a superficial exercise. While this argument holds merit, we shall not explore here the implications of such injustices for the victims and their resultant suffering, as a comprehensive evaluation can only be undertaken once we establish what constitutes a reasonable definition of justice for those who have endured the loss of millions.

For oppressive regimes, the magnitude of suffering inflicted upon victims is inconsequential. Rather, it is their capacity to dominate the rights of other nations that matters most. This reality underscores one fundamental reason why the concept of ''justice'' remains inadequately defined and is often conflated with falsehoods. As a result, the substantive principles of justice inherent in international criminal law will never be realised as intended under the auspices of the ICC. Consequently, both the Court and its prosecutor risk becoming instruments or mere puppets manipulated by deceit - regardless of their intentions. In essence, the International Criminal Court serves as a venue

---

[12] Farhad Malekian, *Conundrums of Paternalism in International Criminal Justice* (New York: Nova Science Publishers, 2024). See also Farhad Malekian, I*mperative Philosophy of International Criminal Justice: Visible Power – Invisible Essence* (New York: Nova Science Publishers, 2022); Farhad Malekian, *Tour de force of Moral Virtue in International Criminal Justice* (New York: Nova Science Publishers, 2022).

where lies may be propagated and institutionalised, compelling governments to adhere to these fabrications.

Once we comprehend the underlying motives behind these falsehoods and their rationalisation, alongside governmental attitudes, we may then discern between terrorist regimes and the legitimately established rights of victims. It is for this reason that essential principles governing international criminal justice - which are vital for fostering genuine justice - are deliberately subordinated to the authority of governments that are not actual signatories to the ICC Statute. Their influence over the ICC derives from provisions enshrined in Chapter VII of United Nations Charter, as established by the Security Council.

The political authority vested in the Security Council exerts such formidable control over any international framework that it compels all governments to acquiesce to decisions made by these authoritarian regimes that label other entities as terrorists.[13] Thus, I reiterate that principles underpinning international criminal justice should first and foremost apply to the foundational aspects that concern the Security Council itself.[14] This assertion stems from an understanding that according to peremptory norms of international *jus cogens*, it is imperative for the Council to exercise its power without infringing upon norms that must remain inviolable and respected at all times, and by all means.

Therefore, *jus cogens* norms, along with *erga omnes* norms, are obligatory and no impunity should be granted to those who violate them. That is one of the most serious problems facing the systems of human rights and criminal justice and has led to the problem of selectivity as well as dependency on the decisions of the powertionist governments of the world - especially of the United States, which compels other nations to follow its lead." "When we use the notion of selectivity regarding the accused, we adopt a particular form of

---

[13] James E. Hickey, *Challenges to Security Council Monopoly Power over the Use of Force in Enforcement Actions: The Case of Regional Organisations, Ius Gentium* (2004), pp. 75.129. "The theory of the big political nations in the Security Council is similar to the theory of Thrasymachus in Plato's *The Republic*. According to Thrasymachus regarding the definition of justice and injustice "An unjust is superior to a just in character and intelligence. Injustice is a source of strength. Injustice brings happiness." This definition of justice is indeed what the permanent members of the United Nations and their allies are imposing upon the traditional Palestinian sovereign state." Farhad Malekian, *Paralysing International Criminal Justice* (New York: Nova Science Publishers, 2021), p. 224.

[14] *Id.*

powertionism that is not recommended by authentic criminal justice procedures and is condemned by all means. [15]

Those norms govern and apply to the recognition of rights for human beings and are therefore sacred in ensuring the protection of human civilisation from the brutalities of powerful entities. This indicates that they are an integral part of the universal moral standard commonly referred to as natural law and the natural rights of all individuals, which should not be monopolised by the authority of any organisation or council. The formulation of these norms within the framework of *jus cogens* suggests that they are complementary principles that deliver both legal and moral justice. These principles presuppose that the moral structure of the international criminal justice system should not be influenced or fragmented by systems that evidently seek to monopolise and distort law and morality. The norms of peremptory law are so clearly defined that they must be respected. However, despite this clarity, we observe how the definitions of justice, human rights, and international crimes are often manipulated. They are interpreted to align with the interests of powerful nations within the international criminal justice system. This reflects the approach taken by certain Western governments regarding the definition and application of justice on a global scale.

6. Lack of Accountability for Violations of Human Rights

The principles of peremptory norms are so clearly defined that they must be adhered to without exception. Nevertheless, it is evident that the interpretations of justice, human rights, and international crimes are subject to manipulation and redefinition in a manner that reflects the prevailing understanding of international criminal justice as dictated by influential powers. This phenomenon illustrates how certain select Western governments frame their definitions of justice and its application on an international scale.

[15] Farhad Malekian, *Powertionism in International Criminal Justice* (New York: Nova Science Publishers, 2022), p. 130 and 240; see aslo Cassese A., 'For an Enhanced Role of Jus cogens' in Cassese, A (ed.), *Realizing Utopia*, (2012); Cassese A., *International Criminal Law* (Oxford: Oxford University Press, 2nd, ed., 2008) ; Cassese A., (ed.), *The New Humanitarian Law of Armed Conflict* (Naples: Editoriale Scientifica, 1979) ; Cassese A., 'First Annual Report of the ICTY,' *Yearbook of International Law Commission*, (1994); Cassese A., On the Current Trends Towards Criminal Prosecution and Punishment of Breaches of International Humanitarian Law, 9 *European Journal of Internaitonal Law* 2 (1998); Cassese A., Albin Eser, Giorgio Gaja and Robert E. Conor, *Justice at Nuremberg* (1980).

It is imperative to assert that the justice system, particularly the international criminal justice framework, should remain free from governmental interference in the pursuit of justice, humanitarianism, and morality.[16] However, I acknowledge that the Security Council possesses veto power over this entire system of justice, which represents a profoundly dangerous and detrimental aspect given that international criminal justice is often directed by individuals who may themselves be among the most egregious criminals globally, including Barack Obama, Joe Biden, both George Bushes, Tony Blair, both Clintons, Keir Starmer, Rishi Sunak, Liz Truss, David Cameron, to name but a few.[17]

Consequently, this situation undermines the integrity of judges and prosecutors worldwide by effectively granting authority over them to those engaged in criminality. As a result, there exists a profound lack of accountability to uphold the principles of humanity and an erosion of freedom among those tasked with evaluating both the nature of crimes committed and their perpetrators. Furthermore, the distinction between arbitrary state accusations against resistant movements labelled as terrorists versus governmental actions framed as freedom fighting becomes obscured within the realm of international criminal justice. This leads to arrests, detentions, and even killings of individuals striving for justice while contravening any established notion of rule of law in the international arena.

The international criminal justice system faces significant challenges in recognising all individuals as equal before the law; every individual should be subject to potential accusation and arrest in order to have their case heard within judicial proceedings. I refer to this as an essential liberty afforded by the ICC, which should treat all subjects under international law with equal consideration - including those entities possessing recognised legal personality on an international scale. The concept of legal personality implies protection against any unwarranted interference regarding matters under investigation at the Court. This principle fosters a doctrinal foundation for independence within the framework of international criminal justice.

Such independence unequivocally supports the Court's autonomy in issuing arrest warrants and rendering final decisions on allegations of international crimes against specific individuals or dismissing such allegations

---

[16] Consult K. R. Vischer, *Martin Luther King Jr. and the Morality of Legal Practice: Lessons in Love and Justice* (2014).

[17] See for instance James E. Hickey, *Challenges to Security Council Monopoly Power over the Use of Force in Enforcement Actions: The Case of Regional Organisations, Ius Gentium* (2004), pp. 75.129.

entirely. In essence, these processes must occur without governmental interference and through complete autonomy granted to judges and prosecutors within the Court. Additionally, no judge or prosecutor associated with the International Criminal Court should allow personal interests to influence their pursuit of justice; adherence to this fundamental principle is crucial for defining a just legal process capable of delivering equitable outcomes based on inherently established rights.

Consequently, a judge's decision or any responsible individual should not influence their income, particularly within a corrupt system. From the outset, the income and wealth of those who uphold justice through its definition and application must remain unaffected by various political influences. Indeed, the concept of justice is intricately linked to these issues; thus, any abuse of power within the courtroom constitutes a distortion and misrepresentation of justice that borders on corruption. Justice demands accountability, which in turn imposes obligations that demand adherence to an appropriate understanding of justice. This underscores why interference from the United Nations Security Council provokes controversy regarding the definition of justice and fosters a counterfeit interpretation that is fundamentally distorted by certain contemporary colonial powers.

While ensuring the equitable distribution of justice is essential for accessing genuine evidence, it is equally vital to preserve the integrity of judicial authority. The definition of justice should not be jeopardised or compromised by those wielding actual authority under the guise of enforcement. The objective is not to restrict the application of international criminal justice principles but rather to reinforce and subsequently implement them. The discrepancies in international law among governments serve as a primary catalyst for empowering modern colonialist Western powers over other nations, contributing significantly to ongoing conflicts and undermining effective enforcement mechanisms for international criminal justice decisions.[18] It is evident that principles related to criminal justice or human rights are distinctly articulated and designed to elucidate and validate concepts of right and wrong in accordance with provisions recognised by the global legal and political community as essential for identifying crimes. Thus, a theory of justice relies on a consistent foundational understanding within the context of human rights or agreements pertaining to criminal justice among a majority of states worldwide.

---

[18] Malekian, F., *International Criminal Vacations: Tears of Justice* (New York: Nova Science Publishers, 2024), pp. 44, 46, 123, 186.

In this regard, it becomes apparent that the system of international criminal justice cannot thrive if we continually seek to redefine what has already been established. This is particularly evident in how definitions surrounding international crimes have been altered through rhetoric and official declarations issued by major terrorist states. A prominent example is found in varying interpretations of genocide as articulated by powerful nations. The implication is that any government opposing these states' criminal assertions may be labelled as terrorist, while those unable to comprehend statements from hegemonic governments face similar scrutiny. A significant number of documents and evidence - including testimonies - regarding the commission of genocide by oppressive regimes are frequently mischaracterised as acts of self-defence. A prominently notable example of this is the egregious actions perpetrated in Gaza by successive Israeli governments over several decades, which continue to be framed as self-defence.[19] The notion that the occupation of a nation and the genocide of its entire population can be deemed permissible is indeed a profound affront to the principles of human rights and international criminal justice.

7. Lies Rendering Legal Values

While I do not intend to limit the discourse on justice solely to the grave and extensive killings of the Gazan populace, it is undeniably offensive to omit reference to this situation, which serves as a stark illustration of the deterioration of global justice standards. This suggests an intentional distortion of the concept of justice, manipulated to facilitate and execute nefarious agendas. At present, it must be acknowledged that although the dual-principle framework governing human rights and criminal justice is sufficiently robust to substantiate claims against major political entities for their crimes, it is often misapplied in ways that undermine its intended purpose - primarily condemning acts framed as self-defence or self-determination.

Consequently, there exist specific instances that necessitate a broader or more nuanced understanding of justice within our discussions; however, when

---

[19] "Israel's military industrial complex uses the occupied Palestinian territories as a testing ground for weaponry and surveillance technology that they then export around the world to despots and democracies. For more than 50 years, the occupation of the West Bank and Gaza has given the Israeli state invaluable experience in controlling an 'enemy' population, the Palestinians. It's here that they have perfected the architecture of control." Antony Loewenstein, *The Palestine Laboratory* (2023).

legal values are rendered meaningless, further examples merely contribute to an endless cycle of falsehoods perpetuated by both historical and contemporary colonial powers. It is imperative to recognise that the foundation for mutual respect within international criminal justice and human rights systems must not rely solely on rigid definitions. The term "genocide" cannot be conflated with military might; unless disparities within these systems are addressed, the core values associated with justice will inevitably lose their binding force.

Injustice within human rights and criminal justice frameworks exemplifies inequalities detrimental not only to individual nations but also serves as a mechanism through which these frameworks are exploited to justify egregious violations - as evidenced in Gaza - interwoven with fabrications from corrupt leaders aimed at annihilating the Palestinian population. Ultimately, while concepts of justice may appear straightforward, they have become increasingly obscured by disinformation propagated by those in power. Any further interpretations or distortions within our understanding of justice risk diverting us from its foundational definitions, leading us into a quagmire, or state of entrapment, where we become ensnared by deceit.

We often become so deeply involved in our perspectives that we distance ourselves from the fundamental definition of genocide, attempting to rationalise our positions regarding what constitutes right and wrong. This tendency indicates a loss of moral and legal clarity in the pursuit of justice, leading us to engage in a tacit endorsement of the injustices propagated by those in power.[20] Such a situation represents an initial step into the realm of deception. Deceptions perpetuated by powerful governments are subsequently accepted as facts, becoming entrenched in the annals of legislation, political rhetoric, and economics. Consequently, these dominant and oppressive governments prevail in defining justice, resulting in an international criminal law system that is fundamentally based on falsehoods and their gradual erosion of objective legal and moral standards during its evolution.

---

[20] For moral faculty consult L. M. Baum, 'Pursuing Justice in a Climate of Moral Outrage: An Evaluation of the Rights of the Accused in the Rome Statute of the International Criminal Court,' 19 *Wisconsin International Law* (2001), p.197; Michael C. Davis, Wolfgang Dietrich, Bettina Schoolman and Dieter Sepp. , *International Intervention in the Post-Cold War World: Moral Responsibility and Power Politics* (New York: M.E. Sharpe, Inc., 2003); M. J. Detmold, *The Unity of Law and Morality: A Refutation of Legal Positivism* (Canada: Law Book Co. of Australasia, 1984); Lon Luvios Fuller, *The Morality of Law* (Virginia: Yale Law University, 2nd ed., 1969); Alasdair MacIntyre, *After Virtue: A Study in Moral Theory* (Notre Dame: University of Notre Dame Press, 1982).

This process shapes how justice is defined and promoted to serve the interests of powerful governments, often at odds with the needs of victims for whom international human rights or criminal justice systems were ostensibly established. Therefore, it is crucial to emphasise that rather than questioning why human rights and criminal justice systems were created, we must focus on their primary objective: to find solutions and impose limitations on acts of barbarity perpetrated by criminals. Although this purpose does not require extensive elaboration, it has been central to all interpretations since the policies enacted by authoritarian governments have profoundly influenced the practical enforcement of justice - an essential aspect when discussing justice itself. In essence, when the enforcement of justice is wielded through coercive means, discussions about politically motivated justice within international conventions or under the authority of the International Criminal Court become fundamentally nonsensical.

Our intention here is not to undermine the value of international criminal justice nor to call for its dissolution due to issues surrounding enforceability. Rather, our aim is to elucidate the original conditions affecting enforcement mechanisms and demonstrate that international criminal justice - as promised - fails to operate effectively; its theoretical stability resembles ice dissolving in boiling water. We contend that politicians from oppressive regimes distort truths to such an extent that their deceptions function as confessions regarding their involvement in crimes. Ideally, one would wish to debate which legal system offers the most optimal model of justice as recorded within jurisprudence frameworks; however, the framework of international criminal law does not function adequately under the auspices of the International Criminal Court; instead, both its concept and scope have officially been reduced to a selective application of justice. Thus, we are compelled to navigate among various potential conceptions of justice and assess whether the ICC fulfils its role when truly necessary – particularly concerning *jus cogens* and *erga omnes* roles.[21]

---

[21] Examine Czaplinski, Wladyslaw 'Concepts of *Jus cogens* and Obligations Erga Omnes in International Law in the Light of Recent Developments' 23 *Polish Yearbook of International Law* (1997–1998), p. 87; G. Danilenko, 'International *Jus cogens*: Issues of Law-Making' 2 (1) *European Journal of International Law* (1991), p. 42; A. D'Amato, 'It's a Bird, It's a Plane, It's *Jus cogens*' 6 *Connecticut Journal of International Law* (1990), p. 1 AJJ de Hoog, 'The Relationship between *Jus cogens*, Obligations Erga Omnes and International Crimes: Peremptory Norms in Perspective' 42 *Österreichische Zeitschrift für öffentliches Recht und Völkerrecht* (1991), p. 183; E de Wet, '*Jus cogens* and Obligations Erga Omnes' in de Wet, E and J. Vidmar (eds.), *Hierarchy in International Law: The Place of Human Rights* (2012); P Dupuy, 'Some Reflections on Contemporary International Law and the Appeal to Universal Values: a Response to Marti Koskenniemi' 16 *European*

Journal of International Law (2005), p. 131; C. Focarelli, 'Promotional *Jus cogens*: A Critical Appraisal of *Jus cogens*' Legal Effects' 77 *Nordic Journal of International Law* (2008), p. 429; Glennon, MJ 'De l'Absurdité du Droit Impératif (*Jus cogens*)' 110 *Revue Générale de Droit International Public* (2006), p. 529; Robledo Gómez, A El Ius Cogens Internacional (Estudio Histórico Crítico) (1982); Gómez, A. Robledo 'Le *Jus cogens* International: Sa Genése, sa Nature, ses Fonctions' 9 *Recueil des Cours de l'Académie de Droit International de la Haye* (1982), p.172; L. Hannikainen, *Peremptory Norms (Jus Cogens) in International Law: Historical Development, Criteria, Present Status* (1988); M. W. Janis, 'The Nature of *Jus cogens*' 3 *Connecticut Journal of International Law* (1988), p. 359; A. Kawasaki 'A Brief Note on the Legal Effects of *Jus cogens* in International Law in International Law' 34 *Hitotsubashi Journal of Law and Politics* (2006), p. 27; A. J. J. de Hoog, 'The Relationship between *Jus cogens*, Obligations *Erga Omnes* and International Crimes: Peremptory Norms in Perspective' 42 *Österreichische Zeitschrift für öffentliches Recht und Völkerrecht* (1991), p. 18; M. Byers, 'Conceptualising the Relationship Between *Jus cogens* and *Erga Omnes Rules*' 66 *Nordic Journal of International Law* (1997), p. 211; A. Cassese, 'For an Enhanced Role of *Jus cogens*' in A. Cassese (ed.), *Realizing Utopia* (2012); C. Chinkin, '*Jus cogens*, Article 103 of the UN Charter and other Hierarchical Techniques of Conflict Solution' *Finnish Yearbook of International Law* (2008), p. 63.

Chapter 7

Empowering Reasoning of the Lies Interpreted in ICC Procedure

1. Closing Any Genuine Opportunity of the Court

Even if we assume there is a viable alternative to the definition of justice presented by the major powers, it remains challenging to articulate how such an alternative does not become entangled with falsehoods. A contemporary example is the genocide occurring in Gaza as I write this work. In this context, the leading political parties of the world base their policies on daily lies, or at the very least, on misleading narratives that justify both the killings and the economic destabilisation of non-Western states. They claim to be working towards a system of international justice and preventing international crimes against the policies of Western governments. Consequently, every act of self-defence is framed as a response to terrorism in the Middle East. However, the reality is that nearly all Western governments support the terrorist actions of the United States and its fabrications, which serve as foundational justifications for their own existence. This indicates a strong connection between the U.S. government and Western governments in their pursuit of a distorted version of justice premised on deception and the subjugation of other nations. The reality is that there is no viable solution to the prevailing injustice due to the strong connection between the laws of the ICC and the regulations of the Security Council.

The ICC operates as an entity that lacks any genuine autonomy. Every significant decision made by the ICC is subject to the legal framework established by the Security Council, which effectively monopolises legal authority. This monopolisation results in a form of subjugation for the ICC, leaving it with no genuine opportunity to assert its own path. The ICC is generally perceived as a tribunal primarily concerned with the prosecution of African leaders. In contrast, when governments such as those of France, Britain, and the United States engage in international crimes while professing to promote justice, they are not held accountable by the ICC. Instead, their actions reflect the geopolitical manoeuvring of modern colonial powers in Africa. This suggests that the ICC's policy lacks genuine independence, being effectively governed by these aforementioned nations; an examination of its prosecutorial records substantiates this assertion.

It raises questions about how the ICC can genuinely pursue justice - specifically, international criminal justice - when it fails to prosecute crimes committed by powerful states or neglects to consider the legitimate claims of self-defence made by certain victimised nations, groups, or governments. The French government's assertions regarding its efforts to combat terrorism within its borders appear disingenuous, particularly given its ongoing interests in African resources. Upon careful reflection, it becomes evident that there exists a fundamental disparity between its articulated commitment to justice and the actual policies enacted in practice by paternalistic governments worldwide - including those in Latin America.

Moreover, it is imperative to scrutinise discussions on definitions of international crimes alongside the reality of international crimes perpetrated by Western governments. While many principles of international criminal justice may be deemed superior to the distorted narratives propagated by powerful governments - often rooted in deception - the true essence of justice remains obscured within the framework established by the ICC. With respect to our understanding of the system of international criminal justice, it appears that a somewhat nebulous set of principles serves as a preferred alternative for dominant governments. This allows them to exert control over various aspects of international criminal law. For instance, the United States has historically refrained from ratifying conventions such as the one on genocide for an extended period and has declared its signature on the Statute of the International Criminal Court invalid - in affect, withdrawing its signature and thus avoiding ratification - a stance shared by several other nations. As long as hegemonic governments maintain control over both military power and legal authority, we find ourselves without viable alternatives to address this issue. Consequently, it is clear that the United States consistently operates under its own definition of justice; all such definitions ultimately reflect its policies concerning international crimes which remain contingent and politically motivated rather than universally binding.

2. Lies Empowering Extensive Obliteration

The manner in which the deceptive practices of the powertionist governments influence the framework of international criminal justice is, in fact, an inadequate approach to addressing issues of justice. It may have been preferable to conceptualise the system of international criminal justice as one governed by force. In such a scenario, we would not have a judicial system operating under the Court's authority but rather one dictated by military might. I contend that this could result in fewer instances of violence, as victims or populations under governmental occupation might refrain from asserting their rights to self-defence and instead comply with legal matters through coercive means. This perspective could also be deemed more logical within the context of international human rights. Currently, however, it is evident that the existing framework for international criminal justice lacks adequate mechanisms for a truly superior conception of such justice. Instead, it reflects a model that consistently aligns with the interests dictated by powerful political entities. At present, we find ourselves without an alternative means to administer effective criminal justice within the Court other than adhering to the stipulations imposed by those who define justice according to their own criteria.

Furthermore, employing mechanisms within the international criminal justice system against those who wield legal authority poses not only a matter of imprudence but also significant risk; it often results in increased violence and the massacre of innocent individuals under the pretext of combating terrorism. Consequently, many governments represented in the General Assembly may oppose this monopolised control over legal power. As we analyse these comparisons between different interpretations of justice, it becomes apparent that arguments put forth by governments advocating for victim rights frequently lack fundamental ethical, legal, or moral foundations. This is primarily due to influential members of the Security Council - such as France, the United States, and Britain - highlighting aspects of international criminal justice that are often undesirable and unacceptable because they do not align with their political, military, or economic agendas. Thus, for these governments, current features of international criminal justice offer neither minimum nor maximum standards for defining justice or establishing peace.

Through this manipulation of international criminal justice, they convey divergent and contradictory understandings of legal principles where moral ethics appear absent.[1] They disproportionately accuse other nations so

---

[1]Consult Farhad Malekian, *Classical Morality in International Peremptory Criminal Law* (Newcastle upon Tyne: Cambridge Scholars Publishing, 2018, republished 2021); Martti Koskenniem, *The Politics of International Law* (Hart, 2011); Martti Koskenniemi, *The Gentle Civilizer of Nations: the Rise and Fall of International Law*, 1870-1960 (Cambridge University Press 2002); Martti Koskenniemi, Mónica García-Salmones Rovira, and Paolo Amorosa, International Law and Religion: Historical and Contemporary Perspectives

extensively that these countries ultimately become perceived as formidable adversaries and opponents to global peace. In doing so, they cultivate and solidify international consensus in response to their malign policies in order to dominate global perspectives and steer the direction of the international community at large. The manner in which they construct an artificial definition of justice serves to underscore their need to project power in order to subjugate individuals who are, in fact, the victims. This approach represents a systematically pervasive and malevolent policy employed in the interpretation of crimes and international criminal justice, leading to increasingly frequent accusations against victims. It is essential to recognise that the more one accuses another, the stronger the implication of self-incrimination by the accused becomes. For instance, any accusation made by the Israeli government can be interpreted as a clear admission of guilt on its part. Consequently, it may not be rational for a government to accuse others without substantial evidence, as this ultimately exacerbates harm inflicted upon the victims and serves only to further its own interests.

While oppressive governments tend to escalate their accusations using various tactics and methods, they do not alleviate their international crimes; rather, they become ensnared in a web of deceit that constitutes their own strategy for waging war. Although some criminal governments may initially evade accountability through deception and destruction of international criminal evidence, the true nature of heinous acts cannot be obscured by lies; the repercussions of such unlawful and immoral actions will endure. A pertinent example includes the falsehoods surrounding alleged beheadings of infants on October 7, 2023, despite no documented instances supporting such claims. They distorted the narrative surrounding that day to such an extent that they justified comprehensive destruction in Gaza and resulted in extensive loss of life among its population. Had these allegations been genuine, they would have been substantiated before the international community; however, no credible evidence has emerged.

It is important to acknowledge that while one cannot definitively characterise or enumerate all potential interpretations within the framework of international criminal justice and its associated concepts, it remains evident that justice often equates to monopolistic power. Therefore, engaging in speculative discourse regarding this system based on misleading narratives

---

(2017); Read also views of Friedrich Nietzsche, *Beyond Good and Evil* (2014); Friedrich Nietzsche, *On the Genealogy of Morality: A Polemic* (19998); Clark, *Maudemarie Nietzsche on Truth and Philosophy* (1991).

propagated by dominant political entities during international assemblies proves unproductive. Any additional arguments merely complicate our understanding of the fundamental issues inherent within international criminal justice systems and ultimately yield no effective solutions for preventing atrocities against victims. In light of current circumstances concerning international criminal justice systems, there is a conspicuous absence of efforts directed at addressing overarching questions related to the motivations behind international crimes - a situation starkly reflected once again in Gaza. Lies upon lies have compounded into perceived truths, diverting global attention towards identifying perpetrators while simultaneously enabling egregious violations - crimes more severe than those witnessed even during World War II - to occur unchecked. The offenses in question include genocide, aggression, piracy, robbery, savagery, rape, torture, plundering, crimes against humanity, violations of cultural heritage, war crimes, apartheid, exploitation, forced migration, and significant breaches of humanitarian law during armed conflicts.[2]

We observe a similar impact of political deceit within the framework of international criminal justice concerning Iraq, where falsehoods propagated by major political entities served as pivotal instruments for the total devastation of the nation and its neighbouring regions. These deceptions were exposed through WikiLeaks publications, in which Julian Assange demonstrated decades of fabricated claims perpetrated by numerous powerful governments globally. The documents released by WikiLeaks indicate that all wars have been predicated upon deliberate misinformation, in which several Western governments have played a substantial role in committing international crimes across various nations such as Libya, Iraq, Afghanistan, Syria, Lebanon, Cuba, Egypt, Vietnam, among others.

I wish to confine my discussion regarding these international crimes committed in those countries to the assertion that the concept of justice has been inscribed within hundreds of thousands of pages of official documentation from the United States. These documents unequivocally establish that deception is a foundational principle within the system of

---

[2] On torture examine also D. Wet, 'The Prohibition of Torture as an International Norm of *Jus Cogens* and Its Implications for National and Customary Law,' 15 *European Journal of International Law* (2004) ; J. Brunnée, 'The Prohibition on Torture: Driving *Jus cogens* Home?' 104 *Proceedings of the Annual Meeting of the American Society of International Law*, (2010); E. de Wet, 'The Prohibition of Torture as an International Norm of *Jus cogens* and its Implementation for National and Customary Law,' 15 (1) *European Journal of International Law* (2014), Vol. 15, No. 1, 97-121; Otterman M., *American Torture: From the Cold War to Abu Ghraib and Beyond* (Pluto Press, 2007).

international criminal justice and serves to define justice favourably for dominant governmental powers. It is noteworthy that former CIA Director Mike Pompeo explicitly stated in 2019: "I was the CIA director. We lied. We cheated. We stole." … "We had entire training courses. It reminds you of the glory of American experiment."[3] This encapsulates the essence of the ideological underpinnings of the system of international criminal justice.

3. Articulating Justice with the Reasoning of Lies

Throughout statements made by powerful nations, the remarks from the former CIA Director provide a clear articulation of justice from multiple perspectives. The term "we" signifies that these three principles - "lies," "cheating," and "stealing" - constitute how political powers effectively define their system of justice within both classified and publicly accessible documents. This suggests that these three tenets can be found throughout documentation produced by influential political entities such as the United States, France, Britain, Netherlands, Germany, and Israel. Such principles stand in stark contrast to truthful notions of justice and fail to actualise equitable liberty for all nations under the auspices of the International Criminal Court. Furthermore, this indicates an absence of equal opportunity among governments or adherence to average utilitarian principles among member states within the United Nations Organisation. Consequently, when access to justice is constrained within an international institution's structure; efforts to promote such justice are similarly limited across other global institutions.[4]

---

[3] He was greeted with applause and a volley of shots! Being above the law and not accountable for crimes against humanity is supposedly a cool thing to do. https://www.youtube.com/watch?v=DPt-zXn05ac; https://www.youtube.com/watch?v=6RmEsPE7iq0; https://www.youtube.com/watch?v=EIwjkt6WeRA;

[4] Article 1 of the United Nations charter states that: The Purposes of the United Nations are:

To maintain international peace and security, and to that end: to take effective collective measures for the prevention and removal of threats to the peace, and for the suppression of acts of aggression or other breaches of the peace, and to bring about by peaceful means, and in conformity with the principles of justice and international law, adjustment or settlement of international disputes or situations which might lead to a breach of the peace;

To develop friendly relations among nations based on respect for the principle of equal rights and self-determination of peoples, and to take other appropriate measures to strengthen universal peace;

To achieve international co-operation in solving international problems of an economic, social, cultural, or humanitarian character, and in promoting and encouraging respect for human

A salient example illustrating this phenomenon is provided by the ICC and its restricted capacity to enforce accountability for grave violations against international criminal law. This underscores a broader failure in our understanding of justice wherein priority is accorded to those who possess greater military capabilities over equitable legal standards ultimately leading us back to square one. The concept of justice will lose its substance, transforming into a mere ornamental phrase rather than an effective instrument within the framework of the International Criminal Court. This also implies that the utility of the justice system diminishes, falling directly under the influence of those who have indefensibly and systematically undermined the principles of justice from various perspectives over decades. Consequently, this leads to an escalation of self-serving interpretations of justice, reducing every victim to a mere pawn in governmental negotiations.

The challenges associated with defining the international criminal justice system or its significant issue of non-applicability stem not only from the deceptions propagated by powerful governments but also from the foundational structure established by the United Nations since its inception, which is rooted in structurally unequal treaties. While the UN Charter emphasises values of equality among its members through various means, it simultaneously establishes one of history's most profound inequities since civilisation's dawn. This occurs because the Charter compels nearly two hundred member states to sign and ratify an international treaty that espouses the insurance of equality among them across different legal and political

---

rights and for fundamental freedoms for all without distinction as to race, sex, language, or religion; and

To be a centre for harmonising the actions of nations in the attainment of these common ends.

Article 55

With a view to the creation of conditions of stability and well-being which are necessary for peaceful and friendly relations among nations based on respect for the principle of equal rights and self-determination of peoples, the United Nations shall promote:

higher standards of living, full employment, and conditions of economic and social progress and development;

solutions of international economic, social, health, and related problems; and international cultural and educational cooperation; and

universal respect for, and observance of, human rights and fundamental freedoms for all without distinction as to race, sex, language, or religion.

Article 56

All Members pledge themselves to take joint and separate action in co-operation with the Organisation for the achievement of the purposes set forth in Article 55.

Article 103

In the event of a conflict between the obligations of the Members of the United Nations under the present Charter and their obligations under any other international agreement, their obligations under the present Charter shall prevail."

dimensions, while concurrently creating a Security Council that not only possesses considerable authority over defining equality among all UN members under stringent legal and political oversight but also empowers certain members to dictate other members' international legal status through resolutions or veto rights.

In light of this context, it becomes evident that although discussions surrounding the impartiality of international criminal justice and the independent nature of the International Criminal Court are prevalent, such independence was compromised even before its establishment. Thus, any discourse regarding the Court's international legal personality becomes fundamentally meaningless when (a) all its members are bound by one of history's most unequal treaties, and (b) when the Security Council wields authority over enforcing court decisions. The judgments or decisions pertaining to arrest warrants for criminals do not fall under ICC jurisdiction; unlike national systems where courts possess enforceability over their rulings - wherein any decision made prompts immediate action by law enforcement against individuals accused of national or international crimes - the ICC operates merely as a framework for rules devoid of actual enforcement power. Even if strong support is extended toward enforcing its decisions, such outcomes remain largely symbolic, with little impact on actual judicial responses.

When the Security Council asserts its authority to enforce any international matter, the decisions of the ICC lose their practical legal weight. Consequently, the Court finds itself in a position of dependency on the Security Council members, which ultimately renders its efforts futile, especially when contemporary governments are unwilling to grant any legitimate authority to the Court's decisions. This situation complicates the definition of justice within the framework of international criminal law, as the traditional theories of justice enforcement become increasingly ineffective. The pursuit of justice for the arrest of criminals becomes a legally and politically daunting challenge. This predicament is exemplified by Israeli leaders who enjoy *de facto* immunity from arrest.[5] Ultimately, the application

[5] Moreover, according to Sipri: "Israel continues to maintain its long-standing policy of nuclear opacity: it neither officially confirms nor denies that it possesses nuclear weapons. In December 2014 the United Nations General Assembly overwhelmingly approved a resolution on nuclear proliferation risks in the Middle East that urged Israel to renounce the possession of nuclear weapons, accede to the 1968 Treaty on the Non-Proliferation of Nuclear Weapons (Non-Proliferation Treaty, NPT) 'without further delay' and place all of its nuclear facilities under International Atomic Energy Agency (IAEA) comprehensive safeguards. It is estimated that Israel has approximately 80 nuclear weapons. Of these,

of genuine international criminal justice to these egregious offenders becomes unattainable.[6] This indicates that the mechanisms of justice have been constrained since the establishment of the United Nations, insofar as the power of the Security Council remains unchallenged. Each of these conceptions of justice - under the ICC and the Security Council - diverges in its approach and operates under distinct legal frameworks. However, the decisions of the Security Council are binding, while the ICC's authority appears to be subsidiary and reliant on the Security Council's overarching power.

There are numerous reasons both for and against the alternate imposition of the international criminal justice system, as administered by the Court for the arrest of criminals. However, all arguments become constrained when considering the issue of applicability. The fact that a particular conception of justice is often monopolised within the international criminal justice system is not merely an illusion. Although the ICC is open to various criticisms, these critiques are not always effectively articulated and require a thorough examination of numerous factors, such as the relationships between state parties and influential political members of the United Nations, as well as their connections to the governments of the accused criminals. This implies that every aspect of justice is inevitably entangled in layers of deception within the justice procedures and, more broadly, within the jurisprudence of international criminal law. Consequently, taking decisive action against criminals is challenging when government officials are threatened by various state-sponsored criminal terrorist organisations. Therefore, we must carefully consider which desirable features of criminal justice to embrace or reject, as their effectiveness can vary significantly depending on the specific circumstances of each case.

---

approximately 30 are gravity bombs for delivery by aircraft. The remaining 50 weapons are for delivery by Jericho II medium-range ballistic missiles, which are believed to be based with their mobile launchers in caves at a military base east of Jerusalem. The operational status of a new Jericho III intermediate-range ballistic missile is unknown. In 2013 Israel conducted a launching test of a 'rocket propulsion system,' which appeared to be for a Jericho III missile." https://www.sipri.org/research/armaments-and-disarmament/nuclear-weapons/world-nuclear-forces/israel.

6 Consult section on *Granting Impunity* in Farhad Malekian, *Conundrums of Paternalism in International Criminal Justice* (New York: Nova Science Publishers, 2024). See also Farhad Malekian, *Imperative Philosophy of International Criminal Justice: Visible Power – Invisible Essence* (New York: Nova Science Publishers, 2022).

4. Illusion of Balance Between Justice and Lies

The decisions made by the prosecutor or judges of the Court in the original position are pivotal to upholding the values of the Court's independence as an international legal entity. Nevertheless, it is imperative to consider, when weighing various factors and circumstances on a case-by-case basis, the intentions of the states involved in relation to the specific situation at hand. In this regard, there exists a compelling appeal to intuition that underpins the philosophy of justice. However, even when all elements within the international criminal justice system have been meticulously calculated and accounted for, it may still appear superficially coherent, wherein an illusion of balanced reasoning concerning justice is presented. This façade often obscures the realities faced by victims who are subjected to falsehoods and injustices, ultimately undermining every aspect of justice. The principles governing international criminal justice and their articulation must consistently remain transparent and devoid of deception. In other words, advocating for particular interpretations within the framework of international criminal justice does not inherently constitute evidence of the Court's authority, especially when confronted with deceit rooted in coercive power.

Furthermore, each interpretation regarding criminal justice in judicial proceedings must be grounded in genuine justice; otherwise, such efforts are compromised. The challenges confronting theories of justice hinge upon certain understandings held by prosecutors or judges within the Court and must clearly be independent from political deceptions perpetuated by the United Nations Security Council. This implies that evaluations pertaining to both general justice systems and specifically international criminal justice necessitate insights from two recognised and established international bodies regarding questions of fairness or injustice. While it may be relatively straightforward to express opinions of the Security Council in judicial rulings, articulating similar perspectives regarding statements issued by the Court proves considerably more complex due to its case-dependent nature. Consequently, decisions rendered by the Court are not invariably insulated from political influences.

A significant issue plaguing the international criminal justice system is that nearly every matter related to justice is susceptible to manipulation by dominant governments. Such manipulation fundamentally hinges on various misrepresentations employed by those orchestrating the entire framework of international criminal justice. It is noteworthy that identifying which political party governs a state holds little intrinsic significance as long as we continue to uphold a system of international criminal justice that evolves according to numerous distorted speculations. As a result, any conception of authentic justice risks stagnation while political lies and their subsequent interpretations acquire legitimacy through legal frameworks governing international criminal law.

In instances where special circumstances arise, these diverse interpretations of the provisions of international criminal law not only serve as the comprehensive, prevailing and mutually contradictory definitions of international criminal justice but also become integral components of the framework governing international criminal law. For instance, one interpretation may assert a particular definition at a specific stage of genocide, while another may propose an alternative understanding of the concept of international criminal justice; thus, the definition of genocide formulated by one perspective diverges from that established by another. Given that lies do not possess a definitive legal foundation, the interpretations surrounding them lead to additional definitions that differ significantly from one another. This phenomenon reflects the nature of legal philosophy, which is grounded in law itself; indeed, the entire system of international criminal law has evolved from its inception within a culture characterised by power dynamics, deceit, coercion, intimidation, and the imposition of authority through force. This historical context illustrates how the system of international criminal justice was developed and perpetuated by both past and present malignantly oppressive political entities.

Consequently, there exists an ongoing variation in conceptualisations of international crimes within this framework, each influenced by differing evidentiary interpretations. Powerful perpetrators may provide disparate definitions regarding international crimes such as genocide, apartheid, torture, crimes against humanity, and war crimes. The rationale behind these varying interpretations is to advance distinct arguments and integrate them into a system of international criminal law that has been largely shaped by those same powers under the guise of defining concepts like genocide or crimes against humanity. Such deceptive policies employed by dominant governments can be regarded as a form of manipulative legal reasoning within international criminal justice and consequently influence the overarching definition articulated in the Convention on Genocide. However, there lacks a definitive finality to the concept of genocide; governmental policies and political figures evolve over time leading to new administrations proposing revised definitions for what constitutes this crime - often diverging significantly from previous understandings.

This indicates that notions surrounding genocide or its definition are essentially composed of interlinked fabrications that connect various misleading assertions in succession. Furthermore, it suggests that perceptions of justice are inherently aligned with the specifics surrounding individual criminal cases and how powerful criminals perpetrate international offenses. Nevertheless, if such definitions of genocide were incorporated into the stipulations of the 1948 Convention on Genocide, then no singular definition would hold validity; consequently, interpreting these provisions would yield numerous conflicting definitions concerning genocide itself. This proliferation could render issues related to international criminal law and justice exceedingly complex - if not entirely unmanageable.

5. Security Council Supervising the Law of ICC

The imposition of falsehoods within the framework of international criminal justice through the use of military force will not yield true justice; rather, it results in a manifestation of injustice and, indeed, culminates in profoundly immoral injustices. Furthermore, there exists a rationale for the definitions provided within the Statute of the ICC concerning international crimes. This rationale is predicated on the intended purpose of the international criminal law system: to minimise controversy within the realm of criminal justice and, most importantly, to avert the commission of international crimes. The overarching intention behind international criminal law, human rights law, and international criminal justice is to eliminate impunity at an international level.[7] We mean "that violators of the system of international peremptory criminal law in the past, present, and future should not receive impunity. This is the only way to achieve to moral force, moral justice, universal moral justice, and the highest stage of categorical imperative justice for all individuals and nations at the same level and to the same degree."[8]

---

[7] Examine also Mary Griffin, Ending the Impunity of Perpetrators of Human Rights Atrocities: A Major Challenge for International Law in the 21st Century, International Review of the Red Cross, Volume 82, Issue 838: Revue Internationale de la Croix-Rouge International Review of the Red Cross, June 2000, pp. 369 - 389. https://www.cambridge.org/core/journals/international-review-of-the-red-cross/article/abs/ending-the-impunity-of-perpetrators-of-human-rights-atrocities-a-major-challenge-for-international-law-in-the-21st-century/E63D5A85F36CDF865B4919F3C0710F92

[8] Farhad Malekian, *Classical Morality in International Peremptory Criminal Law* (Newcastle: Cambridge Scholars Publishing, 2021), p.107.

It is essential to recognise that the international criminal justice system bears the fundamental responsibility for prosecuting individuals who have committed international crimes, thereby establishing international criminal responsibility for violations of established provisions of international law. Notably, there exists no alternative mechanism for enforcing international criminal responsibility other than when major political powers resort to presenting falsehoods and altering foundational principles of international criminal justice to impose their decisions through deception and manipulate the fabric of justice. In this context, it must be acknowledged that any moral or ethical frameworks intended to delineate appropriate principles of justice are rendered ineffective; instead, what prevails is a proliferation of lies imposed upon others. Such distortions can manifest within discussions held in bodies such as the Security Council or during numerous political dialogues led by representatives from oppressive regimes.

A particularly salient example can be found in the ongoing and unmitigated deceptions propagated by leaders of oppressive Israeli governments. Another striking instance involves significant misinformation disseminated globally by leaders from both the United States and British governments, along with their aggressive representatives including Antony Blinken and others. These unrelenting falsehoods emanating from these governments severely undermine the integrity of the international criminal justice system, diminishing its value almost to non-existence. Moreover, this pervasive culture of deceit effectively obliterates any viable alternatives that could foster genuine justice and strengthen the authority of institutions like the ICC. Consequently, we are confronted with a judicial system that fails not only in domestic contexts but also within the procedural norms established by the ICC.

Thus, the lies by the leaders of powertionist governments and their representatives conceal the proper basis of the system of justice and create international criminal instability, as it has been occurring since the establishment of the League of Nations and the United Nations. As long as the principles of international criminal justice are governed by the influence of falsehoods or the coercive force of weapons, we remain unable to attain true justice, and are compelled to disregard the standards of justice in discussions among parties to international conventions or within the ICC.

The rationale behind this is straightforward; many governments, unfortunately, choose to align themselves with powerful criminals in order to safeguard their own interests. Consequently, the definitions surrounding the system of international justice - or indeed, justice as a whole - become devoid of meaning. For numerous governments whose political agendas are supported by significant criminal states, it is far more advantageous to portray their initial stance in a manner that avoids being sanctioned or labelled as terrorist entities by dominant state actors known for perpetrating terrorism themselves. This situation is intricately linked to various political and legal factors, all of which continue to be structured, supported, and guided by diverse interpretations of justice framed as fairness but in reality shaped by the deceptions propagated by criminal regimes worldwide.

However, I shall set this issue aside until we acknowledge that we must not allow ourselves to be governed politically or administratively by subscribing to the criminal ideologies and illicit acts perpetuated by terrorist governments if we aspire to maintain control over our nation's power. Two prominent examples illustrating this point are Anwar Sadat and Abd al-Fattah al-Sisi. Clearly, the international criminal justice system is in dire need of reform if the definitions of justice articulated in various international conventions are implemented through deceit and corruption.

A fundamental aspect inherent in any judicial system is its *integrity*; when we seek justice, we pursue an accurate representation free from deception and falsehoods. A compelling argument supporting the principles of justice relies not on the positions or educational backgrounds of those serving on judicial benches but rather on their commitment to uncovering truth without yielding to the lies propagated by authoritarian governments. Indeed, for any judicial framework - be it national or international - the conception of proper justice as an untainted principle remains vital for both its presentation and practical enforcement. Should we endeavour to alter the authentic definition of justice through various distortions and fabrications, then all discourse regarding its broader implications collapses; thus, not only does justice vanish from national or international courtrooms but it also erodes from the universal moral framework that underpins human equality - a principle often professed yet frequently disregarded in practice by numerous global governments. This observation similarly pertains to all facets concerning the core functions within the international criminal justice system that pledges to uphold victims' rights while holding perpetrators of international crimes accountable.

There exists an extensive array of divergences in the definitions of international crimes and the extent of their applicability. However, it is imperative to note that these differences in understanding regarding the commission of crimes cannot be altered through false representations. Genocide remains genocide, regardless of any misleading portrayals of justice by partisan actors within the Security Council or governmental lobbies.

Consequently, while numerous theories concerning the crime of genocide and its denial may exist, this does not validate definitions that are predicated on falsehoods. The same applies to other offenses. Indeed, there is a moral framework inherent in the system of international criminal justice, whose principles cannot be distorted by deceit; even if such deception proves effective, the essence of moral theory remains unchanged.

6. Empowering Reasoning Based on Immorality

Only a limited number of issues within this context of justice hold philosophical significance regarding the evolution of morality over millennia; nevertheless, the concept of universal morality has remained constant. Even amid our deterioration of Earth's climate, certain fundamental principles endure - much like celestial bodies such as the sun and stars. This consistency extends to international criminal justice and the definition of genocide. Thus, despite acts resulting in millions being killed and countless more subjected to lies, the definition of genocide remains unaltered. As previously stated, genocide is unequivocally genocide, and no alternative discourse exists regarding its definition irrespective of how such definitions are presented.

We must endeavour to avoid peripheral concerns related to international criminal justice while simultaneously steering clear of misunderstandings or influences arising from power politics in our interpretations. This necessitates maintaining focus on the foundational assumptions underpinning arguments for recognising principles of justice and rejecting spurious claims made by inept politicians.

The circumstances surrounding international criminal justice and its definitions can be characterised as fundamentally logical insofar as true justice is impervious to falsehoods and various intrigues. Such conditions are essential for fostering a conception of justice that respects the integrity of victims who have been utterly disregarded. Therefore, although contemporary systems are heavily influenced by powerful political entities globally and have long been monopolised, they persist nonetheless; this monopolisation should not justify the obliteration of life or acts constituting genocide against victims - despite being evident in today's enforcement mechanisms within international criminal justice systems. This reflects a profound lack of enforceability concerning provisions under international criminal law concerning significant offenders or paternalistic governments at present.

It is essential to recognise that a positive and cooperative approach to the multilateral implementation of criminal provisions is not merely important but vital. This collaboration is crucial for the interests of all nations worldwide in the pursuit of justice. Fundamentally, there exists a shared interest among all individuals in seeking the proper application of justice and in avoiding becoming targets of violence from powerful political entities.

As we have emphasised, the purity of justice plays an essential role in presenting accurate results and restoring the rights of victims. Therefore, appropriate principles of justice are necessary for selecting the right measures to restore victims' rights and to approach the fundamental essence of justice, which includes equality, respect, and ethical integrity for all individuals. This indicates that, in the pursuit of justice, we must focus on upholding the ethical philosophy of justice to ensure proper distributive justice. It also suggests that we must avoid any presentation that affirms the false statements of authorities who are empowered by deceitful narratives.

These requirements highlight the importance of an appropriate international criminal justice system that is free from numerous legal, political, and economic falsehoods. The foundational principles of international criminal justice, which distinguish between pure justice and the justice of lies, are fundamentally based on the necessity of presenting an accurate justice and interpreting justice norms independent of political influence. This means that deceitful or fraudulent norms cannot and should not represent the true nature of justice. However, achieving true justice requires both the physical and mental strength of the victims, which is not only difficult to establish but is often fundamentally undermined by the deceit of powerful nations.

This creates a constant psychological struggle between the rights of victims and the threat of force from oppressive governments. The resistance of victims has been evident throughout history, reflecting their varying capacities to combat the brutal power of these governments. Nevertheless, the rights of victims have been obstructed by the coordinated efforts of Western governments, which often collaborate with major criminals. This is the reality faced by those governments that, while appearing judicious and reasonable, claim to uphold the principles of international human rights law and deliver true justice. Consequently, the resources necessary for the functioning of the international criminal justice system are stifled, resulting in harsh and unimaginable conditions for the victims.

7. Widespread Backbone Deficiencies in ICC Parties

While the principles of international criminal justice advocate for the peaceful protection of the rights of victims and the restitution of their lost entitlements, there has been a conspicuous lack of accountability imposed upon powerful governments; indeed, the situation appears to be quite the opposite. Consequently, any proposals for procedural reforms in criminal justice fail to adequately address or enforce the essential rights of victims. Despite widespread recognition among dominant governments and their affiliates regarding their complicity in perpetrating crimes against vulnerable nations and occupying their territories, little progress has been made towards preventing mass atrocities. The prevalence of deceitful intentions has escalated, resulting in egregious harm inflicted upon victims by all possible means. This reality underscores that victims have not only been stripped of their homes and lands but have also suffered the loss of family members and children.[9] Furthermore, the framework of international criminal justice, along with its enforcement mechanisms, has become a vehicle for deception that serves solely the interests of new colonial powers within the United Nations - powers that have secured permanent seats on the Security Council through arrangements enshrined in both the League of Nations' and subsequently the United Nations' Charters.[10]

It is evident that true justice has been supplanted by a distorted interpretation within the realm of international criminal justice due to deliberate and malicious falsehoods propagated by superpowers that undermine its integrity. The situation in Palestine, coupled with the United States' culpability in acts widely perceived as genocidal against this nation,

[9] Examine also Farhad Malekian, *International Criminal Law of Children* (New York: Nova Science Publishers, 2021); Farhad Malekian, 'The Child as an Autonomous Subject of Justice' in Farhad Malekian and Kerstin Nordlöf, *Sovereignty of Children in Law* (Cambridge: Cambridge Scholars Publishing, 2012), pp. 2-55;

[10] "Unfortunately, the structure of Chapter VII of the UN Charter is based on the falsification of truth - presenting the truth as lies, and lies as the truth. This is precisely what the Charter does. It lies and provides provisions of equality in other chapters, but then hangs them out to dry with the provisions of Chapter VII. The political challenges of the true features of the relevant chapter are combined with the causes of injustice. The fact is that the persistent temptation of lawyers and moral philosophers of the truth and truth as the presentation of the entire untainted truth in a jurisdictional statute with the existence of legal thoughts and legalistic assumptions is to give these unjustified provisions the appearance of being justified. Consequently, as an ultimate principle, they are tempted to turn a blind eye to the facts regarding Chapter VII." Farhad Malekian, *Conundrums of Paternalism in International Criminal Justice* (New York: Nova Science Publishers, 2024), pp. 19-20.

exemplifies how falsehoods have infiltrated and adversely shaped international criminal jurisprudence. Although considerations pertaining to both substantive justice and fairness should take precedence, there exists minimal political commitment to actualise these intentions within enforcement practices. Moreover, significant deficiencies are apparent among parties to the Rome Statute of the ICC regarding their capacity to deliver genuine justice for victims' rights.

It is unequivocally evident that the framework governing international criminal justice remains fundamentally deficient in its enforcement capabilities. The significant influence exerted by dominant political powers considerably detracts from the focus on international human rights systems, as well as their legal and humanitarian dimensions. Fundamental rights are frequently overlooked when contrasted with efforts to strengthen global mechanisms through misleading narratives. The judgments rendered by international judicial bodies, along with their reports and statements, are consistently compromised and ultimately biased due to concerns, prejudices, and self-serving definitions of international criminal law that are designed to align with governmental interests. This situation is not merely temporary but rather persistent; it endures unabated as long as substantial contemporary political powers retain decisive control over international legal frameworks, particularly those pertinent to international criminal justice.

The aforementioned issues indicate significant shortcomings within the international criminal justice system, characterised by an instability of power stemming from a lack of enforceability. Some of these deficiencies also arise from the failings of moral responsibility as portrayed by every member state in the General Assembly, particularly those that are parties to the Statute of the ICC based in The Hague.[11] Consequently, not only are state parties fragmented within the United Nations General Assembly, but they also exhibit varying attitudes towards their major powers. This situation has resulted in a multitude of legal, political, economic, and even philosophical and religious divisions that complicate and hinder the enforcement of genuine justice. It is our assertion that the gatherings of different governmental representatives in entities such as the General Assembly, Security Council, International Court of Justice, or International Criminal Court are rendered ineffective when truth

[11] Consult also Francesca Albanese, From Economy of Settler-Colonial Occupation to the Economy of Genocide, Report of the Special Rapporteur on the situation of human rights in the Palestinian territories occupied since 1967; https://www.un.org/unispal/document/a-hrc-59-23-from-economy-of-occupation-to-economy-of-genocide-report-special-rapporteur-francesca-albanese-palestine-2025/.

is equated with justice while falsehood is similarly construed as justice. When corrupt or disingenuous members of the United Nations Security Council operate as perennial offenders and successfully present deceit as an acceptable interpretation of justice, every single norm becomes subject to manipulation.[12]

[12] Mark J Osiel, *Obeying orders: Atrocity, Military Discipline, and the Law of War* (Transaction Publishers, 1999); Timothy L. H McCormack, *The Law of War Crimes: National and International Approaches* (Brill, 1997); Rene Provost, *International Human Rights and Humanitarian Law* (2002); William A. Schabas, *War Crimes and Human Rights: Essays on the Death Penalty, Justice and Accountability* (Cameron May, 2008); Steven R. Ratner, Jason S. Abrams, and James L. Bischoff, *Accountability for Human Rights Atrocities in International Law: Beyond the Nuremberg Legacy*, (3rd ed., Oxford Press, 2009); Eric Stover, *My Neighbour, My Enemy: Justice and Community in the Aftermath of Mass Atrocity* (Cambridge University Press, 2004); Benjamin B. Ferencz, *New Legal Foundations for Global Survival: Security Through the Security Council* (Oceana Publications,1994). See also Farhad Malekian, 'Judging International Criminal Justice in the Occupied Territories,' 12 *International Criminal Law Review* (2012), 827–869; Farhad Malekian, *Trading Virginity of International Criminal Justice* (Nova Sciences Publishers, 2020).

Chapter 8

Criminal Governments Orchestrating Their Bongos of Justice

1. Bongos of Injustice

One could liken the dynamics of international criminal justice to a musical instrument known as the bongo. This analogy suggests that it resonates with the provisions set forth by the ICC whenever powerful governments refer an international conflict concerning criminal justice to the Court, believing it serves their interests in adjudicating cases deemed crucial for those oppressive regimes. Conversely, these same powers may initiate discord when issues under investigation by the ICC do not align with their political agendas. Thus, we contend that principles surrounding justice are employed by these influential powers in fundamentally divergent directions based on their respective policies.

A clear illustration of this orchestration can be observed in two distinct cases presented before the Prosecutor's office: one pertaining to Ukraine and Russia, and another concerning Israel and its occupation of Palestinian rights. This indicates that varying strategies may be utilised by powerful governments regarding both the legal authority of the Court and its interpretation of justice, criminal law, and victim rights.

In both scenarios mentioned above, powerful governments assert claims regarding victims while exacerbating widespread atrocities against populations in Ukraine and Palestine - both orchestrated under U.S. leadership with assertions aimed at delivering justice to Ukraine and Gaza while perpetuating falsehoods through international criminal narratives concerning over half a million casualties among Ukraine's populace.[1] These offenses have

---

[1] One very obvious lie is the United States government claimed that Russia attacked their own pipelines in war between Russia and Ukraine constituting "a significant lie that the system of international criminal justice should not tolerate. The following are some of the reasons which indicate that the United States has carried out the attack:

a) The CIA has long warned that the US powertionist government would damage the pipeline.

b) The president of the United States clearly expressed that he would stop the pipeline.

c) Reopening the pipeline was Russia's only leverage for ending the war and keeping their options open.

been rooted in misrepresentations long devised by various nations including those governed by U.S. and British administrations, among others.[2]

Both of these governments operate in a professional manner, orchestrating a façade of justice through various inhumane rationales and the selective prosecution of criminals. This suggests that they grant impunity for the gravest international offenses and strongly endorse the criminal actions of individuals who have perpetrated mass atrocities, including genocide, aggression, piracy, robbery, brutality, rape, torture, looting, crimes against humanity, violations of cultural heritage, war crimes, apartheid, exploitation, forced migration, and significant breaches of humanitarian law during armed conflicts.[3] Such barbaric acts are not regarded as international crimes but rather as defensive

---

d) The US is one of the few countries in the world that has the ability to carry out underwater attacks.

e) The United States powertionist government has the knowledge of how to damage the pipelines beyond repair.

f) The Russian government benefitted from selling gas to a number of European countries, which would lift sanctions. The US did not want this.

g) The destruction of pipeline was an attack on Russian's own economic interests and benefitted United States powertionist as it led to EU countries being dependent on the US and its economy.

h) The intention of the United States was also de-industrialisation of European Union and having European companies relocate to the United States to benefit the American economy.

j) Above all, United States." Farhad Malekian, *Powertionism in International Criminal Justice* (Nova Sciences Publishers, 2022), pp. 30-31.

[2] "April 2022 presentation drawn up for senior British intelligence officers hashing out an elaborate scheme to blow up Crimea's Kerch Bridge with the involvement of specially trained Ukrainian soldiers. Almost six months after the plan was circulated, Kerch Bridge was attacked in an October 8th suicide bombing apparently overseen by Ukraine's SBU intelligence services. Detailed proposals for providing "audacious" support to Kiev's "maritime raiding operations" were drafted at the request of Chris Donnelly, a senior British Army intelligence operative and veteran high ranking NATO advisor. The wide-ranging plan's core component was "destruction of the bridge over the Kerch Strait." The truck bombing of the Kerch Bridge differed operationally from the plot sketched therein. Yet, Britain's evident interest in planning such an attack underscores the deep involvement of NATO powers in the Ukraine proxy war. At almost precisely the time that London reportedly sabotaged peace talks between Kiev and Moscow in April this year, British military intelligence operatives were drawing up blueprints to destroy a major Russian bridge crossed by thousands of civilians per day. The roadmap was produced by Hugh Ward, a British military veteran. A number of strategies for helping Ukraine "pose a threat to Russian naval forces" in the Black Sea are outlined. The overriding objectives are stated as aiming to "degrade" Russia's ability to blockade Kiev, "erode" Moscow's "warfighting capability," and isolate Russian land and maritime forces in Crimea by "denying resupply by sea and overland via Kerch bridge."" https://thegrayzone.com/2022/10/10/ukrainian-kerch-bridge/.

[3] Martti Koskenniemi, Betwwen Impunity and Show Trials, 6 Max Plank United Nations Year Book (200), pp. 1-35; examine also Otto Kirchheimer, Political Justice: The Use of Legal Procedure for Political Ends (Princeton University Press, 1961).

manoeuvres by powerful governments and thus deemed permissible. However;

Kant taught not only individuals, but also governments, teaching them that they need to make good decisions and not violate the rights of individuals or the basic philosophy of the system of international criminal justice through granting impunity or by committing or supporting international crimes.

Therefore, Kant supported the principle of invisibility which works to protect the principle of visibility. In other words, arresting certain individuals and submitting them to the jurisdiction of international criminal courts serves the purpose of enforcing human rights, however this should not be done selectively and should not be used as a ground for impunity in relation to more serious criminal conducts. Therefore, we should not provide impunity for criminals from big powerful states and let them go free without punishment. The question then becomes: how can the philosophy of the system of international human rights law protect victims and at the same time encourage criminals and protect their "beings"?[4]

Consequently, serious prosecutable international crimes are overlooked due to the assistance, complicity, cooperation, support, abetting, encouragement, and facilitation provided to these criminals which absolves them from the concept of international criminal responsibility. In the absence of such complicity surrounding influential perpetrators, there would be no opportunity for genuine international criminal justice; instead, the notion of authentic justice remains merely aspirational. Thus, the philosophy of justice eludes jurisdictional oversight while conditions akin to threats persist where injustice prevails.

---

[4] Farhad Malekian, *Imperative Philosophy of International Criminal Justice: Visible Power – Invisible Essence* (Nova Sciences Publishers, 2022), p.49. For the philosophy of examine Kant Immanuel, *The Only Possible Argument in Support of a Demonstration of the Existence of God* (1763); Kant Immanuel, *Critique of Pure Reason* (1781); Kant Immanuel, *Prolegomena to Any Future Metaphysics* (1783); Kant Immanuel, *Answering the Question: What is Enlightenment?* (1784); Kant Immanuel, *Perpetual Peace, and Other Essays on Politics, History, and Morals* (1784); Kant Immanuel, *Groundwork of the Metaphysic of Morals* (1785); Kant Immanuel, *Metaphysical Foundations of Natural Science* (1786); Kant Immanuel, *The Critique of Practical Reason* (1788); Kant Immanuel, *Critique of Judgment* (1790); Kant Immanuel, *The Science of Right* (1790); Kant Immanuel, *Religion within the Bounds of Bare Reason* (1793); Kant Immanuel, *Perpetual Peace: A Philosophical Sketch* (1795); Kant Immanuel, *The Metaphysics of Morals* (1797); Kant Immanuel, *Opus Postumum* (1995); Kant Immanuel, 'Religion within the Limits of Reason Alone,' in *Religion and Rational Theology*, ed. and transl. Allen Wood and George di Giovanni (Cambridge University Press, 1996); Kant Immanuel, *Practical Philosophy* (editor: Mary J. Gregor, 1999).

The ongoing threats and violations against victims' rights - exemplified by those endured by Palestinians - continue to manifest within the realm of international relations. It is reasonable to assume that these criminal governments maintain their positions unscathed while their transgressions go unpunished. In this context, impunity is extended to notorious professional criminals who operate under the protective umbrella of dictatorial or neo-colonial powers represented within the Security Council. This situation implies that not only are prominent offenders shielded from prosecution but their capacity for criminality also safeguards their allied nations. Thus arises the question: how can we trust that the system of international criminal justice remains robust when all evidence indicates that major offenders associated with the Security Council and their cooperative allies remain untouched? The current state of international criminal justice lacks any meaningful realisation of true justice; much of what is considered theoretical justice under the auspices of the International Criminal Court devolves into mere illusion. Consequently, any further pursuit or precise definition and application of international criminal justice becomes futile. This signifies that even victims striving to advance their understanding of genuine justice or reclaim their rights to independence will find such pursuits impossible, as their rights continue to be suppressed by the oppressive mechanisms wielded by superpowers.

This scenario illustrates how governments utilise platforms like the Security Council - with representatives from diverse ethnic backgrounds - to project an image intended to convince global populations that they do not embody racism or fascism nor engage in acts constituting international crimes. This illustrates the manner in which we engage with the theory of justice within the international arena, particularly within the domains of the United Nations and the International Criminal Court.

For instance, Judge Julia Sebutinde of the International Court of Justice (ICJ) from Uganda cast her vote against the emergency measures requested by South Africa concerning Israel's alleged war crimes, crimes against humanity, and genocide in Gaza.[5] This occurred despite a prior ruling by the ICJ mandating that the Israeli government take measures to prevent civilian deaths, destruction, and any acts of genocide amidst its military operations in

[5] Sebutinde was born in February 1954 and is presently occupying her second term as a Ugandan judge on the International Court of Justice. She has been a judge at the court since March 2021. She is the first African woman to sit in the ICJ.

Gaza. Surprisingly, however, the Court refrained from issuing an order for a ceasefire.

Consequently, it can be inferred that Judge Sebutinde's perspective was indirectly acknowledged by the Court despite her dissenting vote against her colleagues. This situation further exemplifies how international criminal justice struggles with interpreting "criminal justice" and its fundamental objective of safeguarding victims of international crimes. It raises concerns regarding potential biases or influences affecting judges, including ethical conflicts, notions of inhumanity or immorality, and possible corruption.

Thus, it is perplexing to observe that a significant case involving South Africa regarding allegations of genocide in Palestine is approached with ambiguity while a judge appears to endorse actions perceived as criminal by the Israeli government. This suggests that decisions within international criminal justice systems may have been predetermined even prior to the occurrence of alleged crimes.

Such conclusions are drawn from observations that many judges, prosecutors, attorneys, and politicians appear to be manipulated similarly to certain journalists aligned with Western powers. Consequently, actions taken in defence of a population and their military responses are often labelled as terrorism. This reflects how narratives surrounding criminal justice are constructed and deemed significant in exerting power through criminal jurisdiction.

2. Lies Denying Validity to the Norms of Justice

The inquiry arises as to whether the actions of individuals engaged in criminal activities, particularly those holding governmental positions, contravene the fundamental principles of *jus cogens* and infringe upon the core tenets of human morality, which are encapsulated within pertinent international conventions. This concern is underscored by the fact that all authorities bear duties, obligations, and responsibilities for the implementation of authentic international justice norms. This concept aligns with a broader theory encompassing natural law, *jus cogens* law, and customary international criminal law. Although *jus cogens* norms derive from conventional international criminal law, their significant status endows them with an imperative character within the international legal system that binds all states, irrespective of their participation in specific international conventions. This indicates that non-compliance with *jus cogens* norms is not permissible.[6]

In essence, the framework of *jus cogens* serves as the foundation for all systems of international criminal law and human rights, which are binding on all governments, regardless of their adherence to established rules of international criminal justice. Consequently, no orchestrations of injustice should be tolerated.[7]

To assert that one will act unilaterally without regard for *jus cogens* norms suggests a culpable intent indicative of deliberate planning to breach the established body of international criminal justice.[8] A viable approach to addressing issues surrounding international criminal justice among various governments lies in upholding *jus cogens* norms to mitigate further conflicts

---

[6] "Therefore, *jus cogens* norms, along with *erga omnes* norms, are obligatory and no impunity should be granted to those who violate them. That is one of the most serious problems facing the systems of human rights and criminal justice and has led to the problem of selectivity as well as dependency on the decisions of the powertionist governments of the world - especially of the United States, which compels other nations to follow its lead." "When we use the notion of selectivity regarding the accused, we adopt a particular form of powertionism that is not recommended by authentic criminal justice procedures and is condemned by all means." Farhad Malekian, *Powertionism in International Criminal Justice* (New York: Nova Science Publishers, 2022), p. 130 and 240; examine also Robert Cryer, 'The Doctrinal Foundations of International Criminalisation,' in M. cherif Bassiouni, ed., *International Criminal Law*, Vol. 1, (2008), pp. 107-128. See also Robert Cryer, *Prosecuting International Crimes, Selectivity and the International Criminal Law Regime* (Cambridge University Press, Cambridge, 2005).

[7] On *jus cogens*, consult also A. Verdross, 'Jus dispositivum and jus cogens in international law,' 60 *American Journal of International Law* (1966), 55-63; E. Suy, 'The concept of *jus cogens* in public international law,' in *Lagonissi Conference on International Law* (1967), 17-77; A. Gomez Robledo, "Le ius cogens international: sa genèse, sa nature, ses fonctions," *III RCADI* (1981), 9-217; R. St. J. Macdonald, 'Fundamental norms in contemporary international law,' 25 *Canadian Yearbook of International Law* (1987), 115-149; L. Alexidze, "Legal nature of *jus cogens* in contemporary international law," *III RACADI* (1981), 223-268; G. Gaja "Jus cogens beyond the Vienna Convention," III RACADI (1981), 271-31; G. A. Christenson, '*Jus cogens*: Guarding interests fundamental to international society,' 28 *Virginia Journal of International Law* (1988), 585-628; G. M. Danilenko, 'International *jus cogens*: Issues of law-making,' 2 *European Journal of International Law* (1991), 42-65.

[8] Consult also Farhad Malekian, *Prohibition Governing Child Soldiers Constituting an Integral Part of Jus cogens and Obligatio Erga Omnes*, XVII *World Congress of the International Association of Youth and Family Judges and Magistrates*, Belfast, Northern Ireland, 27 August – 2 September (2006); Farhad Malekian, 'Conundrums of *Jus cogens:* In Case Law' (Part II), No. 13 *Вісник Південного регіонального центру Національної академії правових наук України,* [No. 13 *Journal of the South regional Center of National Academy of Legal Sciences of Ukraine*] (2017), pp. 12-21; Farhad Malekian, 'Conundrums of *Jus cogens*: in International Criminal Law' (Part I), *Вісник Південного регіонального центру Національної академії правових наук України* [*No.12 Journal of the South regional Center of National Academy of Legal Sciences of Ukraine*] (2017), pp. 8-16.

and protect victims. However, this may be perceived by certain governments as subjugation to the authority of international criminal courts. If the pursuit of justice under the framework of international criminal law fails to embody fairness, it implies an attempt to evade our obligations under the laws governing *jus cogens* through expressions that are both immoral and violative; such actions could ultimately manifest as acts leading to immense suffering for countless innocent victims due to self-interest or hegemonic motives.

Thus, it is essential for all nations globally - including those wielding significant influence within bodies such as the Security Council and International Court of Justice - to navigate carefully the potential controversies associated with *jus cogens* or peremptory norms in international criminal law and justice. Regrettably, there exist numerous avenues available for governments seeking to pursue self-interest at the expense of others' rights on both land and sea. Such conduct does not reflect adherence to a legitimate system of international law or human rights but rather embodies self-serving practices motivated by greed - an inclination evident since the inception of global organisations like the League of Nations and subsequently, the United Nations.

Ultimately, while we possess ample discretion in selecting our courses of action and scrutinising any government deemed 'criminal,' this practice persists throughout our engagements in international relations. We may accept any rationale regarding the conception of the international criminal justice system and continue to believe that we are progressing in the right direction toward achieving a true platform of justice. However, this raises the question of whether there exists a definitive understanding of justice that allows for violations of international human rights and international criminal justice in the name of what is deemed legitimate justice. Should such definitions exist, it is evident that they are inherently biased and grounded in falsehoods, presenting a notion of justice as proclaimed by powerful states, which fundamentally constitutes injustice.

Regardless of our actions or destinations, the essence of universal moral justice remains unalterable, although its practical application may often be hindered. An appropriate synthesis of justice principles is not merely a requisite for the framework of international human rights law and international criminal justice; it is also essential to forming an integral part of an ethical representation of natural and moral justice. The absence of moral norms within the construct of justice inevitably leads to various forms of violations within legal systems. Without morality, we lose access to the fundamental tenets of justice, humanity, and peace.

3. Ignoring the Rationale Behind Virtue

It is important to clarify that I do not make obstructive assumptions about the definitions and interpretations related to violations and conceptions of justice that are not tied to erroneous interpretations. The reality is that definitions and descriptions concerning violations and international crimes are sufficiently clear for even a child to recognise them. The aims and definitions associated with these violations and crimes should not be perceived as personal or self-serving interests; rather, they emerge from collective efforts by representatives from numerous governments through negotiation processes under the framework of international criminal law. If government judgments regarding the definition of justice were accurate, we would have succeeded in developing a body of jurisprudence pertaining to international criminal justice that addresses all members of governments who have committed grave international crimes. Despite their claims to adhere to international criminal conventions, substantial evidence suggests that many serious international crimes have been perpetrated by or on behalf of both historical and contemporary colonial powers. Such are violations of:

The Four Geneva Conventions of 12 August 1949 and the First Additional Protocol.

The Vienna Convention on Diplomatic Relations.

The Vienna Convention on Consular Relations.

The Convention on the Rights of the Child and the Optional Protocol to the Convention on the Rights of the Child on the involvement of children in armed conflict.

The Convention on the Elimination of All Forms of Discrimination against Women.

The Hague Convention (IV) respecting the Laws and Customs of War on Land and its annex: Regulations Concerning the Laws and Customs of War on Land.

The Convention on the Rights of Persons with Disabilities.

The Vienna Convention on the Law of Treaties.

The International Convention on the Elimination of All Forms of Racial Discrimination.

The Convention against Torture and Other Cruel, Inhuman or Degrading Treatment or Punishment.

The United Nations Convention against Corruption.

The Convention on the Prevention and Punishment of the Crime of Genocide.

The International Convention on the Suppression and Punishment of the Crime of Apartheid.
The International Covenant on Civil and Political Rights.
The International Covenant on Economic, Social and Cultural Rights.

Whether the system of international criminal justice functions effectively in providing correct definitions and sound guidelines for prosecuting international criminals hinges upon our approach to interpreting our own international conventions. If our objectives are centred on accumulating wealth, gaining positions, or aggressively influencing victims' rights while seeking broad national and international recognition solely to assert our correctness over the alleged wrongdoing of others, then it can be concluded that our conception of justice possesses an inherently self-serving nature.

There exists no inconsistency within the justice system if we adhere to the truth and refrain from accepting the justifications provided by powerful entities regarding their criminal actions, which they claim do not constitute crimes but rather represent the implementation of international norms. This implies that we face a choice: either accept these falsehoods and thereby contribute to the suffering of victims while distorting the concept of true justice, or align ourselves with the truth and safeguard our independence from those who lack a genuine commitment to justice, such as Antony Blinken and Linda Thomas-Greenfield, who perpetuate victimisation. *The perspective one adopts when examining the evolution of jurisprudence fundamentally influences one's assessment of justice and shapes how one scrutinises truth versus deception. As long as ignorance obscures the substantive nature of justice in the Security Council and injustices persist within this framework, there remains a prevailing disinterest in enforcing authentic justice.*

It is crucial to recognise that matters of justice should not be dictated by statements made by governmental representatives. If international criminal justice aims to enhance its foundational principles, then it must embody the principle ideals associated with fairness and virtue while remaining independent of any statement. We do not seek to overstate the significance of justice as an extraordinary achievement; rather, a sound understanding of equitable conditions necessitates moving beyond personal theories of inspiration. The objective is to accurately reflect upon the suffering endured by victims so that true justice can be realised appropriately.

Delivering justice in a proper manner is inherently challenging and may present certain constraints. Judges and prosecutors are afforded discretion, allowing them to apply their authentic knowledge based on their unique circumstances and understanding of justice in accordance with their conscience. The boundaries governing appropriate judgments are not merely matters of choice for judges or lawyers; they are rooted in imperative principles that demand accurate and rightful assertions within judicial decisions.

When I refer to constraints concerning the delivery of just judgments, my intention is to emphasise that the narratives propagated by powerful political entities should not unduly influence written judgments. It is essential for judges to remain cognisant that their rulings should not inadvertently empower malevolent political agendas. Had these powers genuinely acknowledged international criminal justice principles as intended, both the virtues inherent in criminal justice and victims' rights would not have continually suffered degradation. A pertinent illustration of this phenomenon is the monopolisation of the principle of international criminal justice during the Vietnam War.[9] When we refer to constraints, we are indicating the necessity of limiting falsehoods and preventing international crimes.

There exist specific formal conditions in the interpretation of the justice system and its various branches that warrant consideration and enforcement within the framework of international criminal justice, as they serve not only to protect victims' rights but also to uphold the integrity of justice. I do not assert that these conditions are exhaustive; rather, I maintain that justice must always consider certain foundational principles. However, I contend that the principles governing justice - whether under the jurisdiction of the International Criminal Court or influenced by certain authorities within the United Nations Security Council - should never be aligned with the facilitation of falsehoods alongside human rights or criminal justice tenets. Consequently, I have refrained from delving into an examination of concepts related to falsehoods and their detrimental impacts on the justice system as governed by powerful nations. The rationale for this is straightforward: engaging in discourse about such falsehoods risks entangling us within the deceptive narratives perpetuated by entities such as the Biden administration. Indeed, there have been numerous instances where American administrations have exemplified this pattern, a situation mirrored by British governments whose

---

[9] Falk Richard, *The Vietnam War and International Law (*Princeton University Press, 1968); Richard Falk,The Vietnam War and International Law (4 Volumes, 1976); Richard Falk, 'The Accountability of Leaders: A Challenge to Civil Government and Society' in Jeremy Brecher, Jill Cutler, Smith Brendan, *In the Name of Democracy: American War Crimes in Iraq and Beyond* (American Empire Project), (New York: Metropolitan Books, Henry Holt and Company, 2005).

fabrications have pervaded global narratives regarding effective administration and implementation of justice.

4. Conflation of Fabrications Predicated for Self-Interests

There exist numerous philosophical justifications for asserting that the right to justice constitutes a fundamental principle that ought not to be violated under any circumstances. This implies that both the concept of justice and its associated principles should not be subjected to selective interpretations across different systems. The value inherent in any definition of a just system is contingent upon its ability to establish a legacy grounded in truth; if a system fails to foster such a legacy, its definition cannot succeed in fulfilling its intended purpose. The validity of these formal parameters surrounding justice or international criminal justice is derived from humanity's collective obligation to adhere steadfastly to established principles under all circumstances. If international criminal justice principles and those pertaining to the International Criminal Court are to serve their intended roles, then it is imperative that they do not conflate basic victim rights with deceitful narratives or wrongful accusations. Justice cannot be accurately labelled as such while simultaneously being executed through mechanisms rooted in injustice; this has never been nor should it ever be the objective of the establishment or substantive principles of the International Criminal Court.

The prerequisites set forth by the International Criminal Court concerning matters of justice are both natural and indispensable, rendering them invulnerable to critique from any legal philosophy. The principles enshrined in the Rome Statute of the Court are essential for the establishment of just outcomes and the development of satisfactory understandings of justice. Consequently, these principles should not be subjected to negotiations or compromises within governmental corridors, particularly by those administrations that seek to alter and manipulate the definition of justice through persistent falsehoods. It is not an exaggeration to assert that British, American, French, and several other Western governments have long misrepresented the international legal system through a web of lies, fabrications, and deceptions. This observation must also take into account the various manifestations of political, economic, and military self-interest exhibited by these governments as they continuously endeavour to exploit the resources of nations in the Middle East and Asia. Their actions constitute not only a misappropriation of external resources but also an exploitation of cultural assets predicated on deceit.

Numerous Western governments profess to uphold justice and champion international human rights while espousing democratic constitutional frameworks. As previously indicated in this discourse, these administrations rely on deception as a cornerstone of their political strategies to exert moral authority in their international dealings. They engage in arms trading across different regions, fostering conflicts and divisions among diverse national groups. This reality underscores the urgent need to unveil their true moral standing regarding humanity and international criminal justice. The integrity of the international criminal justice system cannot be reinforced by the falsehoods and immorality propagated by certain powerful global leaders. In essence, neither deception nor aggressive military might can be legitimised within any framework that claims to define justice. Thus, an analysis of justice concepts must remain rooted in their fundamental rationale for existence. Furthermore, reasoned discourse within theories of justice does not equate to appeasing those who propagate falsehoods or obstruct efforts to condemn genocide.

Additionally, it is important to note that any definition of justice inherently exposes its association with falsehood - specifically lying. Therefore, I maintain that descriptions pertaining to justice need not be embellished; rather they must present all facts candidly if they are to endure scrutiny. Regrettably, the profound dictatorial influence exerted by major powers such as the United States and Britain - who dominate global perceptions of justice through deception - has generated significant challenges aimed at undermining a coherent understanding of justice itself. In articulating a philosophical theory of justice, one is entitled to examine it from multiple perspectives deemed necessary or conventional.

It is imperative to note that one must not rely on the historical fabrications perpetuated by governments worldwide as a basis for articulating a philosophical definition. Philosophy inherently encompasses a pursuit of truth and wisdom, emphasising the intrinsic value of truth, fairness, and the rights of victims. Even if alternative perspectives on the philosophy of rightful justice exist, such viewpoints ought to remain devoid of political or personal machinations aimed at monopolising justice principles in alignment with self-serving norms that are fundamentally deceptive.

5. Discounting Political and Legal Personalities

In presenting facts and evidence, all governments are effectively compelled to adhere to established principles of international criminal justice and refrain from offering alternative interpretations of truth. However, this notion remains largely aspirational; otherwise, the principles of justice would resemble mere rhetoric crafted within the offices of powerful criminal regimes. These entities subsequently present their narratives as factual rather than fictitious. Indeed, many Latin American nations, particularly Cuba, have endured the falsehoods propagated by successive U.S. administrations and their diplomatic manoeuvrings designed to impose political hegemony based on deception.[10] The use of this coup strategy has been employed in Nicaragua, Bolivia, Argentina, and Venezuela. Consequently, principles of justice often encounter significant opposition from superpower nations. A similar strategy was also planned and executed in Iran by the American and British governments, both of which bear criminal responsibility.

Historically, the Socialist Soviet Union has served as a notable adversary to imperialist governments; thus, we confront an ongoing struggle regarding the definition of justice - not solely within socialist frameworks but also during contemporary times. This suggests that debates surrounding justice definitions are less about elucidating what constitutes justice and more about which political entity possesses superior military might. As such, the understanding of justice continually shifts directions away from its true essence toward accommodating the prevailing conditions dictated by influential powers.

Therefore, comprehending the concept of justice necessitates an engagement with historical contexts relevant to its evolution as a legal and philosophical doctrine. To grasp these international criminal justice principles and their associated requirements adequately requires familiarity with political ideologies as well as insights into governmental lobbying processes. Thus far, it appears that the theory of international criminal justice - ideally an

---

[10] The Cuban clear statement expresses this dreadful situation, rejecting the paternalism character of the United States government's Declaration on Palestine. It clearly states that "Cuba calls on the Security Council to fulfil the responsibility given to it by the UN Charter in the maintenance of international peace and security, to adopt the necessary decisions and to demand from Israel an immediate end to the occupation of the Palestinian territories and of aggressive policies and colonizing practices, as well as compliance with the resolutions adopted by that body on the situation in the Middle East, including the Palestinian issue." *Cuba rejects US recognition of Jerusalem as the capital of Israel* http://www.juventudrebelde.cu/en/internationals/2017-12-08/cuba-rejects-us-recognition-of-jerusalem-as-the-capital-of-israel/print.

independent framework advocating for victims' rights - is not genuinely autonomous. One could argue that it would be exceedingly naïve to assume that the current prosecutor at the International Criminal Court operates without prior or ongoing connections to the British government. His prompt involvement in Ukraine cases, juxtaposed with his questionably delayed response regarding Palestine, serves as clear evidence of influences akin to those experienced by Karim Khan. In reality, scant doctrine on justice remains untainted by political considerations. The concept of institutional bias is so profound and complex within the justice system that it warrants an entire book dedicated to its exploration. This term can be applied in various situations in both courts, namely the International Court of Justice and the International Criminal Court, both of which are located in The Hague.

We must also recognise that the principles of justice have universal applicability. This means that the justice as upheld by the Court should not differentiate between principles, just as it is not permissible to distinguish between criminals. Justice under the ICC system must apply to everyone, based on their moral integrity, until their crimes are proven. However, this expectation is a general guideline for interpreting and applying justice. There are instances where the ICC's jurisdiction is clearly established without the need for formal proceedings, particularly regarding the serious criminality of certain accused individuals. For example, the actions of several U.S. presidents raise questions about the necessity of establishing jurisdiction for the examination of their alleged crimes; this may be more a matter of formality than a lack of evidence. The records provided by Julian Assange already serve as compelling evidence supporting the Court's jurisdiction. How can we assert that Bill Clinton, Hillary Clinton, Barack Obama, or Joe Biden require additional evidence to substantiate their criminality within the framework of international criminal justice?[11] The same applies to several British government leaders.[12]

Thus, I assume that each of us understands that the primary function of the principles of international criminal justice is to distinguish truth from falsehood and to separate rights from wrongdoing. This reality underscores

---

[11] Prince Williams, Barack Obama Is A War Criminal, Havard Political Review (2021), https://harvardpolitics.com/obama-war-criminal/.

[12] Mark Landler, U.K. Special Forces Allowed to 'Get Away With Murder' in Afghanistan, Inquiry Told, Evidence released by an official inquiry into alleged war crimes painted a disturbing picture of an elite fighting force with a culture of impunity (Jan. 8, 2025), https://www.nytimes.com/2025/01/08/world/europe/uk-afghanistan-war-crimes.html; British War Crimes, https://en.wikipedia.org/wiki/British_war_crimes.

the necessity of recognising that justice should not adhere to principles based on deception. Furthermore, a principle of international criminal justice may be deemed invalid if it is self-defeating, self-contradictory, or inconsistent with the theory of justice, particularly with the principles enshrined in the Statutes of the ICC. Similarly, it is a well-established duty of the prosecutors and judges of the Court to refrain from referencing or applying contradictory principles, norms, or provisions that undermine the legal values enshrined in the Court's jurisdiction. This means that all principles within the system of international criminal justice must be reasonable and should not conform to a monopolised definition of justice or the deceptions of authoritarian powers.

The Court should ensure that it does not endorse the power of monopolisation in opposition to the prosecution and punishment of criminals. For example, the actions of Benjamin Netanyahu or any other prominent criminal do not merely require evidence but rather warrant life imprisonment. The principles underlying the international criminal justice system, as articulated in the Court's framework, are intended for implementation rather than mere ornamental purposes. This implies that any individual who has egregiously transgressed international criminal law is subject to the jurisdiction of the Court.[13] According to the statutes of the ICC, every accused party and their superiors must face penalties commensurate with the crimes committed.[14] Relying on falsehoods propagated by powerful nations to shield themselves from accountability under international criminal law diminishes the integrity and respect associated with justice. Autocratic rule cannot be sustained indefinitely, and the mass casualties resulting from conflicts such as the Iraq War should not be misconstrued as a legitimate interpretation of justice.[15] Justice must serve not only to address the grievances of victims but

---

[13] On international criminal law, consult Georg Schwarzenberger, 'The Problem of an International Criminal Law,' 5 Current Legal Problems (1950) 265; Edward M. Wise, 'Prolegomenon to the Principles of International Criminal Law,' 16 New York University Law Review (1970) 562; Farhad Malekian, *International Criminal Law: The Legal and Critical Analysis of International Crimes* (2 vols. 1991); Farhad Malekian, *Principles of Islamic International Criminal Law: A Comparative Search* (2011); Farhad Malekian, *The Monopolization of International Criminal Law in the United Nations: A Jurisprudential Approach* (2nd ed., 1995); M. Cherif Bassiouni (ed.), *International Criminal Law* (5 vols., 1999); Farhad Malekian, 'International Criminal Responsibility,' in M. Cherif Bassiouni (ed.), International Criminal Law, (1999), p.155.

[14] *Id.*

[15] Michael Isikoff and David Corn, Hubris: *The Inside Story of Spin, Scandal, and the Selling of the Iraq War* (Crown Publishers, New York, 2006); Farhad Malekian, 'Emasculating the Philosophy of International Criminal Justice in the Iraqi Special Tribunal,' *Cornell International Law Journal*, 58/5 (2005), pp. 675-725.

also uphold its foundational principles. This is not merely a matter of preference; it constitutes an imperative obligation of the ICC.

6. Contradiction with Rightful Criminal Reasoning

While it may be possible for an entire justice system to operate in accordance with falsehoods perpetuated by authoritarian governments, such an approach would undoubtedly undermine genuine justice and hinder adherence to international criminal justice principles as a whole. The crux of this issue lies in recognising that principles of justice represent universal standards rather arbitrary interpretations held by governments. In essence, these principles are not confined to a select demographic nor exempt those who perpetrate grave international offences such as genocide, crimes against humanity, war crimes, apartheid, and acts of aggression. The legal nature of justice necessitates addressing class disparities among all individuals without regard for their status when accused of committing international crimes. Indeed, throughout judicial proceedings, all individuals bear responsibilities and obligations aligned with principles that ensure equitable treatment for all.

Consequently, numerous duties are imposed upon those who have breached international criminal law; these obligations stem from fundamental tenets of criminal justice that encompass culpability and malevolent intentions rooted in deceitful narratives. It is these deceptive premises that enable the justice system to respond decisively against barbaric violations of international law.[16] Notably, deriving requirements from established

[16] Examine some international conventions such as Declaration on Social Progress and Development, 1969, Universal Declaration on the Eradication of Hunger and Malnutrition, 1974, Declaration on the Elimination of All Forms of Intolerance and of Discrimination Based on Religion or Belief, 1981, Declaration on the Human Rights of Individuals Who are not Nationals of the Country in which They Live, 1985, Vienna Declaration and Program of Action: World Conference on Human Rights, 1993, Draft United Nations Declaration on the Rights of Indigenous Peoples, 1994, Cairo Declaration of Human Rights in Islam, 1990, American Convention on Human Rights, 1969,African Charter on Human and Peoples' Rights, 1981, Arab Charter on Human Rights, 2004, European Convention for the Protection of Human Rights and Fundamental Freedoms of 1950 as amended by Protocol No. 11 of 1998, Charter of Fundamental Rights of the European Union, 2000,Convention on the Reduction of Statelessness, 1961, Supplementary Convention on the Abolition of Slavery, the Slave Trade, and Institutions and Practices Similar to Slavery, 1956, Declaration on the Protection of Women and Children in Emergency and Armed Conflict, 1974, International Covenant on Civil and Political Rights, 1966, International Convention on the Protection of the Rights of All Migrant Workers and Members of Their Families, 1990.

principles of justice often stands in stark contrast to pervasive falsehoods that must be uncovered and prosecuted through sound judicial practices. Therefore, it is imperative for judges and prosecutors alike to maintain clarity regarding evidence related to the commission of crimes while ensuring that their processes effectively distinguish between deception and truth.

It is indeed possible for various forms of evidence to be introduced within the framework of criminal justice; however, the integrity of such evidence must be not only rational and authentic but also wholly truthful and devoid of falsehoods. For instance, when Benjamin Netanyahu claims that infants have been decapitated, this assertion must be substantiated. In the absence of credible proof, such statements constitute a distortion and manipulation of international criminal justice through persistent untruths.

Consequently, the notion that lies can bolster the impunity of offenders should not be utilised to divert attention from the essence of justice or to control the resultant consequences. It is imperative that all governments comprehend and adhere to the principles of genuine justice, which are widely acknowledged or explicitly recognised in the practices of various international criminal courts - whether permanent or *ad hoc*. The fundamental objective of establishing a globally functioning system of international criminal justice is to eradicate all forms of deception, intrigue, and moral ambiguity exhibited by politicians who are publicly lauded through governmental propaganda yet remain deeply corrupt in their professional conduct. This underscores a lack of moral competence inherent in their governance.

There exists no prerequisite for individuals in positions of power to acquiesce to falsehoods that obscure the structure of international criminal justice as dictated by their leaders or legal advisors. Such complicity ultimately undermines the substantive and pure nature of human morality while misrepresenting established facts regarding international criminal conventions through deceptive reasoning that distorts international judicial processes. For these individuals, systems of justice arise directly from their superiors' agendas aimed at countering competing demands. However, there is a challenge in distinguishing between what constitutes deceit and what represents truth due to the necessity for a conception of international criminal justice that aligns with the interests and objectives of politically engaged factions amidst any given conflict as perceived by major powers. This reflects how international criminal justice is interpreted and legitimised through deceptive reasoning.

It stands contrary to any philosophical principle to reserve specific rights for particular governments' political agendas while simultaneously disarming universally recognised rights applicable to all nations globally. Thus, no secret concessions - entirely fabricated - should be permissible within the realm of international criminal justice; such actions fundamentally contradict established human rights frameworks, rendering any political arrangements concerning basic rights invalid. The formal conditions underpinning this system or conception of international criminal justice possess an intrinsic legitimacy; however, they are not always readily demonstrable against the aggressive ambitions and brutal military actions perpetrated by dominant powers.

7. Mendacious Rhetoric and the Subversion of International Criminal Justice by the ICC Council

In analysing the justice system, it is evident that powerful criminal governments present their narratives to the Security Council as authoritative, with the explicit aim of granting additional time to the Israeli government to continue its violent actions. Consequently, it becomes apparent that there is no equitable distribution of time in such presentations, which are largely based on falsehoods. These actions are intrinsically linked to political manoeuvres that seek to orchestrate brutality. The logical progression of deception arises from further deceit; thus, those who amplify these narratives prefer to perpetuate increasingly unjust decisions under the guise of their veto power.

Ultimately, it remains a fact that no representative of victims is allowed to engage with the international criminal justice system or advocate for rights that have been suppressed within the corridors of the British, American, Australian, French, German, and Swedish governments. Collectively, these nations, along with many other Western governments have played a significant role in facilitating acts of genocide in Gaza.[17] It is imperative that the leaders of these governments be held accountable by the ICC, rather than solely focusing on exclusively on Israeli leaders. Providing weapons to individuals who are demonstrably unstable will inevitably lead to misuse; this

---

[17] Israel's Crimes Against Humanity in Gaza, Mass Forced Displacement and Widespread Destruction (November 14, 2024), https://www.hrw.org/news/2024/11/14/israels-crimes-against-humanity-gaza. The Israeli government also commits acts of genocide in Sudan by shipping advanced spying equipment. Examine *inter alia* https://countercurrents.org/2025/11/how-is-israel-involved-in-sudans-genocide-tracing-the-secret-links-to-the-rsf/.

exemplifies how international criminal justice has been manipulated by powerful governments.

Ultimately, military conflicts ought not to be contingent upon individual governmental interpretations regarding international criminal justice but rather on established principles under the Geneva humanitarian conventions, which have emphasised over nearly two centuries. It is imperative that we refrain from fabricating significant falsehoods regarding the rule of law and subsequently using these deceptions as a basis for purported norms of justice, which result in the destruction of essential civilian infrastructure such as hospitals, schools, and emergency vehicles, including ambulances and rescue units.

The primary objective of international humanitarian law governing armed conflicts is to achieve justice and prevent military offenders from major powers from invoking the justification that all civilian facilities can be obliterated under the pretence of pursuing terrorist groups - an assertion that is fundamentally erroneous and barbaric. Instead, the framework of international humanitarian law aims to eschew reliance on coercive falsehoods masquerading as justice while ensuring that the rights of civilians to their essential daily needs and access to justice are prioritised by conflicting parties.

Thus, it must be acknowledged that the concept of justice cannot be shaped solely by individual interpretations during periods of peace or war. It is crucial to uphold significant rules and principles within the justice system - including their meanings and interpretations - at all times. The objective cannot be to annihilate an entire population based on unfounded claims presented as truth. The reliance on deceitful narratives undermines the foundational order required by international criminal law, which is predicated on adherence to established provisions within international conventions. Governments seeking to impose a system built on lies effectively obliterate all potential evidence in a court of appeal through flawed reasoning. The reality is that arguments put forth by oppressive governments cannot withstand scrutiny against any complex standards because the judicial system at the ICC must remain truthful, even if powerful nations do not adhere to such principles.

If we consider a comprehensive theory within international criminal justice that encompasses equitable principles for all parties involved, then such a theory delineates a thorough consideration of applicable legal weights necessary for achieving justice while respecting everyone's rights. Modern colonial powers represented in the Security Council have demonstrated, particularly in instances such as the ongoing genocide in Palestine, a disregard for appropriate justice demands and customary practices alongside an overarching rejection of peremptory norms within international criminal law.

We must confront the reality of justice as it pertains to all states within the framework of international laws - including the principles of international humanitarian law governing armed conflicts. If this understanding eludes us, there exists a pressing need for the reassessment of truths surrounding our codification of the ICC and why certain dominant governments, notably that of the United States as a permanent member of the Security Council, are disinclined to become state parties to this Court under any circumstances.

If the definition of international criminal justice is subject solely to the authority of Security Council members, it follows that they will not permit its evolution; thus, no framework for rational norms can be established. They obstruct the development of fundamental principles of justice that encompass ethical considerations necessary for understanding cases truthfully and exposing all falsehoods. As a result, both the rationale for prosecuting accused individuals and the legal basis for defences against such accusations become increasingly insignificant.

Deceptions surrounding cases divert public opinion towards alternative narratives, as evidenced by numerous military coups orchestrated by American administrations aimed at destabilising existing governments - these coups are strategically designed to propagate falsehoods and achieve specific objectives.

8. New Scenarios Empowering Reasoning of Lies

How can we ascertain which interpretations of international criminal justice are valid and beneficial when its foundational principles seem tailored to serve the interests of major offenders within the United Nations? Clearly, lies within any judicial system should not be tolerated; therefore, we must assume that such falsehoods aim to diminish any potential for holding criminals accountable while simultaneously guiding public sentiment towards trust in systems aligned with repressive and barbaric agendas orchestrated by those instigating coups in politically precarious situations dominated by authoritarian or dictatorial regimes supported by the United States.

These assertions are not solely my own; rather, they are supported by historical evidence and the insights of well-known American scholars such as professors John Mearsheimer and Jeffrey Sachs who have unequivocally highlighted these facts. Addressing the challenges inherent in the international criminal justice system and confronting the political, military, and economic dominance at play is a complex and formidable task. I contend that the principles of justice embedded within both permanent and *ad hoc* tribunals aim to advance the ethical philosophy of good articulated in prior jurisprudence, which was formally initiated with the Nuremberg Trials in 1944. It is my belief that judges and prosecutors at the ICC generally prefer primary authentic legal norms over lesser alternatives. However, this preference is complicated by the persistent external control over justice and a consistent refusal to submit to the jurisdiction of the Court. This issue is particularly evident in the unilateral decisions and actions of U.S. military entities engaged in unlawful and immoral conflicts against sovereign nations.

Furthermore, it may ultimately become apparent that once ignorance is dispelled within the framework of international criminal justice, theories of justice could receive robust support from states that are parties to the Court. Nevertheless, achieving this would require dismantling all military powers globally and reaching a state of complete disarmament - an aspiration that remains highly unrealistic given our current world order and the development of international criminal justice systems rooted in geopolitical power dynamics. From the original perspective of international criminal justice, it would be far more rational for United Nations member states to prioritise disarmament initiatives. In this scenario, definitions of justice would not be distorted by coercion or deception but instead grounded in principled reasoning guided by sound moral judgment. The consequence would be a reduced influence of new colonial influences within the Security Council, whose authority is primarily derived from superior military strength.

Thus, while state parties to the ICC may find themselves largely stripped of their capacity to enforce justice due to monopolistic interpretations of judicial power, they must nonetheless acknowledge that lies have been elevated to authoritative principles or legitimised doctrines. To confront these falsehoods within an international criminal context requires collective action - not necessarily through warfare - which would ultimately prove futile, but rather through legal recourse by leveraging established aims within the ICC's statutory framework to promote strong condemnation against manipulating such a system with deceitful reasoning. States can formulate coherent and judicious decisions embodying essential characteristics inherent in international criminal justice jurisdiction.

Thus, in the current presentation of justice as it exists today, the state parties, judges, and prosecutors of the ICC officially remain largely silent and passive regarding the entrenchment of falsehoods through political reasoning, assessing how many duties remain for them to fulfil. Ultimately, this results in a constrained set of criminal justice norms that are insufficient even to initiate a case.

Judges and prosecutors of the ICC face a critical choice: either uphold a fair and effective criminal justice system for victims or submit to the authority of certain members of the Security Council. Their decisions are clearly visible to all. The approach that best aligns with the principles of international criminal justice is to reinforce the authority of the Court rather than yield to the forces of injustice created by political pressures. This implies that the Court and the justice it administers have a greater chance of being successfully implemented within the framework of the ICC.

I propose that a legitimate and independent Court should not be hindered by deference to the Security Council. The Court must resist external influence that undermines its legal authority, as such manipulation has historically compromised the Court's effectiveness. It is important to remember that the Security Council has a troubling history of making politically motivated and militaristic decisions, as evidenced by the situation in Gaza.

The existence of systematic inequalities among members of the United Nations Organisation clearly reflects a conception of injustice. The ICC prosecutors and judges must not forgo the opportunity to address violations committed by the American and British governments to slip away. The prevailing assumption is that the Court is responsible for delivering justice to victims, and therefore, it cannot evade its obligations.

The question arises: why do the judges and prosecutors of the Court not forgo their salaries for a single month, yet allow the foundational principles of their duty - justice - to be undermined by the Council? This situation leads them to experience professional and institutional humiliation regarding the international legal standing of the ICC.

Furthermore, it is unrealistic to expect Court members to sit on the bench waiting idly in the hope that criminals will come before them. In this context, it is detrimental to have a Court for justice that fails to function during critical historical moments of humanity's legal and moral decline. The reality is that the judges, prosecutors, and other advisors, such as Payam Akavan,[18] possess a heightened sense of their own authority, which deters them from directly confronting the institutional mechanisms that sustain injustice and deceit.

---

[18] Although he claims to be a specialist in genocide and human rights, he has lost his expertise on Gaza because of strong support from Israel and American authorities during his career.

The conception of justice, which in its most critical and contested cases is delivered or obstructed by the Security Council's veto power, eliminates all prospects for advancing a pure philosophy of justice.

Chapter 9

Conclusion

Justice can be described as a mere façade that often conceals lies, while lies frequently masquerade as justice. Regardless of how one defines justice, it is clear that it does not reflect the intentions of honest individuals but rather the deceptive artistry of the dishonest. This observation highlights the fragility of the current state of contemporary international criminal justice. It is not an exaggeration to assert that the definition of international justice today has been shaped, controlled, and promoted throughout history by those who have led or facilitated heinous international crimes. Consequently, the concepts of systemic injustice and the massacre of innocent civilians cannot be overlooked in the evolution of international relations among various civilisations; they are intertwined with the brutality inherent in our power dynamics.

Regrettably, the existing system of international criminal justice suffers from a significant distortion of truth and the substantial prevalence of falsehoods, driven by the influence of military power in the meetings of the United Nations Security Council. Thus, we find ourselves governed by a system entrenched in a bunch of lies, adhered to by all individuals, regardless of their intentions.

The system of international criminal justice is not inherently self-sustaining. Its effectiveness necessitates collaborative efforts to safeguard the rights of victims and to deter international criminals from perpetrating further offenses with global implications. The coordination of roles and regulations within this system is as infrequent as one might play the bongos, as previously noted. It is imperative that we prevent individuals associated with the Security Council and their allies in NATO from asserting their own wills and interests under the pretext of combating manufactured adversaries or threats.[1] Clearly, there are significant flaws within the international criminal justice system, which fails to function as an impartial arbiter. What is fundamentally lacking is a robust foundation for the enforcement mechanisms of international criminal law, one that provides a powerful, just, independent and non-monopolistic means of applying justice.

What we imply by this observation is that the ICC's operations are bound by international criminal law, which in turn is governed by the treaties and legal instruments of the United Nations Organisation. In essence, the organisation's legal framework curtails the provisions of international criminal justice, rendering it a subjugated entity controlled by its internal body known as the Security Council. Consequently, discussions regarding international criminal justice necessitate an understanding of the hierarchical and paternalistic nature inherent in the Security Council law. This indicates a consolidation of power and monopolised definition of the *status quo* articulated in Chapter VII of the Charter, which regrettably garners acceptance from legal, political, and notably morally compromised perspectives.

We cannot simply accept the emergency measures outlined in Chapter VII along with the discretionary powers exercised by permanent members as given realities while expecting to clarify concepts such as conflict, war, fairness, peace, and justice. Such matters appear to be principally determined by negotiations between members of the General Assembly and the permanent members of the Security Council collectively.

In other words, the original design of international criminal justice serves primarily to preserve the strategic interests of permanent Security Council member states. This implies that all member states must adhere to decisions made by the Security Council - particularly those enforced through the application of veto power. When a member exercises its veto power, it compels every other member either to acquiesce or face the potential consequences of economic, political or military repercussions for opposing

[1] "Putative consent is consequently also based on several other deductions. For instance, other members of NATO do not interfere with the statements or activities of the organisation which can be interpreted as expressed consent. A member also may not show any reaction concerning active attacks being carried out by NATO against another state, which in turn represents the expression of tacit putative consent. Thus, a member of NATO can support the actions of NATO through offering their silent complicity. This includes putting forward putative presumptions or acknowledgments of the decisions of NATO. Under other circumstances, the putative consent of a member may be seen through their enforcement of sanctions required by the leadership of NATO or taking certain measures against the diplomats of the enemy government." Farhad Malekian, *Powertionism in International Criminal Justice* (New York: Nova Science Publishers, 2022), p.40.

that decision. This represents one critical issue concerning the inappropriate *status quo* concentration of authority within international criminal justice.

Moreover, this problem extends beyond mere procedural constraints; governments may find themselves subservient to directives from their dominant international overseer counterparts or compelled to endure severe consequences arising from economic, political, and military sanctions imposed through coercive measures. One of the fundamental reasons for the monopolisation of international criminal law by the Council is that it renders the ICC ineffectual precisely when its intervention is most needed. Consequently, the pursuit of justice is obstructed by the manipulated presentation, implementation, and imposition of numerous falsehoods embedded within the Office of the Prosecutor's legal justifications and the judicial deliberations of the Court. The underlying principle remains straightforward: should the Court and global governments remain silent regarding the machinations of powerful modern colonial entities represented by the Security Council, or should they be labelled as terrorists - or categorised as complicit in terrorism?

This precarious situation compels governments worldwide to capitulate to NATO's influence - an organisation established by the United States - which many states either join outright or whose directives they indirectly adhere to. The consequences of these monopolised power structures are inherently based on falsehoods, leading to short-sightedness, narrow decision-making and self-serving interests.

This is not an isolated instance; rather, it reflects a recurring pattern wherein control over international criminal justice is systematically centralised within the framework of powertionist governance. A profound example is the *ongoing genocide occurring in Gaza against the Palestinian people - an atrocity that far exceeds even that perpetrated against innocent Jews during World War II under Nazi Germany*.[2] However, this observation does not suggest that deception has ceased or will cease, nor does it imply that the ICC will acknowledge its institutional failures or take corrective measures.[3]

---

[2] Falk Richard, *Slouching Toward a Palestinian Holocaust*, www.transnational.org/Area.../Falk Palestine Genocide.html, 20 October 2010; Falk Richard, *The Vietnam War and International Law (*Princeton University Press, 1968); Richard Falk,The Vietnam War and International Law (4 Volumes, 1976); Richard Falk, 'The Accountability of Leaders: A Challenge to Civil Government and Society' in Jeremy Brecher, Jill Cutler, Smith Brendan, *In the Name of Democracy: American War Crimes in Iraq and Beyond* (American Empire Project), (New York: Metropolitan Books, Henry Holt and Company, 2005).

[3] *Id.*

It must be made abundantly clear that the Court operates under crippling limitations; its operational capacity is so feeble that its ability to uphold justice is akin to a newborn infant attempting to walk unaided. I do not intend to disregard my own experiences with international criminal justice and its principles; however, it must be acknowledged that lies propagated by dictators within the United Nations illustrate this ineffective system. The structural deficiencies of the UN facilitate an ineffective justice system that remains at the mercy of these dictatorial influences. While the ICC possesses an independent international legal personality akin to that of its state parties, the legal character of its judicial legitimacy is contingent upon decisions made by the Security Council's superpowers, which in turn undermine that legitimacy. Ultimately, only a limited number of norms remain intact - and even these can be readily disregarded when British and American authorities reach a consensus.

It is important to note that both judicial and prosecutorial appointments at the Court are heavily influenced, if not directly determined, by major powers. A pertinent example is Luis Moreno Ocampo, who served as the first prosecutor of the ICC; he not only strategically bartered justice on multiple occasions, but also refrained from initiating any cases against his benefactors. My emphasis here points toward the United States' significant influence over this appointment through covert negotiations alongside British imperialist interests and their historic dominance over Argentina. This exemplifies how international criminal justice remains selectively enforced, failing to prosecute the most prominent criminals of the 21st century.

The assertions regarding international criminal justice and human rights mechanisms are not accurate; however, they resemble fabricated narratives of peacetime rather than a reflection of actual legal practice. In the context of Gaza and the systemic perpetration of international crimes against its Palestinian population, which are characterised by extreme barbarity, it is evident that nearly all Western nations have played an active role in enabling these atrocities. Consequently, the rhetoric surrounding democratic values and human rights protections appears to be little more than a safeguard designed to preserve the self-interest and political self-preservation among Western political powers.

It is unacceptable to continue justifying the deaths of millions worldwide based on the monopolisation of power within the Security Council while attempting to mask our culpability in international criminal law with human rights provisions, particularly when we selectively invoke such principles only when dissatisfied with the outcomes of warfare. If Western governments played a role in perpetrating atrocities against innocent Jews during World War II and have been complicit in the ongoing brutal treatment of Palestinians, such historical records will endure indefinitely. Collectively, these circumstances suggest that the current framework of international criminal justice and its judicial interpretations lead to the conclusion that true, universal rights only exist in rhetoric; in practice, justice remains a construct of those wielding power.

This underscores that the aspiration towards universal moral application and the imperative tenets that construct natural law are fundamentally flawed theories when distorted and imposed upon international legal frameworks. The intention appears to be an invitation to engage in a superficial exploration of human rights norms and criminal justice as if partaking in an extravagant carousel ride - offering a grand performance designed to project legitimacy while serving as an instrument of political expediency. This carefully orchestrated illusion manipulates global perceptions while shielding the most powerful perpetrators from the consequences of their actions. In other words, the nature of this ostensibly enchanting carousel serves only to manipulate perceptions while obscuring true accountability.

The principles governing international criminal justice are ostensibly defined by their specifically prescribed regulations and their applicability to specific categories of offenders within court proceedings. However, it must be emphasised that these rules inherently fail to uphold true universality, as their enforcement remains selective and highly politicised. This is why international criminal justice at The Hague consistently operates under an unspoken principle of selective prosecution - imposing a subjective list dictated by self-serving interests. Cases are adjudicated based on political discretion rather than legal impartiality. Consequently, the intricate judicial mechanisms of the Court do not challenge the authoritarian underpinnings of Chapter VII of the UN Charter; rather, they perpetuate the reinforcement of an existing system of coercion and impunity under the guise of legalism.

Thus, I reiterate that the ICC's framework does not genuinely provide justice but is instead operates under the constraints of Security Council jurisdiction. As a result, cases referred to the Prosecutor's office tend to be selectively chosen based not on the severity of violations but rather on their alignment with dominant state interests. It is essential to recognise that each case presented before the jurisdiction of the Court fundamentally revolves around strategic considerations rather than an impartial application of international legal norms. A rigorously defined concept of justice, accompanied by an effective enforcement mechanism, is a fundamental requirement to uphold legal accountabilityy and the norms of justice. However, under the current legal-political conditions, achieving this remains virtually impossible. The existing framework of international criminal justice is subjugated either to dictatorial regimes or to the alliances between such regimes and purportedly democratic leaders within the Security Council. In reality, both scenarios function symbiotically - akin to rival teams in a football match, where the game itself is rigged by those who control the application of the rules.

The principles of justice articulated in the Statute of the Court may be philosophically defensible and subject to theoretical enforcement through various legal means; however, it remains neither viable nor practically enforceable for any state party to actualise the demand of equal application of these principles at this time. As I conclude this brief work, it is imperative to acknowledge that while the information presented herein remains accurate and verifiable, it is crucial to recognise the underlying realities that reinforce the current power imbalance within international criminal law. The prevailing legal structure of international regulations within the United Nations renders the application of justice principles exceedingly challenging and inherently dysfunctional. Clearly, self-interest driven by deceit and systemic violations of others' rights are unacceptable under general legal principles, particularly within the framework of international human rights law. Yet, it remains an entrenched feature of international criminal justice, despite the purported objectives of international human rights law.

Various forms of egocentric and politically motivated conduct subvert established patterns of justice under the pretence of masquerading as embodiments of democratic values and equitable governance; however, mere adherence to legal formalities cannot remedy the fundamental inequalities entrenched within the mechanisms of international criminal justice.

Nevertheless, a radical reformation - entailing the dissolution of the current United Nations Charter and the establishment of a new global framework that ensures equal recognition of the international legal personality of each state or nation - without any monopolistic authority like that held by the Security Council - could pave the way for genuine reform. This could replace the monopolistic authority with an equitable system that prioritises collective justice over unilateral dominance. This conclusion should not come as a surprise, given this work's extensive critique of the systemic injustices perpetuated by authoritarian regimes, which use military force to shape global affairs.

We must bear in mind that no form of hegemonic governance - whether overt or disguised as democratic paternalism should be tolerated in any newly established global legal framework.[4] In instances where genuine wisdom is absent, societal values diminish, reducing individuals and entire nations to a status resembling *nobodiness*. They become mere instruments of geopolitical manipulation. Consequently, powertionist governments consolidate their control over global justice narratives through calculated deception. However, the suppression of truth is not a permanent condition. The basic theory of *somebodiness* of all individuals - the foundational principle of human dignity and self-determination - must be reaffirmed, protected, and respected within any legitimate international justice system.[5]

---

[4] Farhad Malekian, *Conundrums of Paternalism in International Criminal Justice* (New York: Nova Science Publishers, 2024). See also Farhad Malekian, I*mperative Philosophy of International Criminal Justice: Visible Power – Invisible Essence* (New York: Nova Science Publishers, 2022); Farhad Malekian, *Tour de force of Moral Virtue in International Criminal Justice* (New York: Nova Science Publishers, 2022).

[5] Examine Farhad Malekian, *International Criminal Law, the Law of Somebodiness, the Law of Nobodiness* (New York: Nova Science Publishers, 2021).

Appendix

Chapter VII. Monopolizing the Power of the United Nations Organisation for Equality

Action with Respect to Threats to the Peace, Breaches of the Peace, and Acts of Aggression

Article 39

The Security Council shall determine the existence of any threat to the peace, breach of the peace, or act of aggression and shall make recommendations, or decide what measures shall be taken in accordance with Articles 41 and 42, to maintain or restore international peace and security.

Article 40

In order to prevent an aggravation of the situation, the Security Council may, before making the recommendations or deciding upon the measures provided for in Article 39, call upon the parties concerned to comply with such provisional measures as it deems necessary or desirable. Such provisional measures shall be without prejudice to the rights, claims, or position of the parties concerned. The Security Council shall duly take account of failure to comply with such provisional measures.

Article 41

The Security Council may decide what measures not involving the use of armed force are to be employed to give effect to its decisions, and it may call upon the Members of the United Nations to apply such measures. These may include complete or partial interruption of economic relations and of rail, sea, air, postal, telegraphic, radio, and other means of communication, and the severance of diplomatic relations.

Article 42

Should the Security Council consider that measures provided for in Article 41 would be inadequate or have proved to be inadequate, it may take such action by air, sea, or land forces as may be necessary to maintain or restore international peace and security. Such action may include demonstrations, blockade, and other operations by air, sea, or land forces of Members of the United Nations.

Article 43

1. All Members of the United Nations, in order to contribute to the maintenance of international peace and security, undertake to make available to the Security Council, on its call and in accordance with a special agreement or agreements, armed forces, assistance, and facilities, including rights of passage, necessary for the purpose of maintaining international peace and security.
2. Such agreement or agreements shall govern the numbers and types of forces, their degree of readiness and general location, and the nature of the facilities and assistance to be provided.
3. The agreement or agreements shall be negotiated as soon as possible on the initiative of the Security Council. They shall be concluded between the Security Council and Members or between the Security Council and groups of Members and shall be subject to ratification by the signatory states in accordance with their respective constitutional processes.

Article 44

When the Security Council has decided to use force it shall, before calling upon a Member not represented on it to provide armed forces in fulfilment of the obligations assumed under Article 43, invite that Member, if the Member so desires, to participate in the decisions of the Security Council concerning the employment of contingents of that Member's armed forces.

Article 45

In order to enable the United Nations to take urgent military measures, Members shall hold immediately available national air-force contingents for combined international enforcement action. The strength and degree of readiness of these contingents and plans for their combined action shall be determined within the limits laid down in the special agreement or agreements referred to in Article 43, by the Security Council with the assistance of the Military Staff Committee.

Article 46

Plans for the application of armed force shall be made by the Security Council with the assistance of the Military Staff Committee.

Article 47

1. There shall be established a Military Staff Committee to advise and assist the Security Council on all questions relating to the Security Council's military requirements for the maintenance of international peace and security, the employment and command of forces placed at its disposal, the regulation of armaments, and possible disarmament.
2. The Military Staff Committee shall consist of the Chiefs of Staff of the permanent members of the Security Council or their representatives. Any Member of the United Nations not permanently represented on the Committee shall be invited by the Committee to be associated with it when the efficient discharge of the Committee's responsibilities requires the participation of that Member in its work.
3. The Military Staff Committee shall be responsible under the Security Council for the strategic direction of any armed forces placed at the disposal of the Security Council. Questions relating to the command of such forces shall be worked out subsequently.
4. The Military Staff Committee, with the authorization of the Security Council and after consultation with appropriate regional agencies, may establish regional sub-committees.

Article 48

1. The action required to carry out the decisions of the Security Council for the maintenance of international peace and security shall be taken by all the Members of the United Nations or by some of them, as the Security Council may determine.
2. Such decisions shall be carried out by the Members of the United Nations directly and through their action in the appropriate international agencies of which they are members.

Article 49

The Members of the United Nations shall join in affording mutual assistance in carrying out the measures decided upon by the Security Council.

Article 50

If preventive or enforcement measures against any state are taken by the Security Council, any other state, whether a Member of the United Nations or not, which finds itself confronted with special economic problems arising from the carrying out of those measures shall have the right to consult the Security Council with regard to a solution of those problems.

Article 51

Nothing in the present Charter shall impair the inherent right of individual or collective self-defence if an armed attack occurs against a Member of the United Nations, until the Security Council has taken measures necessary to maintain international peace and security. Measures taken by Members in the exercise of this right of self-defence shall be immediately reported to the Security Council and shall not in any way affect the authority and responsibility of the Security Council under the present Charter to take at any time such action as it deems necessary in order to maintain or restore international peace and security.

Bibliography*

Albanese F., *Anatomy of a Genocide: Report of the Special Rapporteur on the situation of human rights in the Palestinian territories occupied since* 1967, p. 3, https://www.ohchr.org/sites/default/files/documents/hrbodies/hrcouncil/sessions-regular/session55/advance-versions/a-hrc-55-73-auv.pdf (visited 03/11/2024).

Albanese Francesca, *From Economy of Settler-Colonial Occupation to the Economy of Genocide, Report of the Special Rapporteur on the situation of human rights in the Palestinian territories occupied since 1967*; https://www.un.org/unispal/document/a-hrc-59-23-from-economy-of-occupation-to-economy-of-genocide-report-special-rapporteur-francesca-albanese-palestine-2025/

Albanese F. P. and Lex Takkenberg, Palestinian Refugees in International Law (2nd Edition, 2020).

Alexy R., *'Effects of Defects - Action or Argument? Thoughts about Deryck Beyleveld and Roger Brownsword's Law as a Moral Judgment'* (Ratio Juris, 2006), pp. 169–79.

Alexy R., 'The Dual Nature of Law, *Ratio Juris'* (2010), pp. 167–82.

Alexy R., 'The Reasonableness of Law' in *Reasonableness and Law* Ed. Giorgio Bongiovanni, Giovanni Sartor, and Chiara Valentini (Dordrecht: Springer, 2009), pp. 5–15.

Alexy R., Discourse Theory and Fundamental Rights' in *Arguing Fundamental Rights* Ed. Agustín José Menéndez and Erik Oddvar Eriksen (Dordrecht: Springer, 2006), pp. 15–29.

Alexy R., *On the Concept and the Nature of Law* (Ratio Juris, 2008), pp. 21: 281–99.

Allison H., *Kant's Theory of Freedom* (Cambridge University Press, 1990).

Amato A D., 'It's a Bird, It's a Plane, It's *Jus cogens*' 6 *Connecticut Journal of International Law*, (1990).

Ambion B. C., Organisation of a Court of International Criminal Jurisdiction, 29 *Philippine Law Journal* 345 (1954).

Andreopoulos G. J., (ed.), *Genocide: Conceptual and Historical Dimensions* (Philadelphia, 1994).

Annacker C., 'The Legal Régime of erga omnes Obligations in International Law' 46 *Austrian Journal of Public International Law*, (1994), pp. 131–66.

Aquila R. E., *Matter in Mind: A Study of Kant's Transcendental Deduction* (Indiana University Press, 1989).

* *Mention here neither includes nor excludes in the text. It neither confirms nor rejects the work.*

Arts K., Vesselin Popovski. (eds.), *International Criminal Accountability and the Rights of Children* (Heidelberg: Springer, 2006), pp. 37–52 and 53–65.

Austin J., *The Province of Jurisprudence Determined and the Uses of the Study of Jurisprudence* (1954).

Baderin M. A., *International Human Rights and Islamic Law* (New York, NY: Oxford University Press, 2005).

Baderin M., A., 'A Comparative Analysis of the Right to a Fair Trial and due Process under International Human Rights Law and Saudi Arabian Domestic Law,' 10 (3) *The International Journal of Human Rights*, (2006).

Bantekas I., Susan Nash, *International Criminal Law*, (2007).

Barron A., (Legal) Reason and its "Others": Recent DevelopmentinLegal Theory, in *Introduction to Jurisprudence and Legal Theory: Commentary and Materials* (Schiff Penner, and Nobles, eds., 2002), 1038-63.

Bartlett E., *'What's Happening in Syria? The Media 'Kills the Truth,' 'Terrorism' is Described as 'Moderate Opposition.'* (Global Research, February 05, 2017).

Bartlett E., *How We Were Mislead about Syria.*

Bartlett E., *Is Eva Bartlett Credible?* https://www.quora.com/Is-Eva-Bartlett-credible (Accessed: 14th 2016).

Bassiouni C., 'International Crimes: Jus cogens and Obligatio Erga Omnes' 59 *Law and Contemporary Problems*, (1996).

Bassiouni M. Cherif and Benjamin B. Ferencz, The Crime Against Peace and Aggression: From Its Origins to the ICC, in *International Criminal Law,* vol. I, (M. Cherif Bassiouni, ed. 2008), pp. 207-242.

Bassiouni M. Cherif, (ed.), *International Criminal Law* (US: Ocean Publication, 3 vols., 1999).

Bassiouni M. Cherif, (ed.), *International Terrorism and Political Crimes* (1975).

Bassiouni M. Cherif, 'A Comprehensive Strategic Approach on International Cooperation for the Prevention, Control and Suppression of International and Transnational Criminality, Including the Establishment of an International Criminal Cour,' 15 *Nova Law Review*, 353, (1991).

Bassiouni M. Cherif, 'The Discipline of International Criminal Law,' in M. cherif Bassiouni (ed.), *International Criminal Law*, Vol. 1, (2008), pp. 5-40.

Bassiouni M. Cherif, 'The Subjects of International Criminal Law: Ratione Personae' in M. Bassiouni Cherif (ed.), *International Criminal Law*, Vol. 1, (2008), pp. 41-70.

Bassiouni M. Cherif, Benjamin B. Ferencz, *The Crime Against Peace and Aggression: From Its Origins to the ICC, in International Criminal Law*, vol. I, (M. Cherif Bassiouni, ed. 2008).

Bassiouni M. Cherif, *Crimes Against Humanity in International law*, (1999).

Bassiouni M. Cherif, *Criminal Justice in the Time of War and Peace* (Cambridge University Press, Cambridge, 2014).

Bassiouni M. Cherif, *Introduction to International Criminal Law*, (2005).

Bassiouni M. Cherif, The Discipline of International Criminal Law, in *International Criminal Law,* Vol. I (M. Cherif Bassiouni, ed., 2008).

Bassiouni M. Cherif, *The Shariah and Islamic Criminal Justice in the Time of War and Peace* (Cambridge University Press, Cambridge, 2014).

Baum L. M., 'Pursuing Justice in a Climate of Moral Outrage: An Evaluation of the Rights of the Accused in the Rome Statute of the International Criminal Court,' 19 *Wisconsin International Law Journal* (2001).

Beccaria C., *On Crimes and Punishments*, (1764).

Bellamy A., *Responsibility to Protect: the Global Effort to End Mass Atrocities* (Polity Press. Cambridge, 2009).

Bellamy R. (ed.), *C Beccaria, On Crimes and Punishments*. (1995).

Benneh E. Y., 'Sovereignty Immunity and International Crimes,' 22 *Ghana Law Journal*, (2002–2004), 112.

Bennett J., *Kant's Analytic* (Cambridge University Press, 1966).

Bennett J., *Kant's Dialectic* (Cambridge University Press, 1974).

Bennoune K., 'As-Salamu 'Alykum? Humanitarian Law in Islamic Jurisprudence,' 15 *Michigan Journal of International Law*, (1994), pp. 605-643.

Berman S. (ed.), *The Oxford Handbook of Legal Pluralism* (Oxford University Press, 2019).

Berman S., *Global Legal Pluralism: A Jurisprudence of Law Beyond Borders Global* (2012).

Bermann G. A. Roger J. Goebel, William J. Davey, Eleanor M. Fox et al., *Cases and Materials on European Community Law* (1993).

Bernstein R. J. *Radical Evil: A Philosophical Interrogation* (New York: Blackwell Publisher, 2002).

Bianchi A., 'Human Rights and the Magic of Jus cogens,' 19 *European Journal of International Law*, (2008), pp. 491-508.

Bigi G. 'Joint Criminal Enterprise in the Jurisprudence of the International Criminal Tribunal for the former Yugoslavia and the Prosecution of Senior Political and Military Leaders: The Krajišnik Case' 14 *Max Planck United Nations Yearbook*, (2010), pp. 51-83.

Bigi G., 'Joint Criminal Enterprise in the Jurisprudence of the International Criminal Tribunal for the former Yugoslavia and the Prosecution of Senior Political and Military Leaders: The Krajišnik Case' 14 Guyer Paul, *The Cambridge Companion to Kant,* (1992).

Bird G., *Kant's Theory of Knowledge*, (Humanities Press, 1962).

Bix B., 'Natural Law: The Modern Tradition' in Jules Coleman and Schott Shapiro (eds.), *The Oxford Handbook of Jurisprudence and Philosophy of Law*, (2002).

Bloxham Donald, *Genocide on Trial: War Crimes Trials and the Formation of Holocaust History and Memory* (2001).

Boas G., *International Criminal Justice: Legitimacy and Coherence*, (2012).

Boas G., William A. Schabas (eds.), *International Criminal Law Developments in the Case Law of the ICTY* (2005).

Boot M., *Genocide, Crimes against Humanity, War Crimes: Nullum Crimen Sine Lege and the Subjective Matter of Jurisdiction of the International Criminal Court*, (2002).

Brilmayer L., *American Hegemony: Political Morality in a One Superpower World* (1994).

Broomhall B., *International Justice and the International Criminal Court: Between Sovereignty and the Rule of Law* (2003).

Browning C., *The Path to Genocide: Essays on Launching the Final Solution*, (2002).

Browning D. (eds.), *Universalism vs. Relativism: Making Moral Judgements in a Changing, Pluralistic, and Threatening World* (Rowman and Littlefield Publishers, United Kingdom, 2006).

Brownlie I., *International Law and the Use of Force by States* (Oxford: Oxford University Press, 1996).

Brownlie I., *Principles of Public International Law* (Oxford: Clarendon Press, 5th ed., 1998).

Brunnée J., 'The Prohibition on Torture: Driving *Jus cogens* Home?' 104 *Proceedings of the Annual Meeting of the American Society of International Law*, (2010).

Buchanan A., 'Toward a Drone Accountability Regime,' 29 (1) *Ethics and International Affairs*, (2015), pp. 15–70.

Burke-White W. W, 'Implementing a Policy of Positive Complementarity in the Rome System of Justice,' 19 *Criminal Law Forum*, (2008), 59-89.

Burns P. 'An International Criminal Tribunal: The Difficult Union of Principle and Politics,' 5 *Criminal Law Forum*, (1994).

Byers M. 'Conceptualising the Relationship Between *Jus cogens* and *Erga Omnes Rules*' 66 *Nordic Journal of International Law*, (1997).

Caenegem R. C., Van, *European Law in the Past and the Future: Unity and Diversity over Two Millennia* (Cambridge: Cambridge University Press, 2001).

Cançado T., A. '*Jus cogens* in Contemporary International Law,' *UN Audiovisual Library*, (http://www.un.org/law/avl).

Carvin S., 'Getting Drones Wrong,' 19 (2) *International Journal of Human Rights*, (2015), pp. 127–141.

Cassese A. and Albin Eser (eds.), *The Rome Statute of the International Criminal Court: A Commentary* (2002).

Cassese A. and Paola Gaeta, *Cassese's International Criminal Law* (3rd, 2013).

Cassese A., (ed.), *The New Humanitarian Law of Armed Conflict* (Naples: Editoriale Scientifica, 1979).

Cassese A., 'First Annual Report of the ICTY,' *Yearbook of International Law Commission*, (1994).

Cassese A., 'For an Enhanced Role of Jus cogens' in Cassese, A (ed.), *Realizing Utopia*, (2012).

Cassese A., Albin Eser, Giorgio Gaja and Robert E. Conor, *Justice at Nuremberg* (1980).

Cassese A., *International Criminal Law* (Oxford: Oxford University Press, 2nd, ed., 2008).

Cassese A., On the Current Trends Towards Criminal Prosecution and Punishment of Breaches of International Humanitarian Law, 9 *European Journal of Internaitonal Law* 2 (1998).

Chinkin C., '*Jus Cogens*, Article 103 of the UN Charter and Other Hierarchical Techniques of Conflict Solution,' 17 *Finnish Yearbook of International Law* (2008), pp. 63-90.

Chomksy N. and Barsamian D., *Keeping the Rabble in Line.* Boston: Common Courage Press (1994).

Chomsky N., *Media Control: The Spectacular Achievements of Propaganda.* New York: Seven Stories Press (2004).

Chossudovsky M., *War and Globalisation: The Truth Behind September 11* (Global Outlook, 2002).

Christian P., Scherrer, *Iraq: Genocide by Sanctions* (2011).
Clark M., *Nietzsche on Truth and Philosophy* (1991).
Clark R. S , 'The Crime of Apartheid,' in M. Cherif Bassiouni (ed.), *International Criminal Law*, vol. I (1986), pp. 299-323.
Clark R., *War Crimes – A Report on United States War Crimes against Iraq* (Maisonneuve Press, 1992).
Claus K., 'Aggression and the Use of Force in International Law,' *Proceedings of the 108th Annual Meeting of the American Society of International Law,* No. 108, 2014, pp. 325–346.
Cohen M., 'Moral Aspects of the Criminal Law,' 49 *Yale Law Journal* (1949), pp. 987-1026.
Crawford J., Olleson S., 'The Continuing Debate on a UN Convention on State Responsibility,' 54 *ICLQ*, (2005), 959–71.
Cryer R., 'The Doctrinal Foundations of International Criminalisation,' in M. cherif Bassiouni, ed., *International Criminal Law*, Vol. 1, (2008), pp. 107-128.
Cryer R., *Prosecuting International Crimes, Selectivity and the International Criminal Law Regime* (Cambridge University Press, Cambridge, 2005).
Czaplinski W., 'Concepts of *Jus Cogens* and Obligations Erga Omnes in International Law in the Light of Recent Developments,' 23 *Polish Yearbook of International Law* (1997–1998).
D'Amato A., 'It's a Bird, It's a Plane, It's *Jus cogens'* (1990) 6 *Connecticut Journal of International Law*.
D'Amato A., 'The Moral Dilemma of Positivism,' 20 *Valparaiso University Law Review*, (1985-86), 43-53.
D'Amato A., 'The Moral Dilemma of Positivism,' 20 *Valparaiso University Law Review* (1985-86), 43-53.
Danilenko G., 'International Jus cogens: Issues of Law-Making,' 2 *European Journal of International Law* (1991).
Dautricourt J. The Concept of International Criminal Court Jurisdiction-Definition and Limitations of the Subject, in *A Treatise on International Criminal Law* 636 (M. C. Bassiouni & V. P. Nanda eds., 1973).
Davis M. C., Dietrich Wolfgang, Bettina Schoolman and Sepp Dieter, *International Intervention in the Post-Cold War World: Moral Responsibility and Power Politics* (M. E. Sharpe, Inc., 2003).
de Hoog A. J. J., 'The Relationship between *Jus cogens*, *Obligations Erga Omnes* and International Crimes: Peremptory Norms in Perspective,' 42 *Österreichische Zeitschrift für öffentliches Recht und Völkerrecht* (1991).
de Hoogh A., *Obligations Erga Omnes and International Crimes: A Theoretical Inquiry into the Implementation and Enforcement of the International Responsibility of States* (Kluwer The Hague, 1996).
de Wet E., 'The Prohibition of Torture as an International Norm of *Jus cogens* and its Implementation for National and Customary Law,' 15 (1) *European Journal of International Law* (2014), Vol. 15, No. 1, 97-121.
de Wet, E., '*Jus Cogens* and Obligations Erga Omnes' in de Wet, E and Vidmar (eds.), J *Hierarchy in International Law: The Place of Human Rights*, (2012).

Delmas-Marty M., 'The Contribution of Comparative Law to a Pluralist Conception of International Criminal Law,' 1 *Journal of International Criminal Justice*, (2003), pp. 13-25.

DeSon J. S., 'Automating the Right Stuff? The Hidden Ramifications of Ensuring Autonomous Aerial Weapon Systems Comply with International Humanitarian Law,' 72 *Air Force Law Review*, (2015), pp. 85–122.

Detmold M. J., *The Unity of Law and Morality: A Refutation of Legal Positivism* (Canada: Law Book Co. of Australasia, 1984).

Dhanapala J., *Under-Secretary-General for Disarmament Affairs United Nations, International Law, Security, and Weapons of Mass Destruction*, (New York, 9 May 2002).

Dhokalia. 'Problems Relating to *Jus Cogens*,' in S. Agrawala (ed.), *Essays on the Law of Treaties*, (1972).

Dickson J., *Evaluation and Legal Theory*, (2001).

Don P., Jim Hoffman, *Waking Up from Our Nightmare, the 9/11/01 Crimes in New York City* (New York: I/R Press, 2004).

Douzinas C., Peter Goodrich and Yifat Hachamovitch, *Politics, Post modernity and Critical Legal Studies* (1994).

Drost P. N., *The Crime of State: Genocide* (Original from Indiana University, 1959).

Dryer D. P, *Kant's Solution for Verification in Metaphysics* (Allen and Unwin, 1966).

Duffett J., *Against the Crime of Silence* (New York, London, 1968).

Dugard J., 'Lifting the Guise of Occupation and Recourse to Action before the ICJ and ICC,' *Palestine Yearbook of International Law,* Vol. 17, 2013–14, pp. 9–27.

Duncan A. R. C., *Practical Reason and Morality* (Nelson, 1957).

Dupuy P., 'Some Reflections on Contemporary International Law and the Appeal to Universal Values: a Response to Marti Koskenniemi' 16 *European Journal of International Law,* (2005).

Duțu M., *Vespasian V. Pella.* (1897-1952) Founder of International Criminal law, Promoter of the Unification of the Criminal Law, *Architect of the International Criminal Justice* (Universul Juridic, Bucharest, 2012).

Eric D., *Principes de Droit des Conflits Armés*, (2nd, ed. 1999).

Ewald F., 'Unger's Philosophy: A Critical Legal Study,' 5 *Yale Law Journal* 665(1988).

Ewing A. C., *A Short Commentary on Kant's 'Critique of Pure Reason'* (Methuen, 1978).

Falk R. A. & Burns H. Weston, The Relevance of International Law to Palestinian Rights in the West Bank and Gaza: In Legal Defense of the Intifada, 32 Harvard International law Journal (1991), pp. 129-157.

Falk R., 'The Accountability of Leaders: A Challenge to Civil Government and Society' in Jeremy Brecher, Jill Cutler, Smith Brendan, *In the Name of Democracy: American War Crimes in Iraq and Beyond* (American Empire Project), (New York: Metropolitan Books, Henry Holt and Company, 2005).

Falk R., *Slouching Toward a Palestinian Holocaust*, www.transnational.org/Area…/Falk Palestine Genocide.html, 20 October 2010.

Falk R., *The Vietnam War and International Law (*Princeton University Press, 1968).

Farmer J., *The Ground Truth: The Story Behind America's Defense on 9/11* (New York: Riverhead Books, 2009).

Feimpong J. K. & S. Azadon Tiewel, 'Can Apartheid Successfully Defy the International Legal System?' 5 *The Black Law Journal* (1977), pp. 287-311.

Fein B., *'Hillary Clinton's 5 lies about Syria, Terror Threat,'* The Washington Times (25 October, 2016).

Feld W., *The Court of the European Communities: New Dimension in International Adjudication* (1964).

Ferencz B. B. 'Ending Impunity for the Crime of Aggression,' 41 *Case W. Res. J,* (2009), pp. 281-290.

Ferencz B., 'An International Criminal Code and Court: Why They Stand and Where They're Going,' 30 *Columbia Journal of Transnational Law*, (1992), 375.

Ferencz B., *International Criminal Court* (2 vols. 1980).

Findlay E por Mark J, *International and Comparative Criminal Justice: A Critical Introduction* (Routledge, London, 2013).

Finnis J. (ed.), *Natural Law*, (1991).

Finnis J., *Aquinas: Moral, Political and Legal Theory* (1998).

Fischer-Lescano A., Teubner G., 'Regime Collision: The Vain Search for Legal Unity in the Fragmentation of Global Law,' 25 *Michigan Journal of International Law*, (2004), pp. 999-104.

Fitzpatrick P. (ed.), *Dangerous Supplements: Resistance and Renewal in Jurisprudence* (1991).

Focarelli C., 'Promotional Jus cogens: A Critical Appraisal of *Jus Cogens*' Legal Effects' 77 *Nordic Journal of International Law*, (2008), 429.

Fouladvand S., *Complementarity and Cultural Sensitivity: Decision-making by the International Criminal Court (ICC) Prosecutor in Relation to the Situations in the Darfur Region of the Sudan and the Democratic Republic of Congo* (DRC), (2012).

Franck T. M., *Fairness in International Law and Institutions* (1997).

Fuller L. L., *The Morality of Law* (Virginia: Yale Law University, 2nd, ed., 1969).

Fuller S., "Playing Without a Full Deck: Scientific Realism and the Cognitive Limits of Legal Theory," 97 *Yale Law Journal* 549 (1988).

Gebrehana T., Duty to negotiate: An Element of International law (1978).

Gebrehana T., T Arbitration - An Element of International Law (1984).

George J. Andreopoulos, (ed.), *Genocide: Conceptual and Historical Dimensions* (Philadelphia, 1994).

George R. P. (ed.), *The Autonomy Of Law: Essays On Legal Positivism*, (1995).

George R. P., *Natural Law Theory: Contemporary Essays*, (1994).

Gerhard O. W. Mueller & Edward M. Wise (eds), *International Criminal Law* (1965).

Ginsberg Benjamin., The Dark Side of Politics: Essays on the Unpleasant Realities of Political Life (2023).

Glennon M. J., 'De l'Absurdité du Droit Impératif (Jus cogens)'/*On the Absurdity of Imperative Law (Jus cogens)* 110 *Revue Générale de Droit International Public*, (2006), 529.

Goldstone R. J., For Humanity: Reflections of a War Crimes Investigator (2000).

Gómez R., *A., El Ius Cogens Internacional* (Estudio Histórico Crítico), (1982).

Goodrich P., *Languages of Law* (1990).

Gracia-Amador, 'The Crime of Apartheid: Responsibility and Reparations,' *Review of Contemporary Law* (1981), pp. 31-38.

Gray C., *International Law and the Use of Force*, (2000).

Grayeff F., *Kant's Theoretical Philosophy* (Barnes & Noble, 1970).

Green P. J. and Ward, T., State crime, Human rights, and the Limits of Criminology, 27 *Social Justice* (2000), pp. 101–120.

Greenawalt A. K. A., 'The Pluralism of International Criminal Law,' 86 *Indiana Law Journal*, (2011), 1063-1130.

Grover S., *Prosecuting International Crimes and Human Rights Abuses Committed Against Children – Leading International Court Cases*, (2010), pp. 169–279.

Haas J. De, *History of Palestine - The Last Two Thousand Years* (USA: Macmillan, 1934).

Hannikainen L., *Peremptory Norms (jus cogens) in International Law: Historical Development, Criteria, Present Status* (1988).

Haque A. A., *Law and Morality at War* (2017).

Harees L., *The Mirage of Dignity on the Highways of Human 'Progress': the Bystanders Perspective*, (2012).

Harle V., *Ideas of Social Order in the Ancient World* (1998).

Harris J. W., Legal Philosophies, 2 edition (1997).

Harris W., *Tyranny on Trial* (Dallas: Southern Methodist University Press, 1999).

Hart H. L. A., *The Concept of Law*, 2nd ed., (P. A. Bulloch and J. Raz, eds., 1994).

Hartnack J., *Kant's Theory of Knowledge* (Harcourt, Brace and World, 1967).

Heller K. Jon, 'The Shadow Side of Complementarity: The Effect of Article 17 of the Rome Statute on National Due Process,' 17 *Criminal Law Forum* (2006), available at file:///C:/Users/admin/AppData/Local/Temp/SSRN-id907404.pdf.

Heller K. Jon, *The Nuremberg Military Tribunals and the Origins of International Criminal Law* (2010).

Hickey J. E., *Challenges to Security Council Monopoly Power over the Use of Force in Enforcement Actions: The Case of Regional Organisations*, 10 Ius Gentium 75 (2004).

Hitchens C., *The Trial of Henry Kissinger* (London: Verso Books, 2001).

Hoffe O., *Immanuel Kant* (State University of New York Press, 1994).

Hoover J. *Moral Practices: Assigning Responsibility in the International Criminal Court*, 76 *Law and Contemporary Problems* (2014), pp. 263-86.

Hughes G., Validity and the Basic Norm, 59 *California Law Review* 695 (1971).

Huntington C., 'Plato's Theory of Law,' 56 *Harvard Law Review*, (1942), pp. 559-587.

Hurd H., Challenging Authority, 100 *Yale Law Journal* 1611 (1991). https://www.gordogan.com.hr/gordogan/wp-content/uploads/2011/10/2001-Hitchens-The-Trial-of-Henry-Kissinger.pdf.

Hurlock W. L., "The International Court of Justice: Effectively Providing a Long Overdue Remedy for Ending State-Sponsored Genocide (Bosnia-Herzegovina v. Yugoslavia)," 12 *American University Journal of International Law and Policy* (1997).

Husabø E. J., Ingvild Bruce, *Fighting Terrorism through Multilevel Criminal Legislation: Security Council Resolution 1373, the EU Framework Decision on Combating Terrorism and their Implementation in Nordic, Dutch and German Criminal Law* (Martinus Nijhoff Publishers, 2009).

Huskey K. with Aleigh Acerni, Justice at Guantanamo: One Woman's Odyssey and Her Crusade for Human Rights (2009).

Ineke B. 'Towards a Strong System of Supervision: The Human Rights Committee's Role in Reforming the Reporting Procedure under Article 40 of the Covenant on Civil and Political Rights,' *Human Rights Quarterly*, 17. 4, (1995), pp. 766-793.

Isikoff Michael and David Corn, Hubris: *The Inside Story of Spin, Scandal, and the Selling of the Iraq War* (Crown Publishers, New York, 2006).

Jacovides A., *Treaties Conflicting with Peremptory Norms of International Law and the Zurich-London 'Agreements,'* (1966).

James P., Jonathan Friedman, Globalisation and Violence, Vol. 3: *Globalizing War and Intervention* (London: Sage Publications, 2006).

Janis M. W., 'The Nature of *Jus* Cogens' 3 *Connecticut Journal of International Law*, (1988), 59.

Jevons W. S., *The Theory of Political Economy* (London: Macmillan and Co., 1871).

John C. and John R. Pritchard (eds.), *International Humanitarian Law: Origins, Challenges and Prospects* (2000).

Jørgensen, *The Responsibility of States for International Crimes* (OUP Oxford 2000).

Jori M. (ed.), *Legal Positivism* (1992).

Jori M. (ed.), *Legal Positivism,* (1992).

Kairys D.(ed.), *The Politics of Law: A Progressive Critique* (1982).

Kant I., *Answering the Question: What is Enlightenment?* (1784).

Kant I., *Critique of Judgment* (1790).

Kant I., *Critique of Pure Reason* (1781).

Kant I., *Groundwork of the Metaphysic of Morals* (1785).

Kant I., *Metaphysical Foundations of Natural Science* (1786).

Kant I., *Opus Postumum* (1995).

Kant I., *Perpetual Peace, and Other Essays on Politics, History, and Morals* (1784).

Kant I., *Perpetual Peace: A Philosophical Sketch* (1795).

Kant I., *Practical Philosophy* (editor: Mary J. Gregor, 1999).

Kant I., *Prolegomena to Any Future Metaphysics* (1783).

Kant I., *Religion within the Bounds of Bare Reason* (1793).

Kant I., *The Critique of Practical Reason* (1788).

Kant I., *The Metaphysics of Morals* (1797).

Kant I., *The Only Possible Argument in Support of a Demonstration of the Existence of God* (1763).

Kant I., *The Science of Right* (1790).

Kawasaki K., 'A brief Note on the Legal Effects of *Jus Cogens* in International Law,' 34 *Hitotsubashi Journal of Law and Politics* (2006), pp. 27-43.

Kelman M., *A Guide to Critical Legal Studies* (1987).

Kelsen H., 'Will the Judgement of the Nürenberg Trial Constitute a Precedent in International Law,' 1 *International Law Quarterly* (1947), 153.

Kelsen H. 'Will the Judgement of the Nürenberg Trial Constitute a Precedent in International Law,' 1 *International Law Quarterly* (1947), 153.

Kelsen H., *What is Justice? Justice, Law and Politics in the Mirror of Science* (1957).

Kelsen H., *What is Justice? Justice, Law and Politics in the Mirror of Science* (1957);

Kemal S., *Kant's Aesthetic Theory: An Introduction* (St. Martin's Press, 1992).

Khadduri M., *Major Middle Eastern Problems in International Law*, (1972).

Kitcher P., *Kant's Transcendental Psychology* (Oxford University Press, 1990).

Klein D., F., 'A Theory for the Application of the Customary International Law of Human Rights by Domestic Courts,' 13 (2) *Yale Journal of International Law* (1988), pp. 332-365.

Kolb R. 'Jus cogens, Intangibilité, Intransgressibilité, Dérogation 'Positive' et 'Négative' 109 *Revue Générale de Droit International Public* (2005), 305.

Koskenniemi M. 'Solidarity Measures: State Responsibility as a New International Order?' 72 *BYIL*, (2001), pp. 337–56.

Koskenniemi M., "The Politics of International Law," *European Journal of International Law* (2011).

Kos-Rabcewicz-Zubrowski L., The Creation of an International Criminal Court, in *International Terrorism and Political Crimes* 519 (M. Cherif Bassiouni ed., 1975).

Kramer R. C., Michalowski, R. and Kauzlarich, D., 'The origins and development of the concept and theory of state-corporate crime,' 48 *Crime and Delinquency* (2002), pp. 263–282.

Kress C., 'Aggression and the Use of Force in International Law,' *Proceedings of the 108th Annual Meeting of the American Society of International Law* (2014), pp. 325–346.

Kuper L., *International Action against Genocide* (Minority Rights Group Report No. 53, London, 1982).

Kuper L., *The Prevention of Genocide* (New Haven and London, 1985).

Lefenya K., 'Use of Explosive Weapons in Densely Populated Areas: Implications for International Humanitarian Law,' *African Yearbook on International Humanitarian Law* (2014), pp. 68–86.

Leonetti. 'Interprétation des traités et rêgles impératives du droit international général (jus cogens),' 24 *ÖZÖR*, (1973).

Linderfalk U., 'The Creation of Jus cogens – Making Sense of Article 53 of the Vienna Convention,' *Max-Planck-Institut für ausländisches öffentliches Recht und Völkerrecht* (2011), pp. 259-278.

Lippman M., 'Genocide,' in *International Criminal Law*, Vol. I (M. Cherif Bassiouni, ed., 2008) pp. 405-455.

Luper-Foy S., 'Introduction: Global Distributive Justice' in Steven Luper-Foy (ed.), *Problems of International Justice* (London: Westview Press, 1988), pp. 1-24.

Lyons D., 'Moral Aspects of Legal Theory,' in Kenneth Himma and Brian Bix (eds) *Law and Morality* (2005).

MacGregor 'State Immunity and *Jus cogens,*' 55 *International & Comparative Law Quarterly* (2006), 437.

MacGregor D., 'September 11 as 'Machiavellian State Terrorism,' in Paul Zarembka, *The Hidden History of 9-11-2001* (New York: Seven Stories Press, 2008).

MacIntyre A., *A Short History of Ethics: a History of Moral Philosophy from the Homeric Age to the Twentieth Century* (1965).

MacIntyre A., *After Virtue: A Study in Moral Theory* (University of Notre Dame Press, 1982).

Madsen W., Jean-Charles, Guillaume Dasquie. *Forbidden Truth: U.S.-Taliban Secret Oil Diplomacy,* Saudi Arabia and the Failed Search for bin Laden, (2002).

Majd Mohammad Gholi, A Victorian Holocaust: Iran in the Great Famine of 1869–1873 (Hamilton Books, 2017).

Majd Mohammad Gholi, Iran Under Allied Occupation In World War II: The Bridge to Victory & A Land of Famine (University Press of America, 2016).

Majd Mohammad Gholi, The Great Famine & Genocide in Iran 1917-1919 (2nd edition, University Press of America, 2013).

Malekian, F. and Kerstin Nordlöf, 'International Legal Status of Children' in Jay S. Albanese (ed.), *The Encyclopaedia of Criminology & Criminal Justice* (United States: Wiley-Blackwell (5 volumes, 2013), vol. III, pp. 1173-1178.

Malekian, F. and Kerstin Nordlöf, *Prohibition of Sexual Exploitation of Children Constituting Obligation Erga Omnes* (Cambridge: Cambridge Scholars Publishing, 2013).

Malekian, F. and Kerstin Nordlöf, *The Basic documents with Analysis (*Cambridge: Cambridge Scholars Publishing, 2012).

Malekian, F. and Kerstin Nordlöf, *The Sovereignty of Children in Law* (Cambridge: Cambridge Scholars Publishing, 2012).

Malekian, F., 'Armenian Genocide and the Questions of Responsibility of the Turkish Government,' *House of Commons Conference on the Armenian Genocide, Armenian Solidarity, British-Armenian All-Party Parliamentary Group, No Security Publication* (2007), pp. 31-9.

Malekian, F., 'Comparative Substantive International Criminal Justice,' in Ronald Slye (ed.), *The Nuremberg Principles in Non-western Societies: A Reflection on their Universality, Legitimacy and Application* (2017), pp. 10-44.

Malekian, F., 'Conundrums of *Jus Cogens:* In Case Law' (Part II), No. 13 *Вісник Південного регіонального центру Національної академії правових наук України,* (No. 13 *Journal of the South regional Center of National Academy of Legal Sciences of Ukraine)* (2017), pp. 12-21.

Malekian, F., 'Conundrums of *Jus Cogens*: in International Criminal Law' (Part I), *Вісник Південного регіонального центру Національної академії правових наук України (No. 12 Journal of the South regional Center of National Academy of Legal Sciences of Ukraine)* (2017), pp. 8-16.

Malekian, F., 'Emasculating the Philosophy of International Criminal Justice in the Iraqi Special Tribunal,' *Cornell International Law Journal*, 58/5 (2005), pp. 675-725.

Malekian, F., '*International Criminal Responsibility,'* in *International Criminal Law* (M. Cherif Bassiouni, 2ed, ed., 1999).

Malekian, F., 'International Criminal Responsibility: International Criminal Responsibility of Individuals' in M. Cherif Bassiouni, *International Criminal Law,* Vol. *Crimes* (2ed, ed., New York: Transnational Publishers, 1999).

Malekian, F., *'Islamic Law Justice Systems' in* Jay S. Albanese, *The Encyclopaedia of Criminology and Criminal Justice* (United States: Wiley-Blackwell (5 volumes, 2013), vol. III, pp. 1220-1225.

Malekian, F., 'Judging International Criminal Justice in the Occupied Territories,' 12 *International Criminal Law Review* (2012), pp. 627-869.

Malekian, F., 'Mutilating the Philosophy of Justice in the Time of Armed Conflicts,' *Contemporary Journal of International Criminal Law* (2007).

Malekian, F., 'The Canon of Love against the Use of Force in Islamic and Public International Law: Part II: The Anatomy of Love Against Violations,' 15 *International Criminal Law Review*, 2015), pp. 861-895.

Malekian, F., 'The Canon of Love against the Use of Force in Islamic and Public International Law: Part I: The Chamber of Love within Legal Discipline,' 15 *International Criminal Law Review*, 2015), pp. 591-628.

Malekian, F., 'The Child as an Autonomous Subject of Justice' in Farhad Malekian and Kerstin Nordlöf, *Sovereignty of Children in Law* (Cambridge: Cambridge Scholars Publishing, 2012), pp. 2-55.

Malekian, F., 'The Functions of International Criminal Law and the Problem of Positivism and Neutralism Philosophy,' *Contemporary Journal of International Criminal Law* (2007).

Malekian, F., 'The Heaven of Justice with Love,' *The Journal of the Henry Martyn Institute* (2017), pp. 5-29.

Malekian, F., 'The Homogeneity of International Criminal Court with Islamic Jurisprudence,' 9 (4) *International Criminal Law Review* (2009), pp. 595-621.

Malekian, F., 'The Laws Governing Crimes against Women Constituting *Obligatio Erga Omnes*' in David Wingeate Pike, *Crimes Against Women* (2011).

Malekian, F., 'The Miserable Wedding of Naturalism into Positivism,' 2 *ID EST Journal* (2009).

Malekian, F., *Allegations by Political Laundering* (Cambridge Scholars Publishing, 2019).

Malekian, F., *Barrels of Justifications Violating International Criminal Responsibility* (New York: Nova Science Publishers, 2025).

Malekian, F., *Classical Morality in International Peremptory Criminal Law* (Newcastle: Cambridge Scholars Publishing, 2018).

Malekian, F., *Classical Morality in International Peremptory Criminal Law* (Newcastle: Cambridge Scholars Publishing, 2021).

Malekian, F., *Concreting Righteousness in International Criminal Justice* (New York: Nova publishers, 2024).

Malekian, F., *Condemning the Use of Force in the Gulf Crisis* (Almqvist & Wiksell International, 1st ed., 1992).

Malekian, F., *Conscience of Judges in International Criminal Law, the Heart of Judgements* (New York: Nova Science Publishers, 2021).

Malekian, F., *Conscience of Lawyers in International Criminal Law, the Burden of Doppelgängers* (New York: Nova Science Publishers, 2021).

Malekian, F., *Conscience of Prosecutors in International Criminal Law, the Heart of the Matter* (New York: Nova Science Publishers, 2021).

Malekian, F., *Conundrums of Paternalism in International Criminal Justice* (New York: Nova Science Publishers, 2024).

Malekian, F., *Corpus Juris of Islamic International Criminal Justice* (Newcastle: Cambridge Scholars Publishing, 2017).

Malekian, F., *Documents on the Principles of International Human Rights* (Stockholm: Norstedts Juridik AB, 2007).

Malekian, F., *Exploitation of Christian Islamic International Criminal Justice* (New York: Nova Science Publishers, 2024).

Malekian, F., *Gravity of Wisdom in International Criminal Law* (New York: Nova Science Publishers, 2021).

Malekian, F., *Hypocrisy in International Criminal Justice* (New York: Nova Science Publishers, 2025).

Malekian, F., *Imperative Philosophy of International Criminal Justice: Visible Power – Invisible Essence* (Nova Sciences Publishers, 2022).

Malekian, F., *International Crime of Blackboard-Barbarism* ((New York: Nova Science Publishers, 2025).

Malekian, F., *International Criminal Law of Children* (New York: Nova Science Publishers, 2021).

Malekian, F., *International Criminal Law, the Law of Somebodiness, the Law of Nobodiness* (New York: Nova Science Publishers, 2021).

Malekian, F., *International Criminal Law: The Legal and Critical Analysis of International Crimes* (Almqvist & Wiksell International, 2 vols. 1991).

Malekian, F., *International Criminal Responsibility of States: A Study on the Evolution of International Responsibility of States with particular Emphasis on the Concept of Crime and Criminal Responsibility* (Stockholm, 1985).

Malekian, F., *International Criminal Vacations: Tears of Justice* (New York: Nova Science Publishers, 2024).

Malekian, F., *Judgments of Love in Criminal Justice* (Switzerland: Springer: 2017, 2018).

Malekian, F., *Jurisprudence of International Criminal Justice* (Introduction by Professor Benjamin B. Ferencz, the former Prosecutor of the Nuremberg Tribunal (Cambridge: Cambridge Scholars Publishing, 2014).

Malekian, F., *Orchestrating Diversity in International Criminal Justice* (New York: Nova Science Publishers, 2021).

Malekian, F., *Paralysing International Criminal Justice* (New York: Nova Science Publishers, 2021).

Malekian, F., *Powertionism in International Criminal Justice* (Nova Sciences Publishers, 2022).

Malekian, F., *Principles of Islamic International Criminal Law: A Comparative Search* (Netherlands: Brill & Nijhoff, 2011).

Malekian, F., *Prohibition Governing Child Soldiers Constituting an Integral Part of Jus Cogens and Obligatio Erga Omnes*, XVII *World Congress of the International Association of Youth and Family Judges and Magistrates*, Belfast, Northern Ireland, 27 August – 2 September (2006).

Malekian, F., *System of International Law: Formation, Treaties, Responsibility* (Uppsala, 1987).

Malekian, F., *The Concept of Islamic International Criminal Law, A Comparative Study* (Netherlands: Brill, 1994).

Malekian, F., *The Mirage of International Criminal Law*: Kant Metaphysics of *Mens Rea* (Cambridge: Cambridge Scholars Publishing, 2018).

Malekian, F., *The Monopolisation of International Criminal Law in the United Nations, A Jurisprudential Approach* (Stockholm: Almqvist Wiksell International, 1st ed., 1993).

Malekian, F., *The Monopolisation of International Criminal Law in the United Nations, A Jurisprudential Approach* (Stockholm: Almqvist Wiksell International, 2nd ed., 1995).
Malekian, F., *Tour de force of Moral Virtue in International Criminal Justice* (Nova, Science Publishers, 2022).
Malekian, F., *Trading Virginity of International Criminal Justice* (New York: Nova Science Publishers, 2020).
Malekian, F., *Utipolitianist International Crimiminal Court* ((New York: Nova Science Publishers, 2025).
Malekian, F., *Empires of Genocide* (New York: Nova Science Publishers, 2026).
Malekian, F., *Holocaust Against the Children of Palestine* (New York: Nova Science Publishers, 2026).
Malekian, F., *Lies Empowering International Criminal Reasoning* (New York: Nova Science Publishers, 2026).
Malekian, F., *Chronic Criminal Viruses of the United Nations* (New York: Nova Science Publishers, 2026).
Manacorda S., 'Cesare Beccaria e la pena dell'ergastolo' *Jus* (2015), pp. 165–182.
May L., 'Habeas Corpus as *Jus cogens* in International Law' 4 (3) *Criminal Law and Philosophy* (2010), 249–265.
May L., *Aggression and Crimes Against Peace* (New York: Cambridge University Press, 2008).
May L., *Crimes against Humanity: A Normative Account* (New York: Cambridge University Press 2004).
May L., *War Crimes and Just War* (New York: Cambridge University Press, 2007).
Mendus S., 'The Importance of Love in Rawls's Theory of Justice' 29 (1) *British Journal of Political Science* (1999), pp. 57-75.
Meron T., 'On Hierarchy of International Human Rights' 80 *American Journal of International Law*, (1986), 1.
Meron T., *The Humanisation of International Law* (Netherlands: The Hague Academy, 2006).
Meyssan T., *11 September 2001: L'effroyable Imposture*, (2002).
Mokhtar A., '*Nullum Crimen, Nulla Poena, Sine Lege*: Aspects and Prospects,' 26 *Statute Law Review*, pp. 41-55.
Morten B., Emiliano J. Buis, *Philosophical Foundations of International Criminal Law* (2018).
Mosaddeq A., N. (2006), "Terrorism and Statecraft: Al-Qaeda and Western Covert Operations after the Cold War," Zarembka, P. (Ed.) *The Hidden History of 9-11-2001*. (*Research in Political Economy, Vol. 23*), Emerald Group Publishing Limited, Bingley, pp. 149-188. https://doi.org/10.1016/S0161-7230(06)23005-0.
Moyn S., *Not Enough: Human Rights in an Unequal World*, (2018).
Muchnik P., *Kant's Theory of Evil: An Essay on the Dangers of Self-love and the Aperiodicity of History* (Lexington Books, 2010).
Mueller G. O. W., 'International Criminal Law: Civitas Maxima,' 15 *Case Western Reserve Journal of International Law* (1985).

Mullins Christopher W., Kauzlaric David, Rothe Dawn, "The International Criminal Court and the Control of State Crime: Prospects and Problems," 12(3) *Critical Criminology* (2004), pp. 285-308.

Naiman A. *'9/11: The Simple Facts - Why the Official Story can't Possibly be True,'* (US: Soft Skull Press, 2011).

Nieto C., Chris Brandt, Howard Zinn (Foreword), Masters of War: Latin America and U.S. Aggression From the Cuban Revolution Through the Clinton Years (2003).

Nietzsche F. W., *The Will to Power,* https://en.wikisource.org/wiki/The_Will_to_Power.

Nietzsche F., *The Genealogy of Morals: A Polemic* (translated J. M. Kennedy, Vol. 8th, 1913).

Nozary F., *Unequal Treaties in International Law* (Stockholm, 1971).

O'Connor Susan, 'Up in Arms: A Humanitarian Analysis of the Arms Trade Treaty and Its New Zealand Application,' 11 *New Zealand Yearbook of International Law* (2013), pp. 73–105.

O'Neill O., *Constructions of Reason: Explorations of Kant's Practical Philosophy* (Cambridge University Press, 1989).

Ogunfolu A., Oludayo Fagbemi, 'I Have a Drone: The Implications of American Drone Policy for Africa and International Humanitarian Law,' 23 (1) *Revue Africaine de Droit International et Comparé* (2015), pp. 106–128.

Olivecrona K. 'The Imperative Element in Law,' *Rutgers Law Review* (1964).

Olson Peter M., 'The Lawfulness of Russian Use of Force in Crimea,' 53 (1) *Revue de Droit Militaire et de Droit de la Guerre* (2014), pp. 17–40.

Orakhelashvili A., 'The Impact of Peremptory Norms on the Interpretation and Application of United Nations Security Council Resolutions' 16 (1), *The European Journal of International Law* (2005), pp. 59-88.

Orakhelashvili A., *Peremptory Norms in International Law* (2006).

Osiel M. J., Why Prosecute? Critics of Punishment for Mass Atrocity, 22 *Human Rights Quarterly* 118 (2000).

Osiel M., *The End of Reciprocity* (Cambridge University Press, 2009).

Otterman M., *American Torture: From the Cold War to Abu Ghraib and Beyond* (Pluto Press, 2007).

Pardo P. V. S., 'Is International Criminal Law a living discipline?,' 3:4 *The International Journal of Human Rights* (1999), pp. 92-100.

Paris Declaration, International Conference on Sanctions Against South Africa (And Special Declaration on Namibia), 27 May1981, Published by the United Nations Center Against Apartheid.

Parish M., *International criminal law – Justice or Mirage? Transonflict* (2013).

Paton H. J., Kant's Metaphysic of Experience (Humanities Press, 1961).

Patrides C. A., Joseph Anthony Wittreich. *The Apocalypse in English Renaissance Thought and Literature: Patterns, Antecedents, and Repercussions* (Manchester University Press, 1984).

Patterson D.(ed.), *Postmodernism and Law* (1994).

Paulus A., 'Jus cogens in a Time of Hegemony and Fragmentation,' 74 *Nordic Journal of International Law* (2005), pp. 297-334.

Paust J. 'The Reality of Jus cogens,' 7 *Connecticut Journal of International Law* (1991), 83.

Pellet A., 'Comments in Response to Christine Chinking and in Defense of Jus cogens as the Best Bastion against the Excesses of Fragmentation,' 83 *Finnish Yearbook of International Law* (2006).

Pellet A., 'Vive le crime! Remarques sur les degrés de l'illicité en droit international' in United Nations/International Law Commission (ed.), I*nternational Law on the Eve of the Twenty-first Century: Views from the International Law Commission* (United Nations New York 1997), pp. 287–315.

Penrose M. M.'Lest We Fail: The Importance of Enforcement in International Criminal Law An Essay on the Nature and Immutability of Truth,' 15 (2) *American University International Law Review* (1999), pp. 321-394.

Perelman C., *The Idea of Justice and the Problem of Argument* (1963).

Peterson J., 'Unpacking Show Trials: Situating the Trial of Saddam Hussein,' 48 *Harvard International Law Journal* (2007).

Postema G. J., *Bentham and the Common Law Tradition* (1986).

Potter R. B., *War and Moral Discourse* (Richmond, Va., John Knox Press, 1969).

Power J., *Conundrums of Humanity: The Quest for Global Justice* (2007).

Protector J. H.., *Islam and International Relations* (New York, 1965).

Ragazzi M., *The Concept of International Obligations erga omnes* (Clarendon Press Oxford 1997).

Rahmdel M., 'Money Laundering in Iranian Law: Present and Future,' *Journal of Money Laundering Control* (2002).

Rahmdel M., 'The *Ne Bis In Idem* Rule in Iranian Criminal Law,' *Journal of Financial Crime* (2004).

Rahmdel M., The Role of the Courts in the Reform of Iranian Criminal Law Policy,' *Criminal Law Forum*, (2006).

Rawls J., *A Theory of Justice* (1999).

Raz J., 'Why the State?' in N. Roughan and A. Halpin (eds) In *Pursuit of a Pluralist Jurisprudence* (CUP 2017).

Raz J., *Ethics in the Public Domain: Essays in the Morality of Law and Politics* (Oxford: Oxford University Press, 1994).

Raz J., *The Morality of Freedom* (1986).

Reddy E. S., 'India and the Struggle Against Apartheid,' 26 *Indian Journal of International Law* (1986), pp. 551-567.

Reddy E. S., *Apartheid: The United Nations and the International Community* (1986).

Rehman J. *International Human Rights Law* (London and New York: Longman Pub Group, 2nd ed., 2010).

Reisman W. M., 'Legal Responses to Genocide and Other Massive Violations of Human Rights,' 59 *Law and Contemporary Problems* (1996), 75.

Reiss H. S., *Kant: Political Writings*, (2003).

Report of the Independent Inquiry into the actions of the United Nations during the 1994 genocide in Rwanda, UN Doc S/1999/1257, (1999) [Rwanda Report].

Rinceanu J., 'Criminal Liability of Legal Persons in Romania' in Riccardo Borsari, *Responsabilita` da reato deli enti* (Padova: Padova University Press, 2016). pp. 407–418.

Rinceanu J., 'The principle of legality (Nullum crimen sine lege) in Romania' in U. Sieber, S. Forster, & K. Jarvers (Eds.), *National Criminal Law in a Comparative Legal Context*, vol. 2 (1): Max-Planck-Institute für Ausländisches und Internationals Strafrecht, (2011), pp. 89-101.

Robertson G., *Crimes Against Humanity – The Struggle for Global Justice* (Penguin Books, 3rd ed., 2006).

Robinson M., "Genocide, War Crimes, Crimes Against Humanity," *25 Fordham International Law Journal* (1999), p. 275.

Roht-Arriaza N., State Responsibility to Investigate and Prosecute Grave Human Rights Violations in International Law, 78 *California Law Review* 451 (1990).

Roméo Dallaire's, *Shake Hands with the Devil: The Failure of Humanity in Rwanda* (Carroll & Graf, New York, 2003).

Rorty R., *Philosophy and the Mirror of Nature* (1990).

Rosen A. D. Kant's Theory of Justice (Ithaca, London: Cornel University Press, 1996).

Rosenstock R. 'An International Criminal Responsibility of States?,' in United Nations/International Law Commission (ed.), *International Law on the Eve of the Twenty-First Century: Views from the International Law Commission* (United Nations New York, 1997), pp. 265–85.

Ross J. I., *Controlling State Crime* (2nd Edition, New Brunswick, NJ: Transaction Press, 2000).

Ross J. I., *Varieties of State Crime and its Control* (Monsey, NY: Criminal Justice Press, 2000).

Schabas W. A., 'The Banality of International Justice,' 11 *Journal of International Criminal Justice* (2013), pp. 545–551.

Schabas W. A., *An Introduction to the International Criminal Court* (Cambridge University Press, 2011).

Schabas W. A., *Genocide in International Law, the Crime of Crimes* (2000).

Schabas W. A., *Genocide in International Law: The Crimes of Crimes* (Cambridge University Press, 2000 and 2009).

Schabas W. A., Justice, 'Democracy and Impunity in Post Genocide Rwanda: Searching for Solutions to Impossible Problems,' 7 *Criminal Law Forum* (1996).

Schabas W. A., Sentencing by International Tribunals: For a Human Rights Approach, 7:2. *Duke Journal of Comparative & International Law* (1997), pp. 461-518.

Schabas W. A., *The Abolition of the Death Penalty in International Law*, (2002 and 2005).

Schachter O., *International Law in Theory and Practice* (1991).

Schwarzenberger G. 'The Problem of an International Criminal Law,' 5 *Current Legal Problems* (1950).

Schwarzenberger G., *International Jus Cogens?* 43 *Tax. L. Rev* (1965), p. 476.

Schwelb E., *Crimes against Humanity, British Yearbook of International Law* (1946) 178.

Seltzer G., 'The Rule of the South Africa Criminal Code in Implementing Apartheid,' 8 *Georgia Journal of International and Comparative Law* (1978), pp. 176-194.

Sevrine K., 'State Immunity and the Promise of *Jus Cogens*,' *Northwestern Journal of International Human Rights* (2011), Vol. 9, No. 2, pp. 149-183.

Shaffer T. L., 'The Legal Ethics of Radical Individualism,' 65 *Texas Law Review* (1997).

Shelton D., 'Normative Hierarchy of International Law,' 80 *American Journal of International Law* (1986), 1.

Simmonds N., *Law as a Moral Idea* (2008).

Sliedregt E. van., *Pluralism in International Criminal Law*, 25 Leiden Journal of International Law (2012), 847.

Smith N. K., '*Commentary to Kant's 'Critique of Pure Reason'* (Humanities Press, 1962).

Smith T. S., *Lecture Delivered over the Remains of Jeremy Bentham*, Esq., in the Webb-Street School of Anatomy & Medicine, on the 9th June, 1832 (London: Effingham Wilson, 1832).

Sowilet A., *The Problem of the Creation of a Permanent International Criminal Court* (1951).

Spiermann 'Humanitarian Intervention as a Necessity and the Threat or Use of *Jus Cogens*' 71 *Nordic Journal of International Law*, (2002), 523.

Spooner L., *Natural Law; or the Science of Justice: A Treatise on Natural Law, Natural Justice, Natural Rights, Natural Liberty, and Natural Society; showing that all Legislation whatsoever is an Absurdity, a Usurpation, and a Crime.* Part First. [1882], available at http://oll.libertyfund.org/titles/spooner-natural-law-or-the-science-of-justice-1882 (Accessed: on 18 December 2017).

Stern R., *Understanding Moral Obligation: Kant, Hegel, Kierkegaard* (Cambridge, Cambridge University Press, 2012).

Stone J. and Robert Woetzel, *Toward a Feasible International Criminal Court* (1970).

Sugarman D. ed., *Legality, Ideology and the State* (1985).

Sugarman D., (ed.), *Legality, Ideology and the State* (1983).

Svaček O., 'The Human Rights Dimension of the ICC's Complementarity Regime,' *Czech Yearbook of Public and Private International Law,* 2015, Vol. 6, pp. 273-288.

Tunnell K., *Political Crime in Contemporary America* (New York: Garland, 1993).

Unger R., The Critical Legal Studies Movement, *96 Harvard Law Review 561* (1983).

van Schaack B., "The Crime of Political Genocide: Repairing the Genocide Convention's Blind Spot," 106 *Yale Law Journal* (1997).

Van Schaack B., Ronald C. Slye, *International Criminal Law: Intersections and Contradictions* (2020).

Van Schaack B., Ronald C. Slye, *International Criminal Law: The Essentials* (2008).

Van Schaack B., Ronald Sly. (ed.), *International Criminal Law and Its Enforcement* (University Casebook Series, 2nd).

Vanhullebusch M. 'The Arab League and Military Operations: Prospects and Challenges in Syria,' 22 (2) *International Peacekeeping* (2015), pp. 151–168.

Vasilijevic V. A., Crimes against Peace: Between the Past and the Future, 43 *Jugoslovenska Revija Za Medunarodno Pravo* 425 (1996).

Verdross A., 'Forbidden Treaties in International Law: Comments on Professor Garner's Report on 'The Law of Treaties," 31 *American Journal of International Law*, (1937), 571.

Verdross A., 'Jus Dispositivum and *Jus Cogens* in International Law' 60 *American Journal of International Law* (1966), 55.

Vespesian P. V., 'Plan for World Criminal Code,' 17 *Revue Internationale de Droit Penal* (1946).

Vespesian P. V., 'Towards an International Criminal Court,' 44 *American Journal of International Law* (1950), 57.

Vespesian P. V., *La criminalité collective des états et le droit pénal de l'avenir, Bucarest : Imprimerie de l'état* (1925).

Vespesian P. V., *La Guerre-Crime et les Criminels de Guerre/War-Crime and War Criminals* (Paris, 1946).

Vespesian P. V., Plan d'un Code Répressif Mondial, 6 *Rewe International de Droit Pénal* 1948, (1955).

Vespesian P. V., *Revue Internationale de Droit Penal* (1928).

Virally M., 'Réflexions sur le Jus cogens' 12 *Annuaire Français de Droit International* (1966), 5.

Vischer K. R., *Martin Luther King Jr. and the Morality of Legal Practice: Lessons in Love and Justice* (2014).

Vyver J. D. van der, 'Prosecution and Punishment of the Crime of Genocide,' 25 *Fordham International Law Journal* (1999).

Waldock H., 'General Course on Public International Law,' 106 *Recueil Des Course* (1962), pp. 39-103.

Ward I., *An Introduction to Critical Legal Theory* (1998).

Weatherhall T., *Jus cogens International Law and Social Contract* (2015).

Weil P., 'Towards Relative Normativity in International Law,' 77 *American Journal of International Law* (1983).

Weisburd M., 'The Emptiness of the Concept of *Jus Cogens*, As Illustrated by the War in Bosnia-Herzegovina,' 17 *Michigan Journal of International Law* (1995-1996), pp. 1-51.

Weiss, T. G., *Military-Civilian Interactions: Humanitarian Crises and the Responsibility to Protect* (2nd ed., Rowman & Littlefield Publishers Inc., Lanham (MD), 2005).

Weller M., *Iraq and the Use of Force in International Law* (Oxford: Oxford University Press, 2010).

Wet D., 'The Prohibition of Torture as an International Norm of *Jus Cogens* and Its Implications for National and Customary Law,' 15 *European Journal of International Law* (2004).

Whiteman M. M., '*Jus Cogens* in International Law: With a Projected List,' 7 *Georgia Journal of International and Comparative Law* (1977), p. 609.

Wilkes F. Klein & Daniel, United Nations Draft Statute for an International Criminal Court: An American Evaluation, in *International Criminal Law 526* (Gerhard O. W. Mueller & Edward M. Wise eds., 1965).

Wippman D., Atrocities, Deterrence, and the Limits of International Justice, 23 *Forham International Law Journal* 473 (1999).

Wood A., *Kant's Ethical Thought* (Cambridge University Press, 1999).

Wright Q., 'The Scope of International Criminal Law: A Conceptual Framework,' 15 *Virginia Journal of International Law*, (1975).

Wright Q., Proposal for an International Criminal Court, 46 *American Journal of International Law* 60 (1952).

Zaman R., 'Playing the Ace? *Jus Cogens* Crimes and Functional Immunity in National Courts,' 17 *Australian International Law Journal*, (2010), 53.

Zarembka P., *The Hidden History of 9-11-2001* (New York: Seven Stories Press, 2008).

Index

A

aboriginal population, 38
absence of justice, 89
absence of moral norms, 155
accountability, 7, 9, 14, 21, 30, 76, 83, 84, 87, 105, 107, 109, 117, 122, 123, 124, 132, 135, 145, 147, 158, 163, 175, 177, 186, 188, 190
accurate interpretations, 107
achieving justice, 46, 49, 76, 167
achieving moral rectitude, 47
achieving peaceful prosecution, 88
achieving social and international peace, 7
acknowledgment of justice principles, 93
act of genocide, 26
administration of justice, 8, 13, 29, 51, 59, 82, 105, 117
affiliation(s), 10
Afghanistan, 56, 80, 102, 109, 133, 162
Africa, 102, 113, 129, 152, 153, 199, 201
African backgrounds, 61
African leaders, 42, 129
African resources, 130
African(s), 42, 61, 94, 113, 129, 130, 152, 164, 194
aggression, xiv, 15, 23, 79, 81, 82, 91, 96, 97, 101, 118, 133, 134, 150, 164, 181, 186, 189, 191, 194, 198, 199
aggressive, xvi, 54, 55, 57, 60, 61, 63, 64, 82, 141, 160, 161, 166
aggressive ambitions, 166
aggressive force, 82
aggressive military powers, 54
aggressive powers, 57
agreements, 3, 55, 93, 110, 117, 124, 182, 183, 193
Albanese, Francesca, 19, 27, 64, 71, 84, 146, 185, 195
al-Sisi, Abd al-Fattah, 142
alternative definitions, 76
American administrations, 158, 168
American military bases, 111
Americans, 114
annihilating, 32, 126
annihilating the Palestinian population, 126
annihilation of a nation, 26
apartheid, 15, 42, 83, 133, 139, 150, 164, 189, 191, 192, 199, 200, 201
appropriate international criminal justice, 144
appropriate judgments, 158
appropriate judicial functions, 117
appropriate justice in favour, 35
Arab state, 118
arbitrary exercise, 50
architects of colonialism, 98
Argentina, 161, 176
arrest of criminals, 136, 137
arrest warrants for criminals, 136
artificial definition, 132
artificial principles, 97
Asia, 159
atrocities against victims, 133
attaining justice for, 40, 48
audaciously claims, 39
Australia, 38, 56
authentic international justice norms, 153
authentic judgment, 9

authentic justice, 9, 11, 77, 82, 93, 139, 151, 157
authentic nature, 73, 92
authoritarian government(s), 15, 38, 49, 52, 56, 68, 80, 92, 97, 108, 127, 142, 164
authoritarian ideological framework, 107
authoritarian justice, 41
authoritarian political powers, 3
authoritarian regimes, 22, 33, 34, 37, 38, 41, 57, 88, 90, 93, 103, 107, 108, 121, 178
authoritarian states, 60
autocratic rule, 163
autonomous justice, 16

B

barbaric, 30, 56, 80, 81, 82, 87, 150, 164, 167, 168
barbaric acts, 81, 150
barbaric ideologies, 81
barbaric justice, 80, 81
barbaric political powers, 82
barbaric practices, 82
Biden administration, 158
Biden, Joe, 123, 158, 162
Black, 5, 150, 191
Blair, Tony, 64, 123
Blinken, Antony, 141, 157
Bolivia, 161
Bongos, 149, 173
boundaries of morality, 23
Britain, 55, 56, 129, 131, 134, 150, 160
British brutal colonialist power, 4
British colonial governance, 38
British colonial powers, 38
British government leaders, 162
British government(s), xiv, 64, 102, 141, 158, 161, 162, 170
British government's political strategy, 64
British imperialist forces, 38
British Prime Minister, 88
British rule, 4
brutal actions of powerful, 61
brutal military actions, 166
brutal treatment of Palestinians, 177
brutalities of powerful entities, 122
brutality, xi, 2, 3, 4, 56, 63, 79, 103, 150, 166, 173
brutality of wars, 2
Bushes, 123
businesses into the West Bank, 69

C

Cambodia, 100
Cameron, 123, 147
Canada, 7, 11, 25, 56, 126, 190
categorisation among individuals, 52
ceremonies for their actions, 14
champion international human rights, 160
champions of justice, 81
Chapter VII, xiv, xv, 39, 41, 46, 50, 101, 115, 121, 145, 174, 177, 181
characteristic deceptions, 101
characteristics inherent, 67, 169
cheating, 17, 134
children, xiv, xv, 4, 6, 15, 30, 45, 46, 63, 64, 97, 99, 101, 103, 119, 145, 156, 164, 186, 192, 195, 196, 197, 198
CIA Director, 134
civilian facilities, 167
civilian lives, 111
Clinton, Bill, 162, 191, 199
Clinton, Hillary, 162, 191, 199
Clintons, 123
codifications, 3, 36, 100
coercive force of weapons, 141
collaboration, 7, 111, 144
collective authority, 107
collective breach of international law, 119
collective entity, 50
collective interest, 12, 29
collective multilateral obligations, 21
collective rights, 2
colonial British governance, 112
colonial powers, 84, 93, 94, 98, 145, 167
colonialism, 4, 56, 93
colony of powerful political interests, 14
combat terrorism, 118, 130

combating terrorist groups, 72
complex scenario, 68, 94
complicit in terrorism, 175
components of justice, 1, 2
comprehension of justice, 29
conceptualisation of justice, 79, 85
conceptualisation(s), 79, 85, 91, 100, 139
Congo, 115, 191
constitutions, 3, 36, 47, 113
contemporary colonial powers, 99, 108, 109, 113, 124, 126, 156
context of Gaza, 176
control of imperial powers, 83
convention against torture, 156
convention on the elimination of all forms of discrimination, 39, 92, 156
convention on the prevention and punishment of the crime of genocide, 25, 48, 156
convention on the rights of persons with disabilities, 156
convention on the rights of the child, 39, 92, 156
convention(s), 3, 8, 25, 33, 35, 39, 42, 46, 48, 67, 68, 69, 70, 71, 75, 78, 92, 93, 95, 113, 127, 130, 139, 140, 141, 142, 153, 154, 156, 157, 164, 165, 167, 189, 194, 202
corrective mechanisms, 49
corruption, 3, 83, 104, 124, 142, 153, 156
counter-terrorism, 74
court's wall advisory opinion, 70
covert agendas, 58
crimes against humanity, 15, 38, 52, 61, 69, 79, 95, 118, 133, 134, 139, 150, 152, 164
criminal activities, 38, 64, 79, 153
criminal activities of governments, 64
criminal behaviour, 3, 15
criminal elements, 35
criminal government, 39, 45, 52, 58, 59, 60, 61, 64, 95, 119, 132, 152, 166
criminal responsibility, 76, 82, 84, 85, 87, 97, 141, 151, 161
critical challenges, 108
crucial consideration, 25
Cuba, 133, 161
culpability, 145, 164, 176
cultural rights, 9, 10
current global landscape, 23
current legal-political conditions, 178
cycle of falsehoods, 126

D

deaths of millions, 18, 36, 99, 176
deceitful narratives, 105, 113, 144, 159, 164, 167
deceitful narratives of authoritarian regimes, 105
deceitful reasoning, 169
deceitful strategies, 111
deceptions of authoritarian powers, 163
deceptive practices, 120, 130
deceptive reasoning, 165
defenceless, 6, 79
defensive, 40, 66, 150
definition of justice, 1, 4, 11, 17, 26, 29, 31, 51, 55, 60, 67, 68, 71, 77, 78, 82, 87, 91, 95, 100, 103, 105, 110, 111, 120, 121, 124, 129, 130, 136, 142, 156, 159, 160, 161, 163
deliberately provocative, 65
delineating mutual expectations, 105
democratic leaders, 178
democratic values, 176, 178
dependency, 121, 136, 154
desirable features of criminal justice, 137
deterioration of Earth's climate, 143
detrimental outcome, 79
dictatorial influences, 176
dignity of humanity, 6, 28
disarmament, 137, 169, 183, 190
discrimination, 12, 32, 39, 72, 84, 92, 116, 164
discrimination among individuals, 72
disproportionately, 131
dissenting opinion, 38, 50
diverse geopolitical contexts, 49
diverting global attention, 133

domestic Israeli legislation, 69
dominant governments, xiii, 48, 80, 130, 138, 139, 145, 168
dominant nations, 88, 98
dominant political forces, 100
dominant political powers, 74, 146
dominant powers, xvi, 33, 37, 49, 56, 59, 71, 166
dynamics of international criminal justice, 149

E

economic agendas, 77, 131
economic falsehoods, 144
economic practices, 40
egregious injustices, 48
egregiously undermined, 28
Egypt, 102, 133
enforceability of justice, 14
enforcement mechanism(s), 49, 85, 89, 109, 124, 127, 143, 145, 174, 177
enforcement of human rights, 49
equal justice, 16, 18, 48, 92
equality of arms, 52, 98, 104
equitable and fair justice, 27
equitable justice, 7, 21, 45, 48, 96, 110, 116
equitable legal standards, 135
Erga omnes, 70
erroneous, 7, 10, 34, 109, 156, 167
essential principles governing, 121
establishing peaceful relations, 14
ethical dilemmas, 25
ethically wrong, 7
ethnic background, 8, 152
European Union, 91, 150, 164
evaluating the quality of justice, 52
evil, 4, 15, 36, 114, 115, 132, 187, 198
exaggeration, xi, 51, 61, 95, 102, 159, 173
existence of humanity, 7
exploitation, 60, 64, 133, 150, 160, 195, 197
exploitation of the rights, 60
extensive elaboration, 127

F

fabricating falsehoods, 101
fabrication(s), xiii, xiv, xvi, 101, 102, 103, 121, 126, 129, 140, 142, 159, 160
fabrications from corrupt leaders, 126
fail to acknowledge the binding provisions, 114
failings of moral responsibility, 146
family members, 145
fighting for, 9, 45, 162
financial gain, 17, 63
fish, 57, 58
flawed interpretation, 50, 102
football match, 178
force of arms, 111
forced migration, 133, 150
forces of lies, 114
fostering trust, 116
foundation for mutual respect, 126
foundation of moral, 25
foundation of political morality, 119
foundation of universal morality, 74
foundational element of any investigation, 104
foundational legal knowledge, 90
foundational lies inherent in international criminal reasoning, 102
foundational principles, 1, 16, 21, 37, 63, 75, 76, 90, 95, 112, 141, 144, 157, 158, 164, 168, 170
foundational principles of justice, 1, 21, 75, 76, 90
foundational structure of international society, 75
Four Geneva Conventions, 39, 92, 156
France, 3, 4, 56, 118, 129, 131, 134
freedom from deception, 8
French Revolution, 3
fundamental essence of justice, 74, 144
fundamental ethical, 48, 131
fundamental ethical norm, 48
fundamental injustice, 8
fundamental justifications, 76
fundamental philosophy, 51, 53

fundamental principles, 8, 9, 11, 14, 21, 63, 66, 68, 81, 82, 108, 143, 153, 168
fundamental rights, 2, 29, 32, 82, 112, 118, 146
fundamentally impermissible, 25
fundamentally unjust, 109
futile utopian aspiration, 67

G

Gaza, 27, 34, 35, 52, 56, 60, 64, 66, 68, 94, 97, 98, 114, 125, 126, 129, 132, 133, 149, 153, 166, 170, 175, 176, 190
Geneva humanitarian conventions, 167
genocidal against, 145
genocide, xv, 15, 19, 25, 26, 27, 35, 38, 42, 52, 55, 60, 63, 64, 66, 68, 71, 79, 81, 83, 84, 95, 97, 98, 100, 101, 113, 118, 125, 126, 129, 130, 133, 139, 140, 142, 143, 146, 150, 152, 153, 160, 164, 166, 167, 170, 175, 185, 187, 189, 190, 191, 192, 194, 195, 198, 200, 201, 202, 203
genocide against entire populations, 55
genocide in Gaza, 35, 68, 152, 166
genocide's historical narrative, 66
genuine collective beliefs, 73
genuine criminal justice, 82
genuine justice collapses, 79
genuine peace, 5, 8
geopolitical power dynamics, 169
Germany, 30, 55, 56, 85, 134, 175
global affairs, 178
global justice standards, 125
global leaders, 160
global perpetrators, 117
global public, 102
global realities, 22
global scale, 72, 122
gold, 56
good faith, 28, 31, 70, 119
good versus evil, 109
government declarations, 51
governmental lobbies, 142
governmental lobbying processes, 161
governmental mechanisms, 35
governmental propaganda, 165
governments wielding power exploit, 41
grave international offences, 164
greater strength, 58
greater value, 80
Greenfield, 157
guise of legalism, 177

H

Hague, 42, 45, 69, 70, 77, 98, 106, 115, 146, 156, 162, 177, 189, 198
Hague convention, 156
half a million, xiv, 15, 63, 111, 149
harmonious application of justice, 13
harsh reality, 41, 98
hegemonic governments, 48, 125, 130
hegemonic motives, 155
hegemonic principles, 108
hierarchy of individuals, 12
high morality of our actions, 6
Hitler, 25
honouring the rights of other nations, 55
human equality, 142
human morality, 153, 165
human rights, xvii, 1, 6, 19, 27, 28, 30, 33, 36, 37, 39, 41, 46, 47, 48, 49, 50, 54, 58, 60, 61, 62, 63, 65, 66, 67, 73, 74, 75, 79, 80, 83, 84, 93, 94, 95, 101, 102, 105, 108, 112, 115, 116, 119, 121, 122, 124, 125, 126, 127, 135, 140, 146, 151, 154, 155, 158, 166, 170, 176, 177, 185, 192
human shields, 119
humanitarian dimensions, 146
humanitarian law, xv, 15, 27, 30, 36, 54, 58, 70, 71, 113, 133, 150, 167, 168
humanity, 2, 4, 7, 9, 34, 35, 36, 45, 49, 54, 74, 76, 119, 123, 139, 155, 159, 160, 166, 170, 186, 187, 191, 198, 200, 201
human-snaking rights, 81, 87
hypothetical basic framework, 82

I

ideological battles, 28

illegitimate infringements, 18
illusions of prosperity, 58
immoral versus moral justice, 24
impartiality, 9, 16, 41, 82, 113, 136, 177
imperialist governments, 38, 161
impose sanctions, 29, 33, 118
impunity, 33, 45, 65, 79, 97, 121, 137, 140, 150, 151, 152, 154, 162, 165, 177, 191, 201
India, 102, 200
Indigenous peoples, 38
infant beheadings, 103
influence wielded by offenders, 66
influential governments, 33, 59
influential powers, 122, 149, 161
inherently dysfunctional, 178
injustice against victims, 29
injustice to practical justice, 94
innocent children, 15, 30
innocent individuals, 34, 35, 38, 43, 64, 101
institutional mechanisms, 170
institutional regulations, 83
institutionalisation of falsehoods, 113
institutions of criminal justice, 114
institutions of injustice, 82
intentional misinterpretations, 10
interests of specific governments, 110
international community, xv, 15, 19, 45, 46, 53, 62, 67, 75, 132
international convention on the elimination of all forms of racial discrimination, 39, 92, 156
international convention on the suppression and punishment of the crime of apartheid, 157
international court of justice (ICJ), 35, 41, 57, 69, 70, 71, 146, 152, 155, 162, 190, 192
international covenant on civil and political rights, 39, 92, 157, 164
international covenant on economic, social and cultural rights, 39, 92, 157
international crimes akin to blackboard-barbarism, 118
international criminal court (ICC), xvi, 1, 13, 30, 39, 40, 41, 42, 43, 45, 46, 48, 55, 59, 60, 61, 62, 67, 68, 69, 70, 74, 76, 82, 83, 84, 85, 87, 88, 89, 92, 94, 97, 98, 101, 104, 106, 107, 109, 112, 113, 114, 115, 116, 117, 120, 121, 123, 124, 126, 127, 129, 130, 134, 135, 136, 137, 140, 141, 145, 146, 149, 151, 152, 155, 158, 159, 162, 163, 165, 166, 167, 168, 169, 170, 174, 175, 176, 177, 186, 187, 188, 189, 190, 191, 192, 194, 196, 199, 201, 202, 203, 204
international criminal evidence, 132
international criminal justice, xi, xiii, xiv, xv, xvi, 13, 30, 34, 35, 37, 39, 40, 41, 42, 48, 49, 51, 54, 55, 58, 59, 60, 61, 62, 67, 68, 70, 71, 72, 73, 74, 75, 76, 77, 78, 79, 81, 82, 84, 87, 88, 89, 90, 91, 92, 93, 94, 95, 96, 97, 99, 100, 101, 102, 103, 104, 105, 107, 108, 109, 110, 111, 112, 113, 114, 115, 116, 117, 118, 119, 120, 121, 122, 123, 124, 125, 126, 127, 130, 131, 132, 133, 134, 135, 136, 137, 138, 139, 140, 141, 142, 143, 144, 145, 146, 149, 151, 152, 153, 154, 155, 156, 157, 158, 159, 160, 161, 162, 163, 164, 165, 166, 167, 168, 169, 170, 173, 174, 175, 176, 177, 178
international human rights, xvi, 4, 33, 35, 36, 37, 38, 39, 42, 49, 50, 54, 55, 58, 59, 60, 61, 64, 65, 66, 67, 68, 70, 71, 73, 74, 75, 76, 77, 81, 84, 87, 90, 91, 93, 100, 102, 111, 119, 127, 131, 144, 146, 151, 155, 178
international human rights justice, 64
interpretation of justice, 7, 28, 29, 55, 58, 63, 72, 74, 79, 94, 105, 147, 149, 163
interpretations of appropriate justice, 89
interpretations of justice, 6, 22, 33, 48, 59, 76, 79, 82, 96, 99, 122, 131, 142
intrinsic values, 53, 76
Iran, 102, 161, 195
Iraq, xiv, 15, 56, 63, 80, 88, 102, 133, 158, 163, 175, 189, 190, 203
Iraq War, 15, 63, 163

Irish republicanism, 4
isolation of its victims, 41
Israel, 27, 30, 56, 62, 63, 69, 70, 71, 94, 97, 98, 111, 115, 118, 125, 134, 136, 149, 152, 161, 166, 170
Israel's excessive use of force, 70
Israel's systematic failure, 70
Israeli criminal military power, 79
Israeli government, 30, 69, 119, 125, 132, 141, 152, 153, 166
Israeli leaders, 30, 103, 136, 166

J

Jews, 26, 50, 79, 81, 85, 175, 177
judge(s), xvi, 6, 9, 21, 24, 30, 36, 40, 48, 61, 62, 63, 66, 67, 69, 78, 81, 83, 96, 99, 113, 114, 115, 117, 123, 124, 138, 152, 153, 154, 158, 163, 165, 169, 170, 196, 197
judgments, 8, 9, 17, 25, 29, 30, 40, 42, 53, 60, 66, 69, 90, 101, 113, 136, 146, 156, 158, 197
judicial cannibalism, 59
judicial proceedings, 8, 123, 138, 164
judicial responses, 136
judicial theories, 53
jus cogens, 60, 67, 77, 99, 112, 119, 121, 122, 127, 133, 153, 154, 155, 185, 186, 187, 188, 189, 191, 192, 194, 198, 199, 200, 203
justice as aggression, 96
justice as fairness, 94, 96
justice as humiliation, 96
justice as injustice, 96
justice as violations, 96
justice exceedingly complex, 140
justice of truth, 114
justification of killing millions, 7
justifications, 1, 29, 34, 54, 74, 79, 111, 129, 157, 159, 175, 196

K

Kant, Immanuel, 36, 37, 65, 73, 114, 151, 185, 187, 190, 192, 193, 194, 197, 198, 199, 200, 201, 202, 203
Kantian philosophy, 36
Khan, Karim, 162
killer whales, 59

L

label as terrorists, 59
lack justice, 34
lack of choice, 99
largely symbolic, 136
Latin America, xvi, 96, 130, 161, 199
lawbreakers, 8
law-making treaties, xiii
lawyers, xiii, xvi, 21, 37, 40, 63, 65, 66, 71, 74, 75, 78, 95, 145, 158, 196
lawyers are sold, 95
lawyers become similarly commodified, 95
lawyers of corrupt integrity, 71
lawyers selectively, 66
leadership of NATO, 174
leading to the death, 41
league of nations, 98, 141, 145, 155
Lebanon, 56, 133
legal and moral rights, 94
legal duty, 6
legitimate claims of self-defence, 130
legitimate international justice system, 179
legitimate norms, 97
Libya, 56, 102, 133
lies, xi, xiii, xiv, xvi, 1, 3, 12, 14, 16, 21, 26, 30, 33, 37, 43, 59, 64, 67, 68, 71, 76, 78, 80, 82, 93, 95, 96, 98, 102, 103, 107, 110, 112, 114, 116, 121, 125, 129, 130, 132, 133, 134, 138, 139, 141, 142, 143, 144, 145, 153, 154, 159, 164, 165, 167, 168, 169, 173, 176, 191, 198
lies frequently masquerade as justice, 173
lies may be propagated and institutionalised, 121
lies of powerful governments, 43

lifeboat, 45, 46
lobbies of the criminal governments, 95
looting, 150
loss of millions, xv, 120
love, 13, 30, 89, 114, 123, 196, 197, 198, 203
lucrative opportunities, 58

M

major governments, 110, 112
major political factions, 37, 75
major political powers, 67, 101, 102, 113, 141
major powers, 32, 63, 87, 113, 119, 129, 146, 160, 165, 167, 176
major terrorist criminal governments, 62
malevolent governments, 30, 84
malevolent justice, 52
manoeuvres, 151
manufacturing false evidence, 97
marginalisation of victims' rights, 47
mass genocidal actions, 60
massacre of innocent individuals, 131
Mearsheimer, John, 96, 168
mechanisms of justice, 28, 137
metaphor of a tsunami, 21
metaphorical context, 58
metaphorical representation, 58
metaphysical doctrines, 73
Middle East, xvi, 91, 129, 136, 159, 161, 194
military apparatuses, 59
military capabilities, 75, 94, 135
military interests, 73
military leaders, 14
military might, 22, 31, 75, 126, 131, 160, 161
military offenders, 167
military operations, 152
millions losing their lives, 111
millions of innocent individuals, 58
millions suffering globally, 42
minimal assistance, 118
minimal political commitment, 146
minimise controversy, 140
minimum nor maximum standards, 131
misattributing roles of victims, 102
misunderstanding(s), 21, 37, 54, 143
mixture of lies and truths, 78
modern colonial powers, 99, 116, 129, 167
monopolisation, 16, 17, 39, 40, 49, 50, 53, 56, 59, 69, 89, 104, 107, 129, 143, 158, 163, 175, 176, 197, 198
monopolisation of others' rights, 53
monopolisation of victims' rights, 89
monopolising all legal frameworks, 80
monopolising justice, 160
monopolization, 88, 118, 163
moral and philosophical justice, 5
moral attitudes, 29
moral authority, 160
moral dilemma(s), 23, 24, 28
moral force, 140
moral foundation(s), 13, 37, 40, 131
moral frameworks of justice, 19
moral inquiries, 24
moral interpretations, 35
moral judgment, 169
moral justice, 108, 122, 140, 155
moral psychology, 72
moral reasoning, 23, 29, 31, 92
moral recognition, 29
moral responsibilities, 6
moral standards, 126
moral theories, 92
morality, 5, 6, 10, 11, 13, 14, 17, 22, 23, 24, 25, 28, 29, 30, 36, 47, 55, 63, 73, 85, 114, 122, 123, 126, 131, 140, 143, 155, 187, 190, 191, 192, 194, 196, 200, 203
morally compromised perspectives, 174
morally unjustifiable, 18
most perilous criminals, 64
multilateral implementation, 144
multitude of expectations, 93

N

national policies, 90

NATO, 59, 60, 62, 63, 87, 111, 150, 173, 174, 175
NATO countries, 60
NATO governments, 60
natural law, 23, 63, 69, 122, 153, 177
natural rights of humanity, 15
Nazi Germany, 175
negotiation tables, 111
negotiation(s), 2, 53, 56, 97, 110, 111, 135, 156, 159, 174, 176
neo-colonial powers, 152
Netanyahu, Benjamin, 163, 165
Nicaragua, 161
nobodiness, 54, 88, 179, 197
non-Western states, 129
North America, 38
nuclear possessor, 85
Nuremberg trials, 169
Nuremberg tribunal, 88, 98, 104, 197

O

Obama, Barack, 123, 162
objectives of international human rights law, 178
Ocampo, 176
occupied territories, 111, 116
October 7, 2023, 132
office of the prosecutor, 30, 113, 115, 175
official obligations, 50
often insurmountable, 13
oil, 3, 56, 106, 111, 195
opponent(s), 13, 60, 81, 132
opponents of justice, 13
oppressive government(s), xv, 47, 49, 62, 93, 116, 118, 119, 126, 132, 144, 167
oppressive mechanisms, 152
oppressive political entities, 139
oppressive power(s), 41, 75
oppressive regime(s), 55, 56, 60, 61, 63, 91, 111, 120, 125, 127, 141, 149
optimising exploitation, 108
orchestrating deceptive parliamentary, 102
orchestrations of injustice, 154
ornamental regulations, 84
overarching principles, 103

P

Palestine, 28, 68, 70, 80, 95, 97, 118, 119, 125, 145, 149, 153, 161, 162, 167, 175, 190, 192, 198
Palestinian authority, 115
Palestinian nation, 94
Palestinian people, 27, 38, 70, 71, 175
Palestinian rights, 149
Palestinian situation, 25
Palestinians, 26, 27, 30, 50, 69, 71, 119, 125, 152, 177
Palestinians in Gaza, 27
parliamentary politics, 108
passive complicity, 38
paternalistic control, 84
paternalistic governments, 40, 58, 130, 143
paternalistic regimes, 49
peace, 2, 3, 4, 5, 6, 7, 8, 9, 10, 12, 14, 15, 21, 22, 23, 31, 34, 39, 41, 45, 54, 55, 56, 57, 70, 71, 72, 73, 75, 81, 92, 115, 131, 132, 134, 150, 151, 155, 161, 167, 174, 181, 182, 183, 184, 186, 193, 198, 202
peaceful resolutions, 2, 18
perpetration of genocide, 35
perpetrators of international crimes, 79, 114, 142
perpetrators of serious international crimes, 106
perpetuating falsehoods, 149
perpetuating injustice, 89
personal gain, xvii, 58
personal interpretations, 12
personal satisfaction, 38
philosophical theory, 17, 160
philosophical theory of justice, 160
philosophical underpinnings of justice, 105
philosophy of justice, 22, 23, 32, 53, 138, 144, 151, 171
physical strength, 17
piracy, 133, 150
plight of victims, 37, 51
plundering, 133

political affiliations, 9
political characterisations, 80
political community, 76, 124
political governments, 67
political ideologies, 19, 161
political influence(s), 14, 73, 100, 124, 138, 144
political lies, 139
political manoeuvres, 166
political paternalism, 120
political philosophy, 22
political reasoning, 81, 169
political rhetoric, 126
political strategies, 108, 160
political will, 12
politically manipulated, 114
Pompeo, 134
portrayal of victims, 117
potential conceptions of justice, 127
potential errors, 9
potential misinterpretation, 36
power dynamics, 7, 52, 55, 78, 139, 173
powerful criminals, 34, 79, 98, 140, 141
powerful entities, 33, 37, 47, 55, 59, 65, 77, 78, 88, 117, 157
powerful governments, xvi, 36, 39, 48, 50, 52, 53, 54, 55, 57, 58, 61, 63, 72, 78, 83, 87, 89, 91, 98, 99, 102, 105, 126, 127, 133, 145, 149, 151, 167
powerful governments dictating, 57
powerful permanent members, 67
powerful perpetrators, 139, 177
powerful political entities, 64, 74, 75, 89, 131, 143, 144, 158
powertionist, 26, 50, 66, 69, 73, 80, 87, 88, 90, 91, 100, 101, 106, 109, 112, 114, 118, 121, 130, 141, 149, 150, 154, 175, 179
powertionist criminal governments, 66
powertionist governments, 26, 50, 73, 87, 90, 91, 100, 106, 109, 112, 121, 130, 141, 154, 179
practical policies, 35, 54
predatory fishing expedition, 58
prescribed notion of justice, 91
presentation of falsehoods, 91
presentation of justice, 14, 17, 100, 169
presenting falsehoods, 141
President of the United States, 115
pre-trial Chamber I, 66
prevention of injustice, 10
primary catalyst, 124
Prime Minister, 16, 88
principle of equality, 18, 49, 98
principles of peace, 2, 5
principles of righteousness, 114
prioritises fire prevention, 10
processes of criminal justice, 106
proliferation of lies, 6, 141
prolonged abuses, 3
prominent criminals of the 21st century, 176
promotion of justice, 42
promotion of moral rights, 22
propagate falsehoods, 102, 160, 168
propagated by powerful governments, 130, 135
Prosecutor's office, 149, 177
protection of victims, 97
protocol(s), 3, 39, 92, 156, 164
psychological effects, 93
psychological struggle, 144
public grievances, 21
public welfare, 13
punishment, 35, 79, 122, 151, 156, 163, 188, 199, 203
purely hypothetical context, 94
pursuing terrorist groups, 167
pursuit of justice, 4, 21, 30, 51, 63, 72, 92, 110, 123, 124, 126, 136, 144, 155, 175

R

rape, xv, 79, 81, 133, 150
realm of criminal justice, 113, 140
representatives of humanity, 34
representatives of justice, 34
responsibilities, xvi, 6, 21, 46, 97, 112, 153, 164, 183
rightful owners, 27

rights of victims, 5, 27, 38, 40, 42, 51, 60, 67, 72, 90, 121, 144, 145, 160, 173
robbery, 133, 150
robust moral foundation, 48
robust principles, 84
Rome statute, 1, 39, 55, 92, 104, 115, 126, 146, 159, 187, 188, 192
Rome statute of the court, 159
Russia, 111, 149, 150
Russian territories, 111
Rwanda, xv, 39, 79, 85, 92, 100, 113, 200, 201

S

Sachs, Jeffrey, 96, 111, 168
Sadat. Anwar, 142
safeguard all humanity, 75
safeguarding humanity, 65
saltwater crocodiles, 58, 59
sanction(s), xiii, 29, 52, 55, 56, 61, 150, 174, 175, 189, 199
savagery, 133
scenario engenders disparate interpretations, 102
science of justice, 1
scrutinise structural power, 108
scrutiny in legal matters, 62
Sebutinde, Julia, 152, 153
second world war, 26, 79, 85, 95, 100
security council, xi, xiv, xv, xvi, 5, 25, 32, 41, 42, 46, 48, 50, 51, 56, 57, 59, 62, 70, 80, 81, 83, 84, 85, 89, 102, 105, 115, 116, 121, 123, 124, 129, 131, 136, 138, 140, 141, 142, 145, 146, 147, 152, 155, 157, 158, 161, 166, 167, 168, 169, 170, 171, 173, 174, 175, 176, 177, 178, 181, 182, 183, 184, 192, 199
selectivity, 121, 154, 189
self-defence, xvi, 3, 34, 79, 125, 129, 131, 184
self-determination, 15, 70, 71, 118, 119, 125, 134, 135, 179
self-established rules, 29
self-gain, 38
self-interest, 15, 18, 21, 38, 76, 79, 108, 155, 159, 176, 178
self-interpretation, 6
self-satisfaction, 2
self-serving attitudes, 89
self-serving interests, 34, 47, 76, 156, 175, 177
self-serving interpretations of justice, 135
self-serving norms, 160
self-sustaining, 173
serious infringements, 42
service of oppression, 114
severe punishments, 9
sexual violations, 97
shadow of justice, 29
shared conception of justice, 76, 107
sharks, 58
significance of negotiations, 110
significant falsehoods, 105, 113, 167
signifying victims' rightful, 92
situation in Gaza, 170
snaking justice, 87
soldiers, 14, 15, 99, 150, 154, 197
somebodiness, 54, 88, 179, 197
South Africa, 152, 153, 199, 201
specific stage of genocide, 139
Starmer, Kier, 123
statute of the court, 57, 61, 159, 178
stealing, 134
strategic interests, 52, 100, 174
subjective preferences, 104
substantial influence, 80, 91
suffering of the victims, 32
Sunak, Rishi, 123
superior military strength, 169
superior(s), 14, 22, 83, 121, 130, 131, 161, 163, 165, 169
superiority, 5, 71
Swedish, 61, 166
Swedish government's, 61
Syria, 3, 55, 56, 59, 60, 80, 106, 111, 133, 186, 191, 202
systemic violations, 53, 178

T

tangible reality, 67
technological advancements, 72
territories of victims, 117
terroristic political views, 114
terrorist(s), xiii, xvi, 5, 27, 34, 56, 63, 72, 73, 74, 94, 96, 102, 103, 113, 114, 116, 119, 121, 123, 125, 129, 137, 142, 175
theories of humanity, 51
theory of equality, 51, 104
threat of force, 82, 111, 144
torture, 34, 77, 79, 81, 97, 118, 133, 139, 150, 188, 189, 199, 203
traditional theories of justice, 136
trajectory of justice, 96, 106
transcendent power, 12
transgressions against numerous victims, 118
tribunal, 1, 38, 39, 85, 92, 113, 129, 163, 187, 188, 195
true essence of justice, 28, 55, 81, 130
true judicial fairness, 88
true justice, 2, 3, 5, 9, 11, 12, 16, 17, 28, 41, 79, 81, 82, 89, 96, 110, 140, 141, 143, 144, 145, 152, 157
true rights, 107
Truss, Liz, 123
Turkey, 55

U

U.S. aggression, 60
U.S. diplomacy, 112
Uganda, 152
Ukraine, 60, 99, 149, 150, 154, 162, 195
Ukraine cases, 162
Ukraine's situation, 60
Ukrainian lives, 111
UN bureaucracy, 115
unavoidable norm, 51
understanding of justice, xvi, 13, 14, 18, 21, 25, 26, 28, 51, 55, 72, 75, 77, 94, 104, 105, 107, 117, 124, 125, 126, 135, 155, 158, 160, 161
unequal justice, 14
unequivocally genocide, 26, 143
United Kingdom, 16, 63, 102, 188
United Nations, xi, xiii, xiv, xv, 30, 31, 32, 36, 39, 41, 42, 45, 46, 48, 49, 50, 53, 54, 55, 56, 57, 61, 67, 68, 70, 71, 74, 80, 81, 82, 83, 84, 88, 89, 91, 92, 94, 96, 98, 99, 100, 101, 103, 104, 105, 109, 113, 115, 116, 117, 118, 121, 124, 134, 135, 136, 137, 138, 141, 145, 146, 150, 152, 155, 156, 158, 163, 164, 168, 169, 170, 173, 174, 176, 178, 181, 182, 183, 184, 187, 190, 197, 198, 199, 200, 201, 203
United Nations bears the responsibility, 45
United Nations charter, xv, 36, 39, 41, 46, 48, 50, 54, 55, 56, 71, 92, 99, 101, 115, 121, 134, 178
United Nations convention against corruption, 156
United Nations Security Council, xi, 50, 89, 115, 116, 124, 138, 147, 158, 173, 199
United States, xiv, 15, 23, 43, 55, 59, 61, 62, 63, 64, 67, 80, 96, 99, 111, 114, 117, 118, 119, 121, 129, 130, 131, 133, 134, 141, 145, 149, 150, 154, 160, 161, 168, 175, 176, 189, 195
United States government, 15, 23, 43, 67, 80, 96, 111, 114, 117, 118, 149, 161
universal declaration of human rights, 36, 39, 54, 92
universal moral law, 53
universal nature of human rights, 35
universality of justice, 22
unjust interpretation, 80
unscrupulous governments, 108
utilitarian philosophy, 38
utilitarian principles, 134
utilitarianism, xiv, 12, 23, 100
utipolitianist authority, 4

V

value of international criminal justice, 127
various misrepresentations, 138